Additional copies of *Fundamentals of Instructing FAA Knowledge Test* are available from

Gleim Publications, Inc.
P.O. Box 12848 • University Station
Gainesville, Florida 32604
(352) 375-0772
(800) 87-GLEIM or (800) 874-5346
FAX: (352) 375-6940
Internet: www.gleim.com | Email: avmarketing@gleim.com

The price is $14.95 (subject to change without notice). Orders must be prepaid. Call us, order online, or use the order form on page 167. Shipping and handling charges apply to all orders. Add applicable sales tax to shipments within Florida.

Gleim Publications, Inc. guarantees the immediate refund of all resalable texts and unopened software and audios purchased directly from Gleim Publications, Inc. if they are returned within 30 days. Shipping and handling charges are nonrefundable. Returns of books purchased from bookstores and other resellers should be made to the respective bookstore or reseller.

REVIEWERS AND CONTRIBUTORS

Jamie Beckett, CMEL, CFII, MEI, AGI, A&P, is one of our aviation editors. Mr. Beckett researched questions, wrote and edited answer explanations, and incorporated revisions into the text.

Eric L. Crump, CMEL, CFII, AGI, B.S., Middle Tennessee State University, is one of our aviation editors. Mr. Crump researched questions, wrote and edited answer explanations, and incorporated revisions into the text.

John F. Rebstock, B.S., Fisher School of Accounting, University of Florida, specializes in ensuring that our answer explanations and Knowledge Transfer Outlines are user-friendly. Mr. Rebstock reviewed portions of the manuscript.

The CFIs who have worked with us throughout the years to develop and improve our pilot training materials.

The many FAA employees who helped, in person or by telephone, primarily in Gainesville, Orlando, Oklahoma City, and Washington, DC.

The many pilots who have provided comments and suggestions about *Fundamentals of Instructing FAA Knowledge Test* during the past 25 years.

ACKNOWLEDGMENTS

The photograph on the front cover is of a Diamond Air DA40 CS, and it is courtesy of Diamond Aircraft.

A PERSONAL THANKS

This manual would not have been possible without the extraordinary effort and dedication of Allyson Ayers, Jacob Brunny, Kyle Cadwallader, Julie Cutlip, Eileen Nickl, Teresa Soard, and Joanne Strong, who typed the entire manuscript and all revisions and drafted and laid out the diagrams and illustrations in this book.

The authors also appreciate the production and editorial assistance of Ellen Buhl, Daniel Fisher, Katie Goodrich, James Harvin, Jean Marzullo, Shane Rapp, Katie Wassink, and Martha Willis.

Finally, we appreciate the encouragement, support, and tolerance of our families throughout this project.

Groundwood Paper and Highlighters – This book is printed on high quality groundwood paper. It is lightweight and easy to recycle. We recommend that you purchase a highlighter specifically designed to be non-bleed-through (e.g., Avery *Glidestick*™) at your local office supply store.

2010 EDITION

FUNDAMENTALS OF INSTRUCTING

FAA KNOWLEDGE TEST

for the FAA Computer-Based Pilot Knowledge Test

by

Irvin N. Gleim, Ph.D., CFII

and

Garrett W. Gleim, CFII

ABOUT THE AUTHORS

Irvin N. Gleim earned his private pilot certificate in 1965 from the Institute of Aviation at the University of Illinois, where he subsequently received his Ph.D. He is a commercial pilot and flight instructor (instrument) with multiengine and seaplane ratings and is a member of the Aircraft Owners and Pilots Association, American Bonanza Society, Civil Air Patrol, Experimental Aircraft Association, National Association of Flight Instructors, and Seaplane Pilots Association. He is the author of flight maneuvers and practical test prep books for the sport, private, instrument, commercial, and flight instructor certificates/ratings and the author of study guides for the sport, private/recreational, instrument, commercial, flight/ground instructor, fundamentals of instructing, airline transport pilot, and flight engineer FAA knowledge tests. Three additional pilot training books are *Pilot Handbook*, *Aviation Weather and Weather Services*, and *FAR/AIM*.

Dr. Gleim has also written articles for professional accounting and business law journals and is the author of widely used review manuals for the CIA (Certified Internal Auditor) exam, the CMA (Certified Management Accountant) exam, the CPA (Certified Public Accountant) exam, and the EA (IRS Enrolled Agent) exam. He is Professor Emeritus, Fisher School of Accounting, University of Florida, and is a CFM, CIA, CMA, and Registered CPA.

Garrett W. Gleim earned his private pilot certificate in 1997 in a Piper Super Cub. He is a commercial pilot (single and multi-engine), ground instructor (advanced and instrument) and flight instructor (instrument and multi-engine), and he is a member of the Aircraft Owners and Pilots Association and the National Association of Flight Instructors. He is the author of study guides for the sport, private/recreational, instrument, commercial, flight/ground instructor, fundamentals of instructing, and airline transport pilot FAA knowledge tests. He received a Bachelor of Science in Economics from The Wharton School, University of Pennsylvania.

Gleim Publications, Inc.
P.O. Box 12848 · University Station
Gainesville, Florida 32604

(352) 375-0772
(800) 87-GLEIM or (800) 874-5346
FAX: (352) 375-6940
Internet: www.gleim.com
Email: admin@gleim.com

ISSN 1553-6890
ISBN 978-1-58194-780-9

First Printing: July 2009

This is the first printing of the 2010 edition of
Fundamentals of Instructing
FAA Knowledge Test
Please email update@gleim.com with
FOI 2010-1 in the subject or text. You will
receive our current update as a reply. Updates
are available until the next edition is published.

EXAMPLE:

To:	update@gleim.com
From:	*your email address*
Subject:	**FOI 2010-1**

HELP!!

This 2010 edition is designed specifically for pilots who aspire to obtain the flight instructor
certificate and/or ground instructor certificate. Please send any corrections and suggestions for
subsequent editions to the authors, c/o Gleim Publications, Inc. The last page in this book has been
reserved for you to make comments and suggestions. It can be torn out and mailed to Gleim
Publications, Inc.

A companion volume, *Flight/Ground Instructor FAA Knowledge Test*, is available, as is *Flight
Instructor Flight Maneuvers and Practical Test Prep*, which focuses on the FAA practical test, just as
this book focuses on the FAA knowledge test. Save time, money, and frustration--order both books
today! Call us or order online; or use the order form on page 167. Please bring these books to the
attention of flight instructors, fixed-base operators, and others with a potential interest in acquiring their
flight instructor certificates. Wide distribution of these books and increased interest in flying depend on
your assistance and good word. Thank you.

NOTE: ANSWER DISCREPANCIES and UPDATES

Our answers have been carefully researched and reviewed. Inevitably, there will be differences with
competitors' books and even the FAA. If necessary, we will develop an UPDATE for *Fundamentals of
Instructing FAA Knowledge Test*. Send an email to update@gleim.com as described above, and visit our
website for the latest updates and information on all of our products. Updates for this 2010 edition will be
available until December 31, 2010. To continue providing our customers with first-rate service, we request that
questions about our materials be sent to us via <u>mail</u>, <u>email</u>, or <u>fax</u>. The appropriate staff member will give
each question thorough consideration and a prompt response. Questions concerning orders, prices,
shipments, or payments will be handled via telephone by our competent and courteous customer service staff.

TABLE OF CONTENTS

PREFACE

This book has three purposes:

1. To provide you with the easiest and fastest means of passing the Fundamentals of Instructing (FOI) Knowledge Test

2. To help both experienced and inexperienced aviation instructors improve their instruction techniques

3. To assist flight and/or ground instructors in organizing and presenting aviation ground schools that prepare individuals to pass the FAA pilot knowledge tests

FOI Knowledge Test

Successful completion of the FOI knowledge test is required by the FAA for those seeking the flight instructor or ground instructor certificates. The Introduction of this book (beginning on the next page) contains a discussion of the requirements to obtain the flight instructor and ground instructor certificates and a description of the FOI knowledge test, how to prepare for it and take it, and how to maximize your score with minimum effort. Study Units 1 through 6 contain outlines of exactly what you need to know to answer the FAA knowledge test questions, as well as all of the actual FAA test questions, each accompanied by a comprehensive explanation.

NOTE: Appendix A contains a practice test consisting of 50 questions from this book that reflects the subject matter composition of the FAA knowledge test.

Improving Instruction Methods

The FAA has published *Aviation Instructor's Handbook* (FAA-H-8083-9A), which explains the basic principles and processes of teaching and learning. This is the subject matter of the FOI knowledge test. This material is more easily presented and studied in outline format, as it appears in Study Units 1 through 6 of this book. Both experienced and inexperienced aviation instructors will find the study of these outlines very useful in improving their instruction methods.

Appendix B of this book (48 pages in length) is a reprint of chapters 8, 9, and 10 of *Aviation Instructor's Handbook*, which specifically concern flight instruction. It is useful reading and a valuable periodic review for CFIs. It consists of three chapters:

1. Instructor Responsibilities and Professionalism
2. Techniques of Flight Instruction
3. Planning Instructional Activity

Ground School Course Suggestions

Many aviation instructors would like to increase the general public's interest in learning to fly. These instructors also enjoy teaching. Appendix C of this book consists of suggestions on how to find (or become) a sponsor for a "ground school." It also contains suggestions on course organization, lecture outlines, and class presentation.

Enjoy Flying Safely!

Irvin N. Gleim
Garrett W. Gleim
July 2009

INTRODUCTION: THE FAA PILOT KNOWLEDGE TEST

The beginning of this introduction provides an overview of the process to obtain a flight instructor certificate, including a sport pilot rating. The ground instructor certificate is also addressed. The remainder explains the content and procedure of relevant Federal Aviation Administration (FAA) tests. Becoming a Certificated Flight Instructor (CFI) and/or a Certificated Ground Instructor is fun. Begin today!

Fundamentals of Instructing FAA Knowledge Test is one of four related books for obtaining a flight and/or ground instructor certificate. The other three are *Flight/Ground Instructor FAA Knowledge Test*, which is in a format similar to this book, and *Flight Instructor Flight Maneuvers and Practical Test Prep* and *Pilot Handbook*, each in outline/illustration format.

Flight/Ground Instructor FAA Knowledge Test prepares you to pass the FAA's flight and/or ground instructor knowledge test. If you are planning to obtain both the flight and ground instructor certificates, you only need to pass the Fundamentals of Instructing (FOI) test once.

Flight Instructor Flight Maneuvers and Practical Test Prep is a comprehensive, carefully organized presentation of everything you need to know to prepare for your flight training and for your flight instructor practical (flight) test. It integrates material from over 100 FAA publications and other sources.

Pilot Handbook is a complete pilot reference book that combines over 100 FAA books and documents, including *AIM*, FARs, ACs, and much more. This book, more than any other, will help make you a better and more proficient pilot.

FAR/AIM is an essential part of every instructor's library. The Gleim *FAR/AIM* is an easy-to-read reference book containing all the regulations applicable to general aviation, plus the full text of the FAA's *Aeronautical Information Manual (AIM)*.

If you are planning on purchasing the FAA books on aviation weather, purchase the Gleim *Aviation Weather and Weather Services*, which combines all of the information from the FAA's *Aviation Weather* (AC 00-6A), *Aviation Weather Services* (AC 00-45F), and numerous FAA publications into one easy-to-understand book. It will help you study all aspects of aviation weather and provide you with a single reference book.

WHAT IS A FLIGHT INSTRUCTOR CERTIFICATE?

A flight instructor certificate is similar in appearance to your commercial pilot certificate and will allow you to give flight and ground instruction. The certificate is sent to you by the FAA upon satisfactory completion of your training program, two knowledge tests, and a practical test. It expires at the end of the 24th month after issue. A new certificate is sent to you by the FAA upon renewal. A sample flight instructor certificate is reproduced below.

REQUIREMENTS TO OBTAIN A FLIGHT INSTRUCTOR CERTIFICATE

1.   Be at least 18 years of age.

2.   Be able to read, write, and converse fluently in English (certificates with operating limitations may be available for medically related deficiencies).

3.   Hold a commercial or airline transport pilot (ATP) certificate with an aircraft rating appropriate to the flight instructor rating sought (e.g., airplane, glider).

    a.   You must also hold an instrument rating to be a flight instructor in an airplane.

4.   Use this book, *Fundamentals of Instructing FAA Knowledge Test*, *Flight Instructor Flight Maneuvers and Practical Test Prep*, *FAR/AIM*, *Aviation Weather and Weather Services*, and *Pilot Handbook* to learn

    a.   Fundamentals of instructing

    b.   All other subject areas in which ground training is required for recreational, private, and commercial pilot certificates and for an instrument rating

5.   Pass both the FOI and the flight instructor knowledge tests with scores of 70% or better.

    a.   All FAA knowledge tests are administered at FAA-designated computer testing centers.

        1)   See page 9 for an expanded discussion.

    b.   The FOI and flight instructor tests consist of 50 and 100 multiple-choice questions, respectively, selected from the airplane-related questions among the questions in the FAA's flight and ground instructor knowledge test bank.

    c.   Each of the FAA's airplane-related questions is reproduced in this book with complete explanations to the right of each question.

    d.   You are not required to take the FOI knowledge test if you

        1)   Hold an FAA flight or ground instructor certificate,

        2)   Hold a current teacher's certificate authorizing you to teach at an educational level of the 7th grade or higher, or

        3)   Are employed as a teacher at an accredited college or university.

6.   Demonstrate flight proficiency (FAR 61.187).

    a.   You must receive and log flight and ground training and obtain a logbook endorsement from an authorized instructor on the following areas of operations for an airplane category rating with a single-engine or multiengine class rating:

        1)   *Fundamentals of instructing*
        2)   *Technical subject areas*
        3)   *Preflight preparation*
        4)   *Preflight lesson on a maneuver to be performed in flight*
        5)   *Preflight procedures*
        6)   *Airport and seaplane base operations*
        7)   *Takeoffs, landings, and go-arounds*
        8)   *Fundamentals of flight*
        9)   *Performance maneuvers*
        10)   *Ground reference maneuvers*
        11)   *Slow flight, stalls, and spins (single-engine only)*

            a)   *Slow flight and stalls (multiengine only)*

        12)   *Basic instrument maneuvers*
        13)   *Emergency operations*
        14)   *Multiengine operations (multiengine only)*
        15)   *Postflight procedures*

    b.   A CFI who provides training to an initial applicant for a flight instructor certificate must have held a flight instructor certificate for at least 24 months and have given at least 200 hr. of flight training as a CFI.

    c.   You must also obtain a logbook endorsement by an appropriately certificated and rated flight instructor who has provided you with spin entry, spin, and spin recovery training in an airplane that is certificated for spins and who has found you instructionally competent and proficient in those training areas, i.e., so you can teach spin recovery.

7.   Alternatively, enroll in an FAA-certificated pilot school that has an approved flight instructor certification course (airplane).

    a.   These are known as Part 141 schools or Part 142 training centers because they are authorized by Part 141 or Part 142 of the FARs.

        1)   All other regulations concerning the certification of pilots are found in Part 61 of the FARs.

    b.   The Part 141 course must consist of at least 40 hr. of ground instruction and 25 hr. of flight instructor training.

8.   Successfully complete a practical (flight) test which will be given as a final exam by an FAA inspector or designated pilot examiner. The practical test will be conducted as specified in the FAA's Flight Instructor Practical Test Standards (FAA-S-8081-6C, with Change 1, effective November 1, 2006).

    a.   FAA inspectors are FAA employees and do not charge for their services.

    b.   FAA-designated pilot examiners are proficient, experienced flight instructors and pilots who are authorized by the FAA to conduct flight tests. They do charge a fee.

    c.   The FAA's Flight Instructor Practical Test Standards are outlined and reprinted in the Gleim *Flight Instructor Flight Maneuvers and Practical Test Prep.*

REQUIREMENTS TO OBTAIN A GROUND INSTRUCTOR CERTIFICATE

1. To be eligible for a ground instructor certificate, you must

    a. Be at least 18 years of age.

    b. Be able to read, write, and converse fluently in English (certificates with operating limitations may be available for medically related deficiencies).

    c. Exhibit practical and theoretical knowledge by passing the FOI and the appropriate ground instructor knowledge tests.

        1) See item 5.d. on page 3 for information on when the FOI knowledge test is not required.

2. Ground instructor certificates cover three levels of certification:

    a. Basic ground instructor (BGI) may provide

        1) Ground training in the aeronautical knowledge areas required for a sport, recreational, or private pilot certificate

        2) Ground training required for a sport, recreational, or private pilot flight review

        3) A recommendation for the sport, recreational, or private pilot knowledge test

    b. Advanced ground instructor (AGI) may provide

        1) Ground training in the aeronautical knowledge areas required for any certificate or rating issued under Part 61

        2) Ground training required for any flight review

        3) A recommendation for a knowledge test required for any certificate issued under Part 61

    c. Instrument ground instructor (IGI) may provide

        1) Ground training in the aeronautical knowledge areas required for an instrument rating to a pilot or instructor certificate

        2) Ground training required for an instrument proficiency check

        3) A recommendation for the instrument rating knowledge test for a pilot or instructor certificate

    NOTE: See the Gleim *Instrument Pilot FAA Knowledge Test*, which covers the IGI knowledge test. The test consists of 50 questions with a 2.5-hr. time limit.

3. If you are not a CFI, the FARs require you to have a ground instructor certificate to teach ground school or to sign off applicants for the appropriate pilot knowledge test.

Your BGI or AGI knowledge test may have a few non-airplane questions. We have excluded all non-airplane questions from this book. Take your best guess at these questions without worry. It is not worth the few points to study all of the extra questions unless you are going to teach subjects related to rotorcraft, gliders, or lighter-than-air aircraft. Recall that this book has its primary focus on flight instructor -- airplane, and that is why non-airplane questions are excluded.

REQUIREMENTS TO OBTAIN A FLIGHT INSTRUCTOR CERTIFICATE WITH A SPORT PILOT RATING

1. To obtain a flight instructor certificate with a sport pilot rating, you must pass both practical and knowledge tests.

    a. To take the knowledge tests for both the fundamentals of instructing and the aeronautical knowledge areas for a sport pilot certificate, you must receive a logbook endorsement from an authorized instructor who trained you or evaluated your home-study course on the materials. This certifies that you are prepared for the tests.

2. For your convenience, a standard authorization form for the flight instructor sport pilot rating knowledge test is reproduced on page 157. It can be easily completed, signed by a flight or ground instructor, torn out, and taken to the computer testing site.

FAA PILOT KNOWLEDGE TEST

This test book is designed to help you prepare for and successfully take the FAA FOI knowledge test for the flight and/or ground instructor certificate. The remainder of this introduction explains the FAA test procedures.

Follow the suggestions given throughout this introduction and you will have no trouble passing the test the first time you take it.

FORMAT OF THE FAA PILOT KNOWLEDGE TEST

1. The FAA's fundamentals of instructing knowledge test consists of 50 multiple-choice questions.

2. All of the questions in the FAA's flight and ground instructor knowledge test question bank that are applicable to fundamentals of instructing have been grouped into the following 6 categories, which are the titles of Study Units 1 through 6:

   Study Unit 1 -- The Learning Process
   Study Unit 2 -- Barriers to Learning
   Study Unit 3 -- Human Behavior and Effective Communication
   Study Unit 4 -- Teaching Methods
   Study Unit 5 -- Planning Instructional Activity
   Study Unit 6 -- Critique and Evaluation

3. All of the FAA figures are contained in a book titled *Computer Testing Supplement for Flight and Ground Instructor*, which you will be given for your use at the time of your test.

   a. Only one FAA figure is used for the FOI knowledge test, and it is reproduced on page 71.

FAA PRETEST QUESTIONS

1. In an effort to develop better test questions, the FAA frequently **pretests** questions on pilot knowledge tests by adding up to 5 "pretest" questions.

   a. The pretest questions will not be graded.
   b. You will NOT know which questions are "real" and which are "pretest," so you must attempt to answer all questions correctly.

2. When you notice a question NOT covered by Gleim, it is probably a "pretest question."

   a. We want to know about each pretest question you see.

      1) Please call (800 874-5346), email (aviation@gleim.com), or FAX (888-375-6940) with your recollection of any pretest questions so we may improve our efforts to prepare future instructors.

FAA QUESTIONS WITH TYPOGRAPHICAL ERRORS

Occasionally, FAA test questions contain typographical errors such that there is no correct answer. The FAA test development process involves many steps and people and, as you would expect, glitches occur in the system that are beyond the control of any one person. We indicate "best" rather than correct answers for some questions. Use these best answers for the indicated questions.

Note that the FAA corrects (rewrites) defective questions as they are discovered; these changes are explained in our updates--see page iv. However, problems due to faulty or out-of-date figures printed in the FAA Computer Testing Supplements are expensive to correct. Thus, it is important to carefully study questions that are noted to have a best answer in this book. Even though the best answer may not be completely correct, you should select it when taking your test.

REORGANIZATION OF FAA QUESTIONS

1.   In the official FAA knowledge test question bank that contains all of the flight, ground, and fundamentals of instructing questions, the FAA questions are **not** grouped together by topic, i.e., they appear to be presented randomly.

   a.   We have reorganized and renumbered the FAA questions into study units.

2.   Pages 153 and 154 contain a list of all the FAA questions in FAA learning statement code order, with cross-references to the study units and question numbers in this book.

   a.   For example, we have coded question number 12 in Study Unit 3 as PLT204 and 3-12.

      1)   The "PLT204" is the Learning Statement Code that corresponds to the learning statement "*Recall effective communication - basic elements.*"

      2)   The "3-12" means it can be found in Study Unit 3 as question 12.

   b.   Questions relating to helicopters, gliders, balloons, etc., are excluded.

HOW TO PREPARE FOR THE FAA PILOT KNOWLEDGE TEST

1.   Begin by carefully reading the rest of this introduction. You need to have a complete understanding of the examination process prior to initiating your study. This knowledge will make your studying more efficient.

2.   After you have spent an hour analyzing this introduction, set up a study schedule, including a target date for taking your pilot knowledge test.

   a.   Do not let the study process drag on because it will be discouraging, i.e., the quicker the better.

   b.   Consider enrolling in an organized ground school course at your local FBO, community college, etc.

   c.   Determine where and when you are going to take your pilot knowledge test.

3.   Work through each of Study Units 1 through 6.

   a.   All of the questions in the FAA's flight and ground instructor knowledge test question bank that are applicable to fundamentals of instructing have been grouped into the following 6 categories, which are the titles of Study Units 1 through 6:

      Study Unit 1 -- The Learning Process
      Study Unit 2 -- Barriers to Learning
      Study Unit 3 -- Human Behavior and Effective Communication
      Study Unit 4 -- Teaching Methods
      Study Unit 5 -- Planning Instructional Activity
      Study Unit 6 -- Critique and Evaluation

   b.   Within each of the study units listed, questions relating to the same subtopic are grouped together to facilitate your study program. Each subtopic is called a subunit.

   c.   To the right of each question are

      1)   The correct answer

      2)   A reference for the answer explanation (e.g., *AIH Chap I* means *Aviation Instructor's Handbook*, Chapter I)

      3)   A comprehensive answer explanation, including

         a)   A discussion of the correct answer or concept
         b)   An explanation of why the other two answer choices are incorrect

4. Each study unit begins with a list of its subunit titles. The number after each title is the number of FAA questions that cover the information in that subunit. The two numbers following the number of questions are the page numbers on which the outline and the questions for that particular subunit begin, respectively.

5. Begin by studying the outlines slowly and carefully. The outlines in this part of the book are very brief and have only one purpose: to help you pass the FAA knowledge test for the flight and/or ground instructor certificate.

    a. **CAUTION:** The **sole purpose** of this book is to expedite your passing the fundamentals of instructing FAA knowledge test. Accordingly, all extraneous material (i.e., not directly tested on the FAA knowledge test) is omitted even though much more information and knowledge are necessary to be a proficient flight or ground instructor. This additional material is presented in three related Gleim books: *Flight/Ground Instructor FAA Knowledge Test*, *Flight Instructor Flight Maneuvers and Practical Test Prep*, and *Pilot Handbook*.

6. Next, answer the multiple-choice questions under exam conditions. Cover the answer explanations on the right side of each page with the Gleim bookmark provided at the back of this book while you answer the multiple-choice questions.

    a. Remember, it is very important to the learning (and understanding) process that you honestly commit yourself to an answer. If you are wrong, your memory will be reinforced by having discovered your error. Therefore, it is crucial to cover up the answer and make an honest attempt to answer the question before reading the answer.

    b. Study the answer explanation for each question that you answer incorrectly, do not understand, or have difficulty with.

    c. Use our *FAA Test Prep* Software Download to ensure that you do not refer to answers before committing to one AND to simulate actual computer testing center exam conditions.

    d. Go to www.gleim.com to view our FOI Online Ground School. It is a structured course to assist those who have trouble sitting down to books and software.

7. Note that this test book (in contrast to most other question and answer books) contains the FAA questions grouped by topic. Thus, some questions may appear repetitive, while others may be duplicates or near-duplicates. Accordingly, do not work question after question (i.e., waste time and effort) if you are already conversant with a topic and the type of questions asked.

8. As you move from subunit to subunit and study unit to study unit, you may need further explanation or clarification of certain topics. You may wish to obtain and use the following Gleim books described on page 1:

    a. *Flight Instructor Flight Maneuvers and Practical Test Prep*
    b. *Pilot Handbook*
    c. *Aviation Weather and Weather Services*

9. Keep track of your work!!! As you complete each subunit in Study Units 1 through 6, grade yourself with an A, B, C, or ? (use a ? if you need help on the subject) next to the subunit title at the front of the respective study unit.

    a. The A, B, C, or ? is your self-evaluation of your comprehension of the material in that subunit and your ability to answer the questions.

        A　means a good understanding.
        B　means a fair understanding.
        C　means a shaky understanding.
        ?　means to ask your CFI or others about the material and/or questions, and read the pertinent sections in *Flight Instructor Flight Maneuvers and Practical Test Prep* and/or *Pilot Handbook*.

b.   This procedure will provide you with the ability to quickly see (by looking at the first page of Study Units 1 through 6) how much studying you have done (and how much remains) and how well you have done.

c.   This procedure will also facilitate review. You can spend more time on the subunits that were more difficult.

d.   *FAA Test Prep* Software Download and Test Prep for Windows Mobile provides you with your historical performance data.

With this overview of exam requirements, you are ready to begin the easy-to-study outlines and rearranged questions with answers to build your knowledge and confidence and PASS THE FAA's FUNDAMENTALS OF INSTRUCTING KNOWLEDGE TEST.

The feedback we receive from users indicates that our books and software reduce anxiety, improve FAA test scores, and build knowledge. Studying for each test becomes a useful step toward advanced certificates and ratings. If you are taking the BGI knowledge test, answer only 80 questions.

SIMULATED FAA PRACTICE TEST

Appendix A, Fundamentals of Instructing Practice Test, beginning on page 91, allows you to practice taking the FAA knowledge test without the answers next to the questions. This test has 50 questions that have been randomly selected from the airplane-related questions in the FAA's flight and ground instructor knowledge test question bank. Topical coverage in this practice test is similar to that of the FAA fundamentals of instructing test.

It is very important that you answer all 50 questions at one sitting. You should not consult the answers, especially when being referred to figures (charts, tables, etc.) throughout this book where the questions are answered and explained. Analyze your performance based on the answer key which follows the practice test.

Also rely on the Gleim *FAA Test Prep* Software Download to simulate actual computer testing conditions, including the screen layouts, instructions, etc., for CATS and LaserGrade.

For more information on the Gleim *FAA Test Prep* Software Download, see page 14.

PART 141 SCHOOLS WITH FAA PILOT KNOWLEDGE TEST EXAMINING AUTHORITY

The FAA permits some FAR Part 141 schools to develop, administer, and grade their own knowledge tests as long as they use questions from the FAA test bank, i.e., the same questions as in this book. The FAA does not provide the correct answers to the Part 141 schools, and the FAA only reviews the Part 141 school test question selection sheets. Thus, some of the answers used by Part 141 test examiners may not agree with the FAA or with those in this book. The latter is not a problem but may explain why you may miss a question on a Part 141 pilot knowledge test using an answer presented in this book.

AUTHORIZATION TO TAKE THE FAA PILOT KNOWLEDGE TEST

The FAA does not require an instructor endorsement for the FOI or any other instructor knowledge test, except for sport pilot instructor applicants.

WHEN TO TAKE THE FAA PILOT KNOWLEDGE TEST

1.   You must be at least 16 years of age to take the FOI knowledge test.
2.   Take the FAA knowledge test within 30 days.
     a.   Get the test behind you.
3.   You must obtain your flight or ground instructor certificate within 24 months.
     a.   Otherwise, you will have to retake your FOI knowledge test.

WHAT TO TAKE TO THE FAA PILOT KNOWLEDGE TEST

1.   Picture identification of yourself
2.   Proof of age

COMPUTER TESTING CENTERS

The FAA has contracted with several computer testing services to administer FAA knowledge tests. Each of these computer testing services has testing centers throughout the country. You register by calling an 800 number. Call the following testing services for information regarding a location most convenient to you, cost to take the flight instructor (airplane) and/or ground instructor knowledge test, and to confirm the amount of time allowed for the test.

CATS	(800) 947-4228
LASERGRADE	(800) 211-2754

Also, about twenty Part 141 schools use the AvTEST computer testing system, which is very similar to the computer testing services described above.

COMPUTER TESTING PROCEDURES

To register for the pilot knowledge test, you should call one of the computer testing services listed in Computer Testing Centers above, or you may call one of their testing centers. Web links with information about these testing centers and their telephone numbers can be found in the Gleim *FAA Test Prep* Software Download under Test Vendors in the Help menu on the main menu. When you register, you will pay the fee with a credit card.

When you arrive at the testing center, you will be required to provide positive proof of identification and documentary evidence of your age. The identification presented must include your photograph, signature, and actual residential address if different from the mailing address. This information may be presented in more than one form of identification. Next, you will sign in on the testing center's daily log. Your signature on the logsheet certifies that, if this is a retest, you meet the applicable requirements (see "Failure on the FAA Pilot Knowledge Test" on page 11) and that you have not passed this test in the past 2 years.

Next, you will be taken into the testing room and seated at a computer terminal. A person from the testing center will assist you in logging onto the system, and you will be asked to confirm your personal data (e.g., name, Social Security number, etc.). Then you will be prompted and given an online introduction to the computer testing system, and you will take a sample test. If you have used our *FAA Test Prep* Software Download, you will be conversant with the computer testing methodology and environment, and you will breeze through the sample test and begin the actual test soon after. You will be allowed 1.5 hr. to complete the actual test, which equates to 1.8 minutes per question. Confirm the time permitted when you call the testing center to register. When you have completed your test, an Airman Computer Test Report will be printed out, validated (usually with an embossed seal), and given to you by a person from the testing center. Before you leave, you will be required to sign out on the testing center's daily log.

Each testing center has certain idiosyncrasies in its paperwork, scheduling, telephone procedures, as well as in its software. It is for this reason that our *FAA Test Prep* Software Download emulates each of these FAA-approved computer testing companies.

YOUR FAA PILOT KNOWLEDGE TEST REPORT

1. You will receive your Airman Computer Test Report upon completion of the test. An example computer test report is reproduced on the next page.

    a. Note that you will receive only one grade, as illustrated.

    b. The expiration date is the date by which you must take your FAA practical test.

    c. The report lists the FAA learning statement codes of the questions you missed, so you can review the topics you missed prior to your practical test.

2. The following FAA learning statement codes will appear on your test report to identify the topics from the FAA's *Aviation Instructor's Handbook* (FAA-H-8083-9A) with which you had difficulty.

PLT204 Recall effective communication - basic elements
PLT227 Recall FOI techniques - integrated flight instruction
PLT228 Recall FOI techniques - lesson plans
PLT229 Recall FOI techniques - professionalism
PLT230 Recall FOI techniques - responsibilities
PLT231 Recall FOI techniques / human behavior - anxiety / fear / stress
PLT232 Recall FOI techniques / human behavior - dangerous tendencies
PLT233 Recall FOI techniques / human behavior - defense mechanisms
PLT270 Recall human behavior - social / self fulfillment / physical
PLT295 Recall instructor techniques - obstacles / planning / activities / outcome
PLT306 Recall learning process - levels of learning / transfer of learning / incidental learning

PLT307 Recall learning process - memory / fact / recall
PLT308 Recall learning process - principles of learning elements
PLT481 Recall student evaluation - learning process
PLT482 Recall student evaluation - written tests / oral quiz / critiques
PLT487 Recall teaching methods - demonstration / performance
PLT488 Recall teaching methods - group / guided discussion / lecture
PLT489 Recall teaching methods - known to unknown
PLT490 Recall teaching methods - motivation / student feelings of insecurity
PLT491 Recall teaching methods - organizing material / course of training
PLT504 Recall use of training aids - types / function / purpose
PLT505 Recall use of training aids - usefulness / simplicity / compatibility

a. Look them over and review them with your CFI so (s)he can certify that (s)he reviewed the deficient areas and found you competent in them when you take your flight instructor practical test.

3. Keep your Airman Computer Test Report in a safe place because you must submit it to the FAA inspector/examiner when you take your flight instructor practical test.

Federal Aviation Administration
Airman Computer Test Report

EXAM TITLE: Fundamentals of Instructing

NAME: Jones David John

ID NUMBER: 123456789   TAKE: 1

DATE: 07/14/10   SCORE: 82   GRADE: Pass

....

Knowledge area codes in which questions were answered incorrectly. See appropriate knowledge test guide. A code may represent more than one incorrect response.

PLT295   PLT481   PLT504

EXPIRATION DATE: 07/31/12

DO NOT LOSE THIS REPORT

....

Authorized instructor's statement (if applicable).

I have given Mr./Ms. _____ additional instuction in each subject area shown to be deficient and consider the applicant competent to pass the test.

Last _____ Initial _____ Cert. No. _____ Type _____
(Print Clearly)

Signature_____

CTD's Embossed Seal

APPLYING FOR YOUR GROUND INSTRUCTOR CERTIFICATE

Flight instructor applicants will take their Airman Computer Test Reports to their FAA practical tests. A ground instructor applicant (BGI, AGI, or IGI) does not, however, have to take an FAA practical test.

You must take your Airman Computer Test Report and a completed Airman Certificate and/or Rating Application (FAA Form 8710-1) to your local FSDO where you will be issued an appropriate temporary ground instructor certificate. An FAA-designated examiner cannot issue a ground instructor certificate. Also, on FAA Form 8710-1, the Instructor's Recommendation block does not require an instructor's signature.

Your permanent ground instructor certificate will be mailed to you from the FAA in Oklahoma City, OK.

FAILURE ON THE FAA PILOT KNOWLEDGE TEST

1. If you fail (score less than 70%) the pilot knowledge test (which is virtually impossible if you follow the Gleim system), you may retake it after your flight or ground instructor endorses the bottom of your Airman Computer Test Report certifying that you have received the necessary ground training to retake the test.

2. Upon retaking the test, you will find that the procedure is the same except that you must also submit your Airman Computer Test Report indicating the previous failure to the examiner.

3. Note that the pass rate on the FOI written test is about 90%, i.e., 1 out of 10 fail the test initially. Reasons for failure include

    a. Failure to study the material tested (contained in the outlines at the beginning of Study Units 1 through 6 of this book);

    b. Failure to practice working the FAA exam questions under test conditions (all of the FAA questions on airplanes appear in Study Units 1 through 6 of this book); and

    c. Poor examination technique, such as misreading questions and not understanding the requirements.

GLEIM ONLINE GROUND SCHOOL

1. Gleim Online Ground School (OGS) course content is based on the Gleim Knowledge Test books, *FAA Test Prep*, FAA publications, and Gleim reference books. The delivery system is modeled on the Gleim FAA-approved online *Flight Instructor Refresher Course.*

    a. Online Ground School courses are available for

        1) Private Pilot
        2) Sport Pilot
        3) CFI/CGI
        4) FOI
        5) Instrument Pilot
        6) Commercial Pilot
        7) ATP
        8) Flight Engineer
        9) Canadian Certificate Conversion

    b. OGS courses are airplane-only and have lessons that correspond to the study units in the Gleim FAA Knowledge Test books.

    c. Each course contains study outlines that automatically reference current FAA publications, the appropriate knowledge test questions, FAA figures, and Gleim answer explanations.

    d. OGS is always up to date.

    e. Users achieve very high knowledge test scores. In fact, if you complete the course satisfactorily, we guarantee that you will PASS!

    f. **Gleim *Online Ground School* is the most flexible course available!** Access your OGS personal classroom from any computer with Internet access--24 hours a day, seven days a week. Your virtual classroom is never closed!

Number	Study Unit	Status	Score	Time Started	Time Completed	Outline	Action
1	The Learning Process	Not Started	N/A	N/A	N/A		Start
2	Barriers to Learning	Not Started	N/A	N/A	N/A		Start
3	Human Behavior and Effective Communication	Not Started	N/A	N/A	N/A		Start
4	Teaching Methods	Not Started	N/A	N/A	N/A		Start
5	Planning Instructional Activity	Not Started	N/A	N/A	N/A		Start
6	Critique and Evaluation	Not Started	N/A	N/A	N/A		Start
	End-of-Course Test	Not Started	N/A	N/A	N/A	N/A	
	Practice Test 1	Not Started	N/A	N/A	N/A	N/A	
	Practice Test 2	Not Started	N/A	N/A	N/A	N/A	
	Practice Test 3	Not Started	N/A	N/A	N/A	N/A	
	Practice Test 4	Not Started	N/A	N/A	N/A	N/A	
	Practice Test 5	Not Started	N/A	N/A	N/A	N/A	

g. **Save time and study only the material you need to know!** the Gleim Online Ground School Certificate Selection will provide you with a customized study plan. You save time because unnecessary questions will be automatically eliminated.

h. **We are truly interactive. We help you focus on any weaker areas.** Answer explanations for wrong choices help you learn from your mistakes.

Register for Gleim *Online Ground School* today: www.gleim.com/OGS

GLEIM *FAA TEST PREP* SOFTWARE DOWNLOAD/TEST PREP FOR WINDOWS MOBILE

Computer testing is consistent with modern aviation's use of computers (e.g., DUATS, flight simulators, computerized cockpits, etc.). All FAA knowledge tests are administered by computer.

Computer testing is natural after computer study. Computer-assisted instruction is a very efficient and effective method of study. Gleim *FAA Test Prep* Software Download is designed to prepare you for computer testing because our software can simulate both CATS and LaserGrade. We make you comfortable with computer testing!

FAA Test Prep Software Download contains all of the questions in this book, context-sensitive outline material, and on-screen charts and figures. It allows you to choose either Study Mode or Test Mode.

In Study Mode, the software provides you with an explanation of each answer you choose (correct or incorrect). You design each study session:

Topic(s) and/or FAA learning statement codes you wish to cover	Questions marked and/or missed from last session -- test, study, or both
Number of questions	Questions marked and/or missed from all sessions -- test, study, or both
Order of questions -- FAA, Gleim, or random	
Order of answers to each question -- Gleim or random	Questions never seen, answered, or answered correctly

In Test Mode, you decide the simulation -- CATS, LaserGrade, or Gleim. When you finish your test, you can study the questions missed and access answer explanations. The software emulates the operation of FAA-approved computer testing companies. Thus, you have a complete understanding of how to take an FAA knowledge test and know exactly what to expect before you go to a computer testing center.

Study Sessions and Test Sessions

Study Sessions give you immediate feedback on why your answer selection for a particular FAA question is correct or incorrect and allow you to access the context-sensitive outline material that helps to explain concepts related to the question. Choose from several different question sources: all questions available for that library; questions from a certain topic (study units and subunits from Gleim books); questions that you missed or marked in the last sessions you created; questions that you have never seen, answered, or answered correctly; questions from certain FAA learning statement codes, etc. You can mix up the questions by selecting to randomize the question and/or answer order so that you do not memorize answer letters.

You may then grade your study sessions and track your study progress using the performance analysis charts and graphs. The Performance Analysis information helps you to focus on areas where you need the most improvement, saving you time in the overall study process. You may then want to go back and study questions that you missed in a previous session, or you may want to create a study session of questions that you marked in the previous session, and all of these options are made easy with *FAA Test Prep*'s Study Sessions.

After studying the outlines and questions in a Study Session, you can switch to a Test Session. In a Test Session, you will not know which questions you have answered correctly until the session is graded. You can further test your skills with a Standard Test Session, which gives you the option of taking your pilot knowledge test under actual testing conditions using one of the simulations of the major testing centers.

Recommended Study Program

1. Start with Study Unit 1 and proceed through study units in chronological order. Follow the 3-step process below.

   a. First, carefully study the Gleim Outline.

   b. Second, create a study session of all questions in the study unit. Answer and study all questions in the study session.

   c. Third, create a test session of all questions in the study unit. Answer all questions in the test session.

2. After each study session and after each test session, create a new study (review/feedback) session from questions answered incorrectly. This is of critical importance to allow you to learn from your mistakes.

Example Question Screen

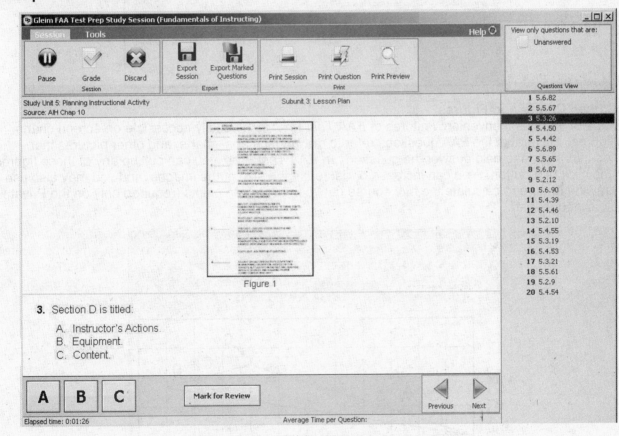

Practice Test

Take an exam in the actual testing environment of either of the major testing centers: CATS or LaserGrade. *FAA Test Prep* Software Download simulates the testing formats of these testing centers, making it easy for you to study FAA questions under actual exam conditions. After studying with *FAA Test Prep* Software Download, you will know exactly what to expect when you go in to take your pilot knowledge test.

On-Screen Charts and Figures

One of the most convenient features of *FAA Test Prep* is the easily accessible on-screen charts and figures. Several of the FAA questions refer to drawings, maps, charts, and other pictures that provide information to help answer the question. In *FAA Test Prep*, you can pull up any of these figures with the click of a button. You can increase or decrease the size of the images, and you may also use our drawing feature to calculate the true course between two given points (required only on the Private Pilot knowledge test).

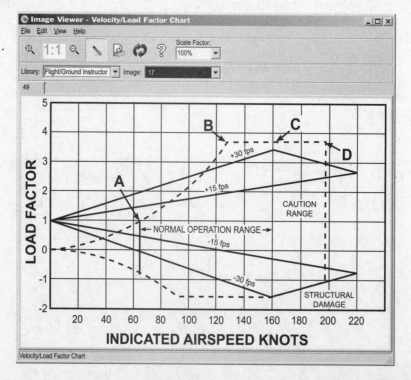

Instructor Print Options

FAA Test Prep Software Download is also a useful tool for instructors who want to create quizzes and assignments for their students. An instructor may mark questions in a session and then choose to print marked questions to create a quiz or test. (S)he may select to print a correct answer sheet, a blank answer sheet, and a renumbered printout of questions marked and any instructions that go along with the quiz or test.

Order *FAA Test Prep* today.
(800) 874-5346
gleim.com

FAA Test Prep Software Download also contains a link to a listing by state of all major testing center locations for CATS and LaserGrade, as well as instructor sign-off forms needed to take the FAA knowledge tests (if required). The Gleim *FAA Test Prep* Software Download is an all-in-one program designed to help anyone with a computer, Internet access, and an interest in flying to pass the pilot knowledge tests.

FREE UPDATES AND TECHNICAL SUPPORT

Gleim offers FREE technical support to all registered users of the current version. Call (800) 874-5346, send email to support@gleim.com, or fill out the technical support request form online (www.gleim.com/support/form.php). The Gleim new Online Updates feature makes updating your *FAA Test Prep* Software Download and test banks easy. Simply connect to the Internet, start the Gleim software, and select Online Updates from the Test Prep Tools screen. For more information on our update service for books by email, turn to page iv.

STUDY UNIT ONE
THE LEARNING PROCESS

(5 pages of outline)

1.1 CHARACTERISTICS OF LEARNING

1. Learning can be defined as a change in behavior as a result of experience.

   a. The behavior change can be physical and overt (a better glide path, for instance), or psychological and attitudinal (better motivation, more acute perceptions, insights).

2. The learning process may include any (or all) of the following elements: verbal, conceptual, perceptual, motor skills, emotional, and problem solving.

3. While learning the subject at hand, the student may be learning other useful things as well. This learning is called incidental and can have a significant impact on the student's total development.

1.2 THE PRINCIPLES OF LEARNING

1. Educational psychology professor Edward L. Thorndike has suggested several "principles of learning" that apply to the learning process. While these principles are not absolute, they do give important insight into effective teaching.

2. The **principle of readiness** states that if a student is ready to learn, and has a strong purpose, clear objective, and well-fixed reason for learning, (s)he will make more progress than if (s)he lacks motivation. Readiness implies single-mindedness.

3. The **principle of exercise** states that those things most often repeated are best remembered or performed.

   a. The basis of the principle is to provide opportunities for a student to practice and then direct this process towards a goal.

4. The **principle of effect** relates to the emotional reaction of the learner:

   a. Learning is strengthened when accompanied by a pleasant or satisfying feeling.
   b. Learning is weakened when associated with an unpleasant feeling.

5. The **principle of primacy** states that those things learned first often create a strong, almost unshakable impression.

   a. This principle means that bad habits learned early are hard to break. Instructors must thus insist on correct performance from the outset of maneuvers.

6. The **principle of intensity** states that a vivid, dramatic, or exciting experience teaches more than a routine or boring experience.

   a. The principle of intensity thus implies that a student will learn more from the real thing than from a substitute.

7.   The **principle of recency** states that the things most recently learned are best remembered.

    a.   Instructors recognize the principle of recency when they determine the sequence of lectures within a course of instruction.

1.3 PERCEPTION AND INSIGHT

1.   Perceiving involves more than the reception of stimuli from the five senses. Perceptions result when the person gives meaning to sensations being experienced.

    a.   Thus, perceptions are the basis of all learning.

2.   It takes time and opportunity to perceive.

    a.   A properly planned training syllabus allows sufficient time and opportunity for key perceptions to occur.

3.   A person's basic need is to maintain, enhance, preserve, and perpetuate the organized self.

    a.   Thus, all perceptions are affected by this basic need.

4.   Self-concept, or self-image, has a great influence on the total perceptual process.

5.   Fear or the element of threat narrows the student's perceptual field.

    a.   The resulting anxiety may limit a person's ability to learn from perceptions.

6.   Insight occurs when associated perceptions are grouped into meaningful wholes, i.e., when one "gets the whole picture."

    a.   Evoking insights is the instructor's major responsibility.

    b.   Instruction speeds the learning process by teaching the relationship of perceptions as they occur, thus promoting the development of insights by students.

    c.   An instructor can help develop student insights by providing a secure and nonthreatening environment in which to learn.

1.4 MEMORY

1.   Memory is an integral part of the learning process. It includes three parts: the sensory register, the short-term or working memory, and the long-term memory.

    a.   The **sensory register** receives input from the environment and quickly processes it according to the individual's preconceived concept of what is important. This occurs on a subconscious level.

        1)   **Precoding** is the selective process by which the sensory register recognizes certain stimuli and immediately transmits them to the working memory for action.

            a)   Irrelevant stimuli are discarded by the sensory register.

    b.   The **short-term memory** (or working memory) is the receptacle of the information deemed important by the sensory register.

        1)   The information may temporarily remain in the short-term memory, or it may rapidly fade.

            a)   Retention of information by the short-term memory is aided when the information is initially categorized into systematic chunks in a process known as **coding**.

            b)   Retention is also aided by repetition or rehearsal of the information (rote learning).

2)   Information remains in the short-term memory for longer periods when it can be related to an individual's previous knowledge or experiences through a process known as recoding.

    a)   **Recoding** may be described as a process of relating incoming information to concepts or knowledge already in memory.

    b)   Methods of recoding vary with the subject matter, but they typically involve some type of association, such as rhymes or mnemonics.

       i)   The use of associations such as rhymes and mnemonics is best suited to the short-term memory.

  c.   The **long-term memory** is where information is stored for future use.

    1)   For the stored information to be useful, some special effort must have been expended during the recoding process.

1.5 FORGETTING AND RETENTION

1.   The following are three theories of forgetting:

  a.   The **theory of disuse** states that a person forgets those things that are not used. Students are saddened by the small amount of actual data retained several years after graduation.

  b.   The **theory of interference** holds that people forget because new experiences overshadow the original learning experience. In other words, new or similar subsequent events can displace facts learned previously.

  c.   The **theory of repression** states that some forgetting is due to the submerging of ideas or thoughts into the subconscious mind. Unpleasant or anxiety-producing material is forgotten by the individual, although not intentionally. This is a subconscious and protective response.

2.   Responses that produce a pleasurable return are called praise.

  a.   Praise stimulates remembering because responses that give a pleasurable return tend to be repeated.

1.6 TRANSFER OF LEARNING

1.   The student may be either aided or hindered by things learned previously. This process is called transfer of learning.

  a.   Positive transfer occurs when the learning of one maneuver aids in learning another.

    1)   EXAMPLE: Flying rectangular patterns to aid in flying traffic patterns.

  b.   Negative transfer occurs when a performance of a maneuver interferes with the learning of another maneuver.

    1)   EXAMPLE: Trying to steer a taxiing plane with the control yoke as one drives a car.

    2)   Negative transfer thus agrees with the interference theory of forgetting.

2.   By making certain the student understands that what is learned can be applied to other situations, the instructor helps facilitate a positive transfer of learning.

  a.   This is the basic reason for the building-block technique of instruction in which each simple task is performed acceptably and correctly before the next learning task is introduced.

  b.   The introduction of instruction in more advanced and complex operations before the initial instruction has been mastered leads to the development of poor habit patterns in the elements of performance.

1.7 LEVELS OF LEARNING

1.   Learning may be accomplished at any of four levels.

  a.   The lowest level, **rote learning**, is the ability to repeat back what one has been taught without necessarily understanding or being able to apply what has been learned.

  1)   EXAMPLE: Being able to cite the maneuvering speed of an airplane.

  b.   At the **understanding** level, the student not only can repeat what has been taught but also comprehends the principles and theory behind the knowledge.

  1)   EXAMPLE: Being able to explain how gross weight affects maneuvering speed.
  2)   Being able to explain (not demonstrate) is the understanding level.

  c.   At the **application** level, the student not only understands the theory but also can apply what has been learned and perform in accordance with that knowledge.

  1)   This is the level of learning at which most instructors stop teaching.

  d.   At the **correlation** level, the student is able to associate various learned elements with other segments or blocks of learning or accomplishment.

  1)   EXAMPLE: Know what to do if, during the flight portion of the practical test, the examiner closes the throttle and announces "simulated engine failure."

1.8 DOMAINS OF LEARNING

1.   In addition to the four basic levels of learning discussed above, learning can be categorized in other ways.

2.   Three **domains of learning** have been identified based on what is learned:

  a.   The **cognitive domain** deals with knowledge (e.g., facts, concepts, or relationships).
  b.   The **affective domain** relates to attitudes, beliefs, and values.
  c.   The **psychomotor domain** concerns physical skills.

3.   Each of the domains of learning has a hierarchy of educational objectives.

  a.   A listing of the hierarchy of objectives is often referred to as a taxonomy.

  1)   A **taxonomy of educational objectives** is a systematic classification scheme for sorting possible learning outcomes into the three domains of learning and ranking them in a developmental hierarchy from least complex to most complex.

  a)   Each of the three domains of learning has several distinct learning outcomes. These outcomes are equivalent to the educational objective levels.

  2)   The following are hierarchical taxonomies for the three domains of learning:

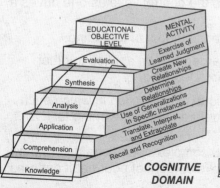

COGNITIVE DOMAIN

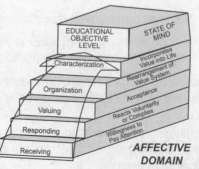

AFFECTIVE DOMAIN

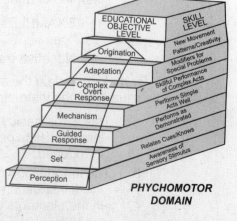

PHYCHOMOTOR DOMAIN

b. The educational objectives/learning outcomes become more complex from bottom to top.

1.9 LEARNING SKILLS AND THE LEARNING CURVE

1. The best way to prepare a student to perform a task is to provide a clear, step-by-step example. Students need a clear picture of what they are to do and how they are to do it.

2. Learning typically follows a pattern which, if shown on a graph, would be called the learning curve. The first part of the curve indicates rapid early improvement. Then the curve levels off.

a. This normal leveling-off of an individual's learning rate is called a learning plateau.

QUESTIONS AND ANSWER EXPLANATIONS

All of the FAA questions from the Fundamentals of Instructing knowledge test relating to the learning process outlined above are reproduced on the following pages in the same subunits as the outlines. To the immediate right of each question are the correct answer and answer explanation. You should cover these answers and answer explanations while responding to the questions. Refer to the general discussion in the Introduction on how to take the FAA pilot knowledge test.

Remember that the questions from the FAA knowledge test bank have been reordered by topic, and the topics have been organized into a meaningful sequence. Also, the first line of the answer explanation gives the citation of the authoritative source for the answer.

QUESTIONS
1.1 Characteristics of Learning

1. A change in behavior as a result of experience can be defined as

A. learning.

B. knowledge.

C. understanding.

Answer (A) is correct. *(AIH Chap 2)*
 DISCUSSION: Learning can be defined as a change in behavior as a result of experience.
 Answer (B) is incorrect because knowledge is awareness as a result of experience but not necessarily a change in behavior. Answer (C) is incorrect because understanding is only one of the four levels of learning.

2. The learning process may include some elements such as verbal, conceptual, and

A. habitual.

B. experiential.

C. problem solving.

Answer (C) is correct. *(AIH Chap 2)*
 DISCUSSION: The learning process involves many elements. Verbal, conceptual, perceptual, motor skill, problem solving, and emotional elements may be used at the same time.
 Answer (A) is incorrect because habits are the customary or usual way of doing things and can be changed by the learning process. Answer (B) is incorrect because all learning is by experience, but it takes place in different forms in different people.

3. While learning the material being taught, students may be learning other things as well. This additional learning is called

A. residual.

B. conceptual.

C. incidental.

Answer (C) is correct. *(AIH Chap 2)*
 DISCUSSION: While learning the subject at hand, students may be learning other things as well. They may be developing attitudes (good or bad) about aviation depending on what they experience. This learning is called incidental, but it may have a great impact on the total development of the student.
 Answer (A) is incorrect because residual is not a term used to define any type of learning. Answer (B) is incorrect because conceptual learning is an element of learning the subject at hand, not other incidental things.

1.2 The Principles of Learning

4. Individuals make more progress learning if they have a clear objective. This is one feature of the principle of

    A. primacy.

    B. readiness.

    C. willingness.

Answer (B) is correct. *(AIH Chap 2)*
    DISCUSSION: One feature of the principle of readiness is that when a student has a strong purpose, a clear objective, and a well-fixed reason to learn something, (s)he will make more progress than if (s)he lacks motivation.
    Answer (A) is incorrect because the principle of primacy states that first experiences create a strong, almost unshakable impression. Answer (C) is incorrect because there is no principle of willingness.

5. Things most often repeated are best remembered because of which principle of learning?

    A. Principle of effect.

    B. Principle of recency.

    C. Principle of exercise.

Answer (C) is correct. *(AIH Chap 2)*
    DISCUSSION: The principle of exercise states that those things most often repeated are best remembered. This is the basis of practice and drill.
    Answer (A) is incorrect because the principle of effect relates to the learner's emotional reaction to the learning experience. Answer (B) is incorrect because the principle of recency states that things most recently learned are best remembered.

6. Providing opportunities for a student to practice and then directing this process towards a goal is the basis of the principle of

    A. exercise.

    B. learning.

    C. readiness.

Answer (A) is correct. *(AIH Chap 2)*
    DISCUSSION: The principle of exercise states that those things most often repeated are best remembered. You must provide opportunities for your student to practice and then direct this process towards a goal.
    Answer (B) is incorrect because learning is a change in behavior as a result of experience. The principle of exercise is part of the learning process. Answer (C) is incorrect because the principle of readiness states that individuals learn best when they are ready to learn, not practicing a task.

7. The principle that is based on the emotional reaction of the learner is the principle of

    A. effect.

    B. primacy.

    C. intensity.

Answer (A) is correct. *(AIH Chap 2)*
    DISCUSSION: The principle of effect is the one which directly relates to the learner's emotional reaction. Pleasant experiences strengthen the learning process, whereas unpleasant experiences tend to weaken it.
    Answer (B) is incorrect because the principle of primacy states that a strong, almost unshakable impression is created by first experiences. Answer (C) is incorrect because the principle of intensity states that dramatic or exciting experiences teach more than routine experiences.

8. Which principle of learning often creates a strong impression?

    A. Principle of primacy.

    B. Principle of intensity.

    C. Principle of readiness.

Answer (A) is correct. *(AIH Chap 2)*
    DISCUSSION: Primacy, the state of being first, often creates a strong, almost unshakable impression. For the instructor, this means that what is taught must be right the first time. The first experience should be positive and functional and should lay the foundation for all that is to follow.
    Answer (B) is incorrect because the principle of intensity means that a student will learn more from the real thing than from a substitute. Answer (C) is incorrect because the principle of readiness means that a student must be willing and eager to learn.

9. Which principle of learning implies that a student will learn more from the real thing than from a substitute?

   A. Principle of effect.

   B. Principle of primacy.

   C. Principle of intensity.

Answer (C) is correct. *(AIH Chap 2)*
DISCUSSION: The principle of intensity states that a vivid, dramatic, or exciting learning experience teaches more than a routine or boring experience. Thus, the principle of intensity implies that a student will learn more from a real thing than from a substitute.
   Answer (A) is incorrect because the principle of effect is based on the emotional reaction of the student. Thus, pleasant experiences strengthen the learning, while unpleasant experiences weaken the learning. These may be experienced by learning from either the real thing or a substitute. Answer (B) is incorrect because the principle of primacy states that a strong, almost unshakable impression is created by first experiences. These experiences may be from either a real thing or a substitute.

10. Which principle of learning often determines the sequence of lectures within a course of instruction?

   A. Principle of primacy.

   B. Principle of recency.

   C. Principle of intensity.

Answer (B) is correct. *(AIH Chap 2)*
DISCUSSION: The principle of recency states that the things most recently learned are best remembered. The farther a student is removed time-wise from a new fact or understanding, the more difficult it is to remember it. The principle of recency often determines the sequence of lectures within a course of instruction.
   Answer (A) is incorrect because the principle of primacy means to the instructor that what is taught must be right the first time. Answer (C) is incorrect because the principle of intensity means that a student will learn more from the real experience than a substitute.

1.3 Perception and Insight

11. What is the basis of all learning?

   A. Perception.

   B. Motivation.

   C. Positive self-concept.

Answer (A) is correct. *(AIH Chap 2)*
DISCUSSION: Initially, all learning comes from perceptions that are directed to the brain by one or more of the five senses. Perceptions result when a person gives meaning to sensations.
   Answer (B) is incorrect because motivation is the dominant force that governs a student's progress and ability to learn, not the basis for all learning. Answer (C) is incorrect because positive self-concept is a factor that affects an individual's ability to learn, not the basis of all learning.

12. Perceptions result when a person

   A. gives meaning to sensations being experienced.

   B. is able to discern items of useful information.

   C. responds to visual cues first, then aural cues, and relates these cues to ones previously learned.

Answer (A) is correct. *(AIH Chap 2)*
DISCUSSION: Perceptions occur when a person gives meaning to sensations being experienced. This is the difference between just seeing something and understanding what is seen.
   Answer (B) is incorrect because a person who is able to discern items of useful information has learned, not just perceived. Answer (C) is incorrect because it describes the rote level of learning, i.e., memorization without concern for meaning.

13. A basic need that affects all of a person's perceptions is the need to

   A. maintain and enhance the organized self.

   B. accomplish a higher level of satisfaction.

   C. avoid areas that pose a threat to success.

Answer (A) is correct. *(AIH Chap 2)*
DISCUSSION: A person's basic need is to maintain and enhance the organized self. The self is a person's past, present, and future and is both physical and psychological. A person's most fundamental need is to preserve and perpetuate this self. Thus, all perceptions are affected by this need.
   Answer (B) is incorrect because accomplishing a higher level of satisfaction is a goal, not a basic need. Answer (C) is incorrect because avoiding areas that are a threat to success is a defense mechanism, not a basic need that affects perceptions.

14. Which factor affecting perception has a great influence on the total perceptual process?

    A. Self-concept.

    B. Goals and values.

    C. Time and opportunity.

Answer (A) is correct.   *(AIH Chap 2)*
    DISCUSSION: A student's self-concept (or self-image) has a great influence on the total perceptual process. Negative self-concepts inhibit the perceptual process by introducing psychological barriers, which tend to keep a student from perceiving. Positive self-concepts allow the student to be less defensive and more ready to digest experiences by assimilating all of the instructions and demonstrations offered.
    Answer (B) is incorrect because perceptions depend on one's goals and values in that every experience is colored by the individual's own beliefs and value structures, but they do not have a great influence on the total perceptual process. Answer (C) is incorrect because it takes time and opportunity to perceive, but it is not a great influence on the total perceptual process.

15. Which factor affecting perceptions is based on the effectiveness of the use of a properly planned training syllabus?

    A. Basic need.

    B. Time and opportunity.

    C. Goals and values.

Answer (B) is correct.   *(AIH Chap 2)*
    DISCUSSION: It takes time and opportunity to perceive. Learning some things depends on other perceptions that have preceded these learnings and on the availability of time to sense and relate these new things to the earlier perceptions. Thus, sequence and time are necessary to learn; a properly planned training syllabus facilitates sequencing and timing. The effectiveness of using a properly planned training syllabus is proportional to the consideration given by the instructor to the need for sufficient time and opportunity for perception to occur.
    Answer (A) is incorrect because a person's basic need is to maintain and enhance the organized self, which does not relate to a properly planned training syllabus. Answer (C) is incorrect because goals and values are the basis for perceptions. Every experience and sensation that gets funneled into one's central nervous system is colored by the individual's beliefs and value structures, which do not relate to a properly planned training syllabus.

16. In the learning process, fear or the element of threat will

    A. narrow the student's perceptual field.

    B. decrease the rate of associative reactions.

    C. cause a student to focus on several areas of perception.

Answer (A) is correct.   *(AIH Chap 2)*
    DISCUSSION: Fear or the element of threat will impair the student's perceptual field. This is because one tends to limit attention to the threatening object or condition rather than to what should be learned.
    Answer (B) is incorrect because the element of threat causes stress and anxiety; the mind tends to race, often irrationally, thereby increasing, not decreasing, the rate of associative reactions. Answer (C) is incorrect because fear or the element of threat will cause a student to focus only on the threatening object or condition, not on several areas of perception.

17. Which is one of the ways in which anxiety will affect a student?

    A. Anxiety may limit the student's ability to learn from perceptions.

    B. Anxiety will speed up the learning process for the student if properly controlled and directed by the instructor.

    C. Anxiety causes dispersal of the student's attention over such a wide range of matters as to interfere with normal reactions.

Answer (A) is correct.   *(AIH Chap 8)*
    DISCUSSION: Anxiety is a state of mental uneasiness arising from fear of anything, real or imagined, which threatens the person who experiences it. Anxiety may have a potent effect on actions and on the ability to learn from perceptions.
    Answer (B) is incorrect because perceptions blocked by anxiety will tend to slow, not speed up, the learning process. Answer (C) is incorrect because anxiety narrows, not disperses, a student's attention.

18. The mental grouping of affiliated perceptions is called

    A. insights.

    B. association.

    C. conceptualization.

Answer (A) is correct. *(AIH Chap 2)*
    DISCUSSION: Many principles, theories, and learned tasks can be treated as pieces relating to other pieces in the overall pattern of the task to be learned. This mental relating or grouping of associated perceptions is called insight.
    Answer (B) is incorrect because association is not the final, completed mental picture, although it is a necessary process to connect the affiliated perceptions. Answer (C) is incorrect because it refers only to the formation of individual ideas.

19. Insights, as applied to learning, involve a person's

    A. association of learning with change.

    B. grouping of associated perceptions into meaningful wholes.

    C. ability to recognize the reason for learning a procedure.

Answer (B) is correct. *(AIH Chap 2)*
    DISCUSSION: Insights, as applied to learning, involve a person's grouping of associated perceptions into meaningful wholes. As perceptions increase in number and are grouped to become insights by the student, learning becomes more meaningful and permanent.
    Answer (A) is incorrect because insights involve the grouping of perceptions into meaningful wholes, not the association of learning with change. Answer (C) is incorrect because the ability to recognize the reason for learning a procedure is a feature of the principle of readiness, not insight.

20. Instruction, as opposed to the trial and error method of learning, is desirable because competent instruction speeds the learning process by

    A. motivating the student to a better performance.

    B. emphasizing only the important points of training.

    C. teaching the relationship of perceptions as they occur.

Answer (C) is correct. *(AIH Chap 2)*
    DISCUSSION: Competent instruction speeds the learning process by teaching the relationship of perceptions as they occur, thus promoting the development of insights by the student.
    Answer (A) is incorrect because motivating a student to a better performance is just one element of instruction. Answer (B) is incorrect because instructors must emphasize all points of training, not just the major, important points.

21. Name one way an instructor can help develop student insights.

    A. Provide a secure and nonthreatening environment in which to learn.

    B. Point out various items to avoid during the learning process.

    C. Keep learning blocks small so they are easier to understand.

Answer (A) is correct. *(AIH Chap 2)*
    DISCUSSION: Pointing out the relationships of perceptions as they occur, providing a secure and nonthreatening environment in which to learn, and helping the student acquire and maintain a favorable self-concept are most important in fostering the development of insights.
    Answer (B) is incorrect because the instructor should point out the relationships of perceptions as they occur, not point out various items to avoid during the learning process. Answer (C) is incorrect because insights develop when a student's perceptions increase in number and are assembled into larger, not smaller, blocks of learning.

1.4 Memory

22. Which memory system processes input from the environment?

    A. Working.

    B. Long-term.

    C. Sensory register.

Answer (C) is correct. *(AIH Chap 2)*
    DISCUSSION: The sensory register receives input from the environment and quickly processes it according to the individual's preconceived concept of what is important (i.e., it recognizes certain stimuli as significant). The sensory register processes inputs or stimuli from the environment within seconds, discards what is considered extraneous, and processes what is considered by the individual to be relevant.
    Answer (A) is incorrect because the working, or short-term, memory is the receptacle for the information determined to be relevant by the sensory register. Once in the short-term memory, the information may temporarily remain for immediate use, or it may fade rapidly. Answer (B) is incorrect because the long-term memory is where information is stored for future use.

23. The use of some type of association, such as rhymes or mnemonics is best suited to which memory system?

A. Short-term.

B. Sensory.

C. Long-term.

Answer (A) is correct.   *(AIH Chap 2)*
DISCUSSION: For information to remain in the short-term memory for a significant amount of time, it must be categorized in some way. The information is initially grouped into systematic chunks in a process called coding. It must then be related to concepts or knowledge already in memory in a process called recoding. The use of some type of association, such as rhymes or mnemonic devices, is well suited to this task.
Answer (B) is incorrect because the sensory register detects and processes stimuli on a subconscious level. They are then discarded or transferred to the short-term memory according the individual's preconceived concept of what is important.
Answer (C) is incorrect because, in order for information stored in long-term memory to be useful, some special effort must have been expended during the recoding process while the information was in short-term memory.

24. How can recoding be described?

A. The relating of incoming information to concepts or knowledge already in memory.

B. The initial storage of information in short-term memory.

C. The selective process where the sensory register is set to recognize certain stimuli.

Answer (A) is correct.   *(AIH Chap 2)*
DISCUSSION: Recoding takes place in the short-term memory, when new information is adjusted to individual experiences. Recoding may be described as a process of relating incoming information to concepts or knowledge already in memory.
Answer (B) is incorrect because the initial storage of information in short-term memory is coding, not recoding.
Answer (C) is incorrect because the selective process where the sensory register is set to recognize certain stimuli is precoding, not recoding.

25. Where is information for future use stored?

A. Short-term memory.

B. Sensory register.

C. Long-term memory.

Answer (C) is correct.   *(AIH Chap 2)*
DISCUSSION: Information for future use is stored in the long-term memory.
Answer (A) is incorrect because short-term memory is where information is temporarily stored, not stored for future use, after the sensory register deems it to be significant. Answer (B) is incorrect because the sensory register processes stimuli from the environment according to the individual's preconception of what is important. Significant information is sent to the short-term memory for immediate, not future, use.

1.5 Forgetting and Retention

26. When a person has difficulty recalling facts after several years, this is known as

A. disuse.

B. repression.

C. poor retention.

Answer (A) is correct.   *(AIH Chap 2)*
DISCUSSION: The theory of disuse states that a person forgets those things that are not used or, at least, not used frequently.
Answer (B) is incorrect because repression is the practice of submerging an unpleasant experience into the subconscious. Answer (C) is incorrect because poor retention results in forgetting due to disuse, interference, or repression.

27. When the learning of similar things overshadows other learning experiences, it is called

A. suppression.

B. correlation.

C. interference.

Answer (C) is correct.   *(AIH Chap 2)*
DISCUSSION: The theory of interference states that new or similar events can often replace previously learned facts. Most susceptible to this replacement by interference are closely similar materials and materials not well learned to begin with.
Answer (A) is incorrect because suppression is not a consideration (or theory) as to why a person forgets. Answer (B) is incorrect because correlation is the highest level of learning, which means that it is resistant to forgetting.

28. According to one theory, some forgetting is due to the practice of submerging an unpleasant experience into the subconscious. This is called

    A. blanking.

    B. immersion.

    C. repression.

Answer (C) is correct. *(AIH Chap 2)*
    DISCUSSION: The theory of repression states that some forgetting is due to the submersion of ideas or thoughts into the subconscious mind. For instance, information learned during an unpleasant experience may be buried out of reach of memory.
    Answer (A) is incorrect because blanking refers to a temporary inability to remember, not to a theory of forgetting. Answer (B) is incorrect because immersion is not a theory of forgetting.

29. Responses that produce a pleasurable return are called

    A. reward.

    B. praise.

    C. positive feedback.

Answer (B) is correct. *(AIH Chap 2)*
    DISCUSSION: Responses that give a pleasurable return, called praise, tend to be repeated, thus stimulating and encouraging retention.
    Answer (A) is incorrect because rewards are motivators and are not usually responses (e.g., praise); that is, they are normally financial, self-interest, or public recognition. Answer (C) is incorrect because positive feedback (e.g., constructive criticism) is part of the learning, not retention, process. Positive feedback teaches a student how to capitalize on things done well and to use them to compensate for lesser accomplishments.

1.6 Transfer of Learning

30. The performance of rectangular patterns helps a student fly traffic patterns. What type transfer of learning is this?

    A. Lateral.

    B. Positive.

    C. Deliberate.

Answer (B) is correct. *(AIH Chap 2)*
    DISCUSSION: Transfers of learning can be negative or positive. Since the learning of Task A (flying rectangular patterns) helps in the learning of Task B (flying traffic patterns), it is advantageous and therefore a positive transfer of learning.
    Answer (A) is incorrect because there is no lateral transfer of learning, only positive or negative. Answer (C) is incorrect because there is no deliberate transfer of learning, only positive or negative.

31. Which transfer of learning occurs when the performance of a maneuver interferes with the learning of another maneuver?

    A. Adverse.

    B. Positive.

    C. Negative.

Answer (C) is correct. *(AIH Chap 2)*
    DISCUSSION: Transfers of learning can be negative or positive. If the learning of Task A helps in the learning of Task B, the transfer of learning is deemed to be positive. If, on the other hand, Task A interferes with Task B, the transfer is a hindrance to learning and is thus negative.
    Answer (A) is incorrect because there is no adverse transfer of learning, only positive or negative. Answer (B) is incorrect because the transfer of learning is a hindrance and is thus negative.

32. To ensure proper habits and correct techniques during training, an instructor should

    A. use the building block technique of instruction.

    B. repeat subject matter the student has already learned.

    C. introduce challenging material to continually motivate the student.

Answer (A) is correct. *(AIH Chap 2)*
    DISCUSSION: The building-block technique of teaching insists that each simple task be performed correctly before the next is introduced. This technique fosters thorough and meaningful performance and good habits, which will be carried over into future learning.
    Answer (B) is incorrect because too much repetition can lead to boredom. The instructor must mix teaching methods to sustain interest and promote learning. Answer (C) is incorrect because complex or difficult tasks introduced before simpler ones are mastered can be frustrating, not motivating, for the student. This approach will not ensure proper habits; the student will likely develop bad habits from trying to perform tasks not completely understood.

1.7 Levels of Learning

33. What level of knowledge is being tested if asked, "What is the maneuvering speed of the aircraft listed in the owner's manual?"

A. Rote.

B. Application.

C. Understanding.

Answer (A) is correct.   *(AIH Chap 2)*
DISCUSSION: The lowest level, rote learning, is the ability to repeat something back that one has been taught without understanding or being able to apply what has been learned. An example of rote learning is to be able to cite the maneuvering speed of the aircraft listed in the owner's manual.
Answer (B) is incorrect because application is the ability of a student to apply what has been taught. This is the third level of learning and is achieved after the student understands, has practiced, and can consistently perform a task. Answer (C) is incorrect because the second level of learning is understanding, which has been achieved when a student can put together a block of learning and develop an insight into the performance of a task.

34. During the flight portion of a practical test, the examiner simulates complete loss of engine power by closing the throttle and announcing "simulated engine failure." What level of learning is being tested?

A. Application.

B. Correlation.

C. Understanding.

Answer (B) is correct.   *(AIH Chap 2)*
DISCUSSION: When the examiner simulates complete loss of engine power by closing the throttle and announcing "simulated engine failure," the examiner is testing at the correlation level of learning. The applicant must be able to correlate (associate) the engine failure with the requirements to perform the elements of an emergency approach and landing; e.g., establish best-glide speed, select a field, perform restart checklist, plan a flight pattern to the selected field, complete all appropriate checklists, etc.
Answer (A) is incorrect because the application level of learning is tested when the examiner closes the throttle and tells the applicant to perform an emergency approach and landing. Answer (C) is incorrect because the understanding level of learning is tested when the examiner asks the applicant to explain the elements of an emergency approach and landing.

35. At which level of learning do most instructors stop teaching?

A. Application.

B. Correlation.

C. Understanding.

Answer (A) is correct.   *(AIH Chap 2)*
DISCUSSION: Most instructors stop teaching at the application level of learning. Discontinuing instruction on an element at this point and directing subsequent instruction exclusively to other elements is characteristic of piecemeal instruction, which is usually inefficient. It violates the building block concept of instruction by failing to apply what has been learned to future learning tasks.
Answer (B) is incorrect because correlation is the highest level of learning and should be the goal of each instructor. Instructors all too often stop at the application level. Answer (C) is incorrect because understanding is the second level of learning, and at this point, a student understands a task but may not be able to do it. Instructors will usually continue teaching to the next level, which is application.

36. When asking a student to explain how gross weight affects maneuvering speed, what level of learning is being tested?

A. Application.

B. Correlation.

C. Understanding.

Answer (C) is correct.   *(AIH Chap 2)*
DISCUSSION: At the understanding level of learning, a student will be able to explain how gross weight affects maneuvering speed (V_A). Understanding is the next level after rote memorization and the level before acquiring the skill to apply knowledge, which is application (correlation is the fourth and highest level of learning). Being able to explain (not demonstrate) is the understanding level of learning, not the application or correlation level.
Answer (A) is incorrect because, at the application level, a student will be able to apply the knowledge that gross weight affects maneuvering speed when determining the appropriate airspeed for entering turbulent air or maneuvers that require an airspeed at or below V_A. Answer (B) is incorrect because, at the correlation level, a student has developed the ability to correlate the elements of maneuvering speed with other concepts, such as gust loads, accelerated stalls, load factors, acceleration forces in the aircraft, etc.

1.8 Domains of Learning

37. Which domain of learning deals with knowledge?

- A. Affective.
- B. Cognitive.
- C. Psychomotor.

Answer (B) is correct. *(AIH Chap 2)*
DISCUSSION: Domains of learning are classified based on what is to be learned. The cognitive domain of learning deals with knowledge (e.g., facts, concepts, or relationships).
Answer (A) is incorrect because the affective domain deals with attitudes, beliefs, and values, not knowledge. Answer (C) is incorrect because the psychomotor domain deals with physical skills, not knowledge.

38. Affective domain relates to

- A. physical skills.
- B. knowledge.
- C. attitudes, beliefs, and values.

Answer (C) is correct. *(AIH Chap 2)*
DISCUSSION: Domains of learning are classified based on what is to be learned. The affective domain relates to attitudes, beliefs, and values.
Answer (A) is incorrect because the psychomotor domain, not the affective domain, relates to physical skills. Answer (B) is incorrect because the cognitive domain, not the affective domain, relates to knowledge.

39. The educational objective levels for the cognitive domain are

- A. receiving, responding, valuing, organization, and characterization.
- B. perception, set, guided response mechanism, complex overt response, adaptation, and origination.
- C. knowledge, comprehension, application, analysis, synthesis, and evaluation.

Answer (C) is correct. *(AIH Chap 2)*
DISCUSSION: Each domain of learning has multiple educational objective levels. The six educational objective levels of the cognitive domain are knowledge, comprehension, application, analysis, synthesis, and evaluation.
Answer (A) is incorrect because receiving, responding, valuing, organization, and characterization are the five educational objective levels of the affective, not cognitive, domain. Answer (B) is incorrect because perception, set, guided response mechanism, complex overt response, adaptation, and origination are the seven educational objective levels of the psychomotor, not cognitive, domain.

40. The listing of the hierarchy of objectives is often referred to as a

- A. taxonomy.
- B. skill.
- C. domain.

Answer (A) is correct. *(AIH Chap 2)*
DISCUSSION: Each of the domains of learning has a hierarchy of educational objectives. The listing of the hierarchy of objectives is often called a taxonomy.
Answer (B) is incorrect because a skill is what is learned in the psychomotor domain of learning. It is not a hierarchy of educational objectives. Answer (C) is incorrect because domains of learning contain, but are not, hierarchies of educational objectives.

41. The most complex outcome in the affective domain is

- A. organization.
- B. characterization.
- C. valuing.

Answer (B) is correct. *(AIH Chap 2)*
DISCUSSION: A taxonomy of educational objectives is a systematic classification scheme for sorting learning outcomes into the three domains of learning (cognitive, affective, and psychomotor) and ranking the desired outcomes in a developmental hierarchy from least complex to most complex. The most complex learning outcome in the affective domain is characterization in which the learner incorporates a value or attitude into his/her life.
Answer (A) is incorrect because organization (in which the learner rearranges his/her value system to accommodate a new value or attitude) is the second-most-complex, not the most complex, learning outcome in the affective domain. Answer (C) is incorrect because valuing (in which the learner accepts a new value or attitude) is the third-most-complex, not the most complex, learning outcome in the affective domain.

42. The least complex outcome in the psychomotor domain is

A. adaptation.

B. mechanism.

C. perception.

Answer (C) is correct.   *(AIH Chap 2)*
DISCUSSION: A taxonomy of educational objectives is a systematic classification scheme for sorting learning outcomes into the three domains of learning (cognitive, affective, and psychomotor) and ranking the desired outcomes in a developmental hierarchy from least complex to most complex. The least complex learning outcome in the psychomotor domain is perception in which the learner has awareness of sensory stimuli.

Answer (A) is incorrect because adaptation (in which the learner modifies his/her performance of a skill for special problems) is the second-most-complex, not the least complex, learning outcome in the psychomotor domain. Answer (B) is incorrect because mechanism (in which the learner performs simple acts well) is the fourth-least-complex, not the least complex, learning outcome in the psychomotor domain.

1.9 Learning Skills and the Learning Curve

43. The best way to prepare a student to perform a task is to

A. explain the purpose of the task.

B. provide a clear, step-by-step example.

C. give the student an outline of the task.

Answer (B) is correct.   *(AIH Chap 2)*
DISCUSSION: The best way to prepare a student to perform a task is to provide a clear, step-by-step example. Having a model to follow permits a student to get a clear picture of each step in the sequence (e.g., what it is, how to do it).

Answer (A) is incorrect because, while a student should know the purpose of a task, (s)he must be provided with a clear, step-by-step example showing how to perform the task. Answer (C) is incorrect because an outline is not as useful as a clear, step-by-step example.

44. A learning plateau may be defined as the

A. point in the learning curve at which skill proficiency retrogresses.

B. normal leveling-off of an individual's learning rate.

C. achievement of the highest possible level of competence for a particular individual.

Answer (B) is correct.   *(AIH Chap 2)*
DISCUSSION: A learning plateau may be defined as the normal leveling-off of an individual's learning rate. This is normal and should be expected by you and your student after an initial period of rapid improvement.

Answer (A) is incorrect because a learning plateau is the normal leveling-off of an individual's rate of learning, not retrogression. Answer (C) is incorrect because a learning plateau is the normal leveling-off of an individual's rate of learning, not achievement of the highest possible level of competence.

END OF STUDY UNIT

STUDY UNIT TWO
BARRIERS TO LEARNING

(2 pages of outline)

2.1 SELF-CONCEPT

1. Self-concept is how one pictures oneself.

   a. This is the most powerful determinant in learning.
   b. Self-concept has a great influence on the total perceptual process.

2. Negative self-concept contributes most to a student's failure to remain receptive to new experiences and creates a tendency to reject additional training.

3. Thus, an instructor can foster the development of insights by helping the student acquire and maintain a favorable self-concept.

2.2 DEFENSE MECHANISMS

1. Certain behavior patterns are called defense mechanisms because they are subconscious defenses against the reality of unpleasant situations. People use these defenses to soften feelings of failure, alleviate feelings of guilt, and protect feelings of personal worth and adequacy.

2. Although defense mechanisms can serve a useful purpose, they can involve some degree of self-deception and distortion of reality.

   a. They alleviate symptoms, not causes.

3. Common defense mechanisms:

   a. **Rationalization** -- When a person cannot accept the real reasons for his/her own behavior, this device permits the substitution of excuses for reasons. Rationalization is a subconscious technique for justifying actions that otherwise would be unacceptable.

   b. **Flight** -- Students escape from frustration by taking physical or mental flight.

      1) To flee physically, students may develop symptoms or ailments that give them excuses for removing themselves from the frustration.
      2) More frequent than physical flight is mental flight or daydreaming.

   c. **Aggression** -- A person can avoid a frustrating situation by means of aggressive behavior. Shouting and accusing others are typical defense mechanisms. Social pressure usually forces student aggressiveness into more subtle forms. Typically, students may

      1) Ask irrelevant questions,
      2) Refuse to participate in class activities, or
      3) Disrupt activities.

   d. **Resignation** -- Students become so frustrated that they lose interest and give up.

      1) They may no longer believe it profitable or even possible to work further.
      2) Resignation usually occurs when the student has completed early lessons without grasping the fundamentals and then becomes bewildered and lost in the advanced phase.

2.3 STRESS AND ANXIETY

1. Normal individuals react to stress by responding rapidly and exactly, often automatically, within their experience and training.

    a. This underlines the need for proper training prior to emergency situations.

    b. The effective individual thinks rapidly, acts rapidly, and is extremely sensitive to his/her surroundings.

2. Some abnormal reactions to stress include

    a. Inappropriate reactions, such as extreme overcooperation, painstaking self-control, inappropriate laughter or singing, and very rapid changes in emotion.

    b. Marked changes in mood (e.g., high spirits followed by deep depression).

    c. Severe, unreasonable anger toward the flight instructor, service personnel, or others.

3. Anxiety is probably the most significant psychological barrier affecting flight instruction. It is the extreme worry brought on by stressful situations (e.g., an emergency, an exam, etc.). Anxiety can be countered by

    a. Treating fears as a normal reaction rather than ignoring them,

    b. Reinforcing the student's enjoyment of flying, and

    c. Teaching students to cope with fears.

2.4 THE OVERCONFIDENT OR IMPATIENT STUDENT

1. Impatience is a greater deterrent to learning pilot skills than is generally recognized.

    a. The impatient student fails to understand the need for preliminary training. (S)he seeks only the final objective without considering the means necessary to reach it.

    b. Impatience can be corrected by the instructor by presenting the necessary preliminary training one step at a time, with clearly stated goals for each step.

2. Because they make few mistakes, apt students may assume that the correction of those errors is unimportant.

    a. This overconfidence soon results in faulty performance.

    b. For apt students, a good instructor will constantly raise the standard of performance for each lesson, demanding greater effort.

QUESTIONS AND ANSWER EXPLANATIONS

All of the FAA questions from the *Fundamentals of Instructing* knowledge test relating to the barriers to learning material outlined above are reproduced on the following pages in the same subunits as the outlines. To the immediate right of each question are the correct answer and answer explanation. You should cover these answers and answer explanations while responding to the questions. Refer to the general discussion in the Introduction on how to take the FAA pilot knowledge test.

Remember that the questions from the FAA knowledge test bank have been reordered by topic, and the topics have been organized into a meaningful sequence. Also, the first line of the answer explanation gives the the citation of the authoritative source for the answer.

QUESTIONS

2.1 Self-Concept

1. The factor which contributes most to a student's failure to remain receptive to new experiences and which creates a tendency to reject additional training is

    A. basic needs.

    B. element of threat.

    C. negative self-concept.

Answer (C) is correct. *(AIH Chap 2)*
    DISCUSSION: A student with a negative self-concept is resistant to new experiences and may reject additional training. People tend to avoid experiences that contradict their self-concept.
    Answer (A) is incorrect because a student's basic needs can be used by the instructor to promote learning. For instance, personal safety is one of the most important basic needs, and aviation training heavily emphasizes this need. Answer (B) is incorrect because an element of threat will cause a student to limit his/her attention to the threatening object or condition. Once this is removed, the student will be able to learn.

2. An instructor may foster the development of insights by

    A. helping the student acquire and maintain a favorable self-concept.

    B. pointing out the attractive features of the activity to be learned.

    C. keeping the rate of learning consistent so that it is predictable.

Answer (A) is correct. *(AIH Chap 2)*
    DISCUSSION: Especially in a field such as aviation training, the instructor can foster the development of insights by helping the student acquire and maintain a favorable self-concept. The student who feels sure of his/her knowledge, skills, and judgments learned in class will also feel better about actual performance and his/her own ability to fly.
    Answer (B) is incorrect because the attractive features in a learning situation tend to increase motivation rather than insight. Answer (C) is incorrect because learning rates will vary, not stay constant, with each training lesson.

2.2 Defense Mechanisms

3. Although defense mechanisms can serve a useful purpose, they can

    A. provide feelings of adequacy.

    B. alleviate the cause of problems.

    C. involve some degree of self-deception and distortion of reality.

Answer (C) is correct. *(AIH Chap 1)*
    DISCUSSION: Although defense mechanisms can serve a useful purpose, they can also be hindrances. Because they involve some self-deception and distortion of reality, defense mechanisms do not solve problems.
    Answer (A) is incorrect because defense mechanisms mask and protect feelings of adequacy rather than provide them. Answer (B) is incorrect because defense mechanisms alleviate symptoms, not causes, of problems.

4. When a student uses excuses to justify inadequate performance, it is an indication of the defense mechanism known as

    A. flight.

    B. aggression.

    C. rationalization.

Answer (C) is correct. *(AIH Chap 1)*
    DISCUSSION: Rationalization is a subconscious technique for justifying unacceptable actions or performance. This allows a student to substitute excuses for reasons and make those excuses plausible and acceptable to themselves.
    Answer (A) is incorrect because flight is the defense mechanism in which the student escapes (either physically or mentally) from a frustrating experience. Answer (B) is incorrect because aggression is the defense mechanism in which the student uses aggressive behavior to deal with feelings of frustration.

5.   Taking physical or mental flight is a defense mechanism students use when they

    A.   want to escape from frustrating situations.

    B.   cannot accept the real reasons for their behavior.

    C.   lose interest during the advanced stages of training.

Answer (A) is correct.   (AIH Chap 1)
    DISCUSSION: The defense mechanism of flight allows a student to escape from a frustrating situation. This escape can be physical flight (absenteeism, illness, etc.) or mental flight (daydreaming).
    Answer (B) is incorrect because, if a student cannot accept the real reasons for his/her behavior, (s)he may rationalize, not take flight. Answer (C) is incorrect because a student who loses interest during the advanced stages of training may resign, not take flight, and give up. This is common if a student has not understood the fundamentals.

6.   When students subconsciously use the defense mechanism called rationalization, they

    A.   use excuses to justify acceptable behavior.

    B.   cannot accept the real reasons for their behavior.

    C.   develop symptoms that give them excuses for removing themselves from frustration.

Answer (B) is correct.   (AIH Chap 1)
    DISCUSSION: Rationalization is a subconscious technique for justifying unacceptable actions or performance. This allows a student to substitute excuses for reasons and make those excuses plausible and acceptable to themselves.
    Answer (A) is incorrect because, in rationalization, excuses are used to justify unacceptable, not acceptable, behavior. Answer (C) is incorrect because, when students develop symptoms that give them excuses for removing themselves from frustration, they are using the defense mechanism of physical flight.

7.   When a student engages in daydreaming, it is the defense mechanism of

    A.   flight.

    B.   fantasy.

    C.   avoidance.

Answer (A) is correct.   (AIH Chap 1)
    DISCUSSION: A student engaging in daydreaming is an example of flight or mental escape.
    Answer (B) is incorrect because fantasy is not a defense mechanism in and of itself, yet it is involved in the defense mechanism of flight: fantasy in mental flight (daydreaming). Answer (C) is incorrect because avoidance is not a defense mechanism in and of itself, yet it is involved in the defense mechanism of flight: avoidance in physical flight.

8.   When students display the defense mechanism called aggression, they

    A.   become visibly angry, upset, and childish.

    B.   may refuse to participate in class activities.

    C.   attempt to justify actions by asking numerous questions.

Answer (B) is correct.   (AIH Chap 1)
    DISCUSSION: Examples of subtle aggression include students who ask irrelevant questions, refuse to participate in class activities, or disrupt activities within the group. Aggressive behavior is used to avoid facing failure.
    Answer (A) is incorrect because, although such behavior is characteristic of aggression, it is relatively uncommon in a classroom due to social pressure. Student aggressiveness is usually more subtle in nature and will thus be expressed less obviously. Answer (C) is incorrect because attempting to justify actions is an example of rationalization.

9.   When a student asks irrelevant questions or refuses to participate in class activities, it usually is an indication of the defense mechanism known as

    A.   flight.

    B.   aggression.

    C.   resignation.

Answer (B) is correct.   (AIH Chap 1)
    DISCUSSION: Examples of subtle aggression include students who ask irrelevant questions, refuse to participate in class activities, or disrupt activities within the group. Aggressive behavior is used to avoid facing failure.
    Answer (A) is incorrect because flight is the defense mechanism when a person removes him/herself, physically or mentally, from a frustrating situation. Answer (C) is incorrect because resignation is a process of becoming frustrated and not believing that continuing will be worthwhile, i.e., the person is resigned to failure and gives up.

10.   When a student becomes bewildered and lost in the advanced phase of training after completing the early phase without grasping the fundamentals, the defense mechanism is usually in the form of

    A.   submission.

    B.   resignation.

    C.   rationalization.

Answer (B) is correct.   (AIH Chap 1)
    DISCUSSION: When a student has become frustrated, lost interest, given up, and no longer believes it profitable or possible to work further, resignation has taken place. A student in this frame of mind accepts defeat. Typically, such a student has not grasped the fundamentals and is bewildered by later lessons.
    Answer (A) is incorrect because submission is not a defense mechanism but may be characteristic of resignation. Answer (C) is incorrect because rationalization is a process of making excuses for unacceptable behavior.

2.3 Stress and Anxiety

11. When under stress, normal individuals usually react

- A. by showing excellent morale followed by deep depression.
- B. by responding rapidly and exactly, often automatically, within the limits of their experience and training.
- C. inappropriately such as extreme overcooperation, painstaking self-control, and inappropriate laughing or singing.

Answer (B) is correct. *(AIH Chap 1)*
DISCUSSION: When under stress, normal individuals begin to respond rapidly and exactly, within the limits of their experience and training. Many responses are automatic, which indicates the need for proper training in emergency operations prior to an actual emergency.
Answer (A) is incorrect because marked changes in mood, e.g., excellent morale followed by deep depression is an abnormal, not a normal, reaction to stress. Answer (C) is incorrect because inappropriate reactions, such as extreme overcooperation, painstaking self-control, and inappropriate laughter or singing, are abnormal, not normal, reactions to stress.

12. Which would most likely be an indication that a student is reacting abnormally to stress?

- A. Slow learning.
- B. Inappropriate laughter or singing.
- C. Automatic response to a given situation.

Answer (B) is correct. *(AIH Chap 1)*
DISCUSSION: Inappropriate laughter or singing is an abnormal reaction to stress. The instructor should be alert for other inappropriate (and possibly dangerous) reactions.
Answer (A) is incorrect because slow learning is a normal, not an abnormal, reaction to stress. Answer (C) is incorrect because automatic response to a given situation is a normal, not an abnormal, reaction to stress.

13. One possible indication of a student's abnormal reaction to stress would be

- A. a hesitancy to act.
- B. extreme overcooperation.
- C. a noticeable lack of self-control.

Answer (B) is correct. *(AIH Chap 1)*
DISCUSSION: Extreme overcooperation is an indication that a student is reacting abnormally to stress. The abnormally tense or anxious student may be noticeably over-agreeable.
Answer (A) is incorrect because a hesitancy to act is an indication of anxiety, not an abnormal reaction to stress. Answer (C) is incorrect because painstaking self-control, not a lack thereof, is an indication of an abnormal reaction to stress.

14. The instructor can counteract anxiety in a student by

- A. treating the student's fears as a normal reaction.
- B. discontinuing instruction in tasks that cause anxiety.
- C. allowing the student to decide when he/she is ready for a new maneuver to be introduced.

Answer (A) is correct. *(AIH Chap 1)*
DISCUSSION: Psychologists tell us that a student's fear is a normal reaction and should be treated as such by an instructor. Treating fear as normal will help in counteracting anxiety.
Answer (B) is incorrect because discontinuing instruction in stressful tasks will not help the student to overcome the anxiety. Perhaps a different approach to the task is necessary. Answer (C) is incorrect because it describes an example of negative motivation, which would tend to contribute to the student's anxiety.

2.4 The Overconfident or Impatient Student

15. Students who grow impatient when learning the basic elements of a task are those who

- A. are less easily discouraged than the unaggressive students.
- B. should have the preliminary training presented one step at a time with clearly stated goals for each step.
- C. should be advanced to the next higher level of learning and not held back by insisting that the immediate goal be reached before they proceed to the next level.

Answer (B) is correct. *(AIH Chap 8)*
DISCUSSION: Impatient students fail to see why they must learn one step thoroughly before they move to the next. Presenting the preliminary training with clearly stated goals for each step will minimize student impatience.
Answer (A) is incorrect because impatient students are often aggressive and more easily discouraged than unaggressive students. Answer (C) is incorrect because it is necessary to hold a student until (s)he masters the basics if the whole task is to be performed competently and safely. This is the basis of the building block technique of instruction.

16. Which obstacle to learning is a greater deterrent to learning pilot skills than is generally recognized?

A. Anxiety.

B. Impatience.

C. Physical discomfort.

Answer (B) is correct. *(AIH Chap 8)*
DISCUSSION: Failing to understand the need for preliminary training, the impatient student can only see the ultimate objective of flying an airplane. This impatience can be detrimental to the usual, careful acquisition of pilot skills.
Answer (A) is incorrect because, although anxiety may be detrimental to the learning process, it is generally recognized as such, whereas impatience has an equal effect and is not widely recognized. Answer (C) is incorrect because, although physical discomfort may be detrimental to the learning process, it is generally recognized as such, whereas impatience has an equal effect and is not widely recognized.

17. Should an instructor be concerned about an apt student who makes very few mistakes?

A. No. Some students have an innate, natural aptitude for flight.

B. Yes. The student may assume that the correction of errors is unimportant.

C. Yes. The student will lose confidence in the instructor if the instructor does not invent deficiencies in the student's performance.

Answer (B) is correct. *(AIH Chap 7)*
DISCUSSION: Because apt students make few mistakes, they may assume that the correction of errors is not important. Such overconfidence soon results in faulty performance. For such students, a good instructor will constantly raise the standard of performance for each lesson, demanding greater effort.
Answer (A) is incorrect because, regardless of natural gift, apt students may assume that the correction of errors is not important. Such overconfidence soon results in faulty performance. Answer (C) is incorrect because the instructor should not invent deficiencies in order to diminish a student's confidence. On the contrary, a good instructor will constantly raise the standard of performance for each lesson, demanding greater effort.

18. What should an instructor do with a student who assumes that correction of errors is unimportant?

A. Divide complex flight maneuvers into elements.

B. Try to reduce the student's overconfidence to reduce the chance of an accident.

C. Raise the standard of performance for each lesson, demanding greater effort.

Answer (C) is correct. *(AIH Chap 7)*
DISCUSSION: Because apt students make few mistakes, they may assume that the correction of errors is not important. Such overconfidence soon results in faulty performance. For such students, a good instructor will constantly raise the standard of performance for each lesson, demanding greater effort.
Answer (A) is incorrect because dividing complex tasks into simpler elements should be done with students whose slow progress is due to a lack of confidence, not apt students. Answer (B) is incorrect because reducing students' overconfidence would be inefficient for properly motivating the apt student. After realizing the impatience of such students comes only from improperly paced instruction, instructors should give them challenges fitting their abilities.

19. The overconfidence of fast learners should be corrected by

A. high praise when no errors are made.

B. raising the standard of performance for each lesson.

C. providing strong, negative evaluation at the end of each lesson.

Answer (B) is correct. *(AIH Chap 7)*
DISCUSSION: Because apt students make few mistakes, they may assume that the correction of errors is not important. Such overconfidence soon results in faulty performance. For such students, a good instructor will constantly raise the standard of performance for each lesson, demanding greater effort.
Answer (A) is incorrect because high praise will only lead the student to become more overconfident. Answer (C) is incorrect because a strong, negative evaluation should not be used to diminish a student's confidence. On the contrary, a good instructor will constantly raise the standard of performance for each lesson, demanding greater effort.

20. Faulty performance due to student overconfidence should be corrected by

A. increasing the standard of performance for each lesson.

B. praising the student only when the performance is perfect.

C. providing strong, negative evaluation at the end of each lesson.

Answer (A) is correct. *(AIH Chap 7)*
DISCUSSION: Because apt students make few mistakes, they may assume that the correction of errors is not important. Such overconfidence soon results in faulty performance. For such students, a good instructor will constantly raise the standard of performance for each lesson, demanding greater effort.
Answer (B) is incorrect because students need consistent, fair critique of every performance, perfect or not. Overly high standards also frustrate students by making them work too hard without reward (and for an unrealistic goal). Answer (C) is incorrect because the principle of effect states that learning is weakened when associated with an unpleasant feeling. Aside from being unfair, the continual negative evaluations will also increasingly frustrate students.

STUDY UNIT THREE
HUMAN BEHAVIOR AND EFFECTIVE COMMUNICATION

(4 pages of outline)

3.1 HUMAN NEEDS

1. Human needs can be organized into a series of levels. The "pyramid of human needs" has been suggested by Abraham Maslow. For instance, physical needs must be satisfied before so-called "higher" needs can be used as motivators. He suggests that needs must be satisfied in the following ascending order:

    a. **Physical needs** pertain to food, rest, exercise, sex, etc. Until these needs are satisfied to a reasonable degree, a student cannot concentrate on learning.

    b. **Safety needs** include shelter and protection against danger, threat, and deprivation.

    c. **Social needs** are the needs to belong and to associate with other people.

    d. **Egoistic needs** will usually have a direct influence on the student-instructor relationship. Egoistic needs are of two kinds:

        1) Relating to one's self-esteem: needs for self-confidence, independence, achievement, and knowledge.

        2) Relating to one's reputation: needs for status, power, prestige, appreciation, and the deserved respect of one's fellow beings.

    e. **Self-fulfillment needs** are at the top of the hierarchy of human needs. These are the needs for realizing one's own potentialities, for continued development, and for being creative.

        1) This need of a student should offer the greatest challenge to an instructor.

        2) Helping students realize self-fulfillment is perhaps the most worthwhile accomplishment an instructor can achieve.

3.2 MOTIVATION

1. Motivation is probably the dominant force governing the student's progress and ability to learn.

    a. Slumps in learning very often go hand-in-hand with slumps in motivation.

2. Positive motivations are provided by the promise or achievement of rewards.

3. Negative motivations are those that cause a student to react with fear and anxiety.

    a. Negative motivations in the form of reproof and threats should be avoided with all but the most overconfident and impulsive students.

4. It is important for an instructor to make the student aware that a particular lesson can help him/her reach an important goal.

    a. When students are unable to see the benefits or purpose of a lesson, they will be less motivated.

    b. Confusion, disinterest, and uneasiness on the part of the student could happen as a result of not knowing the objective of each period of instruction.

5.   Motivations may be

a.   Positive or negative
b.   Tangible or intangible
c.   Obvious or subtle and difficult to identify

6.   A student is like any worker in wanting tangible returns for his/her efforts. If such motivation is to be effective, students must believe that their efforts will be suitably rewarded. Instructors should remember always to tailor individual lessons to the objective.

7.   An instructor can most effectively maintain a high level of student motivation by making each lesson a pleasurable experience.

3.3 EFFECTIVE COMMUNICATION

1.   The process of communication is composed of three dynamically interrelated elements:

a.   A source (instructor)
b.   The symbols used in composing and transmitting the message (e.g., words)
c.   The receiver (student)

2.   Communication takes place when one person transmits ideas or feelings to another person or to a group of people.

a.   The effectiveness of communication is measured by the similarity between the idea transmitted and the idea received.
b.   Effective communication has taken place when, and only when, the receivers react with understanding and change their behavior accordingly.
c.   Instruction has taken place when a procedure has been explained and the desired student response has occurred.

3.   The effectiveness of persons acting in the role of communicators is related to at least three basic factors.

a.   First, their ability to select symbols that are meaningful to the listener.
b.   Second, communicators consciously or unconsciously reveal attitudes toward themselves, toward the ideas they are trying to transmit, and toward their receivers.

1)   Thus, to communicate effectively, instructors must reveal a positive attitude while delivering their message.

c.   Third, to be more likely to communicate effectively, communicators should speak or write from a broad background of accurate, up-to-date, stimulating material.

4.   To understand the process of communication, at least three characteristics of receivers must be understood.

a.   First, they exercise their ability to question and comprehend the ideas that have been transmitted.
b.   Second, the receiver's attitude may be one of resistance, willingness, or of passive neutrality. Communicators must gain the receiver's attention and then retain it.

1)   The communicator will be more successful in this area by using a varied communicative approach.

c.   Third, the receiver's background, experience, and education frame the target at which communicators must aim.

3.4 BARRIERS TO EFFECTIVE COMMUNICATION

1. Probably the greatest single barrier to effective communication is the lack of a common core of experience between communicator and receiver.

    a. A communicator's words cannot communicate the desired meaning to another person unless the listener or reader has had some experience with the objects or concepts to which these words refer.

2. Overuse of abstractions should be avoided.

    a. Concrete words refer to objects that human beings can experience directly.

    b. Abstract words stand for ideas that cannot be directly experienced or things that do not call forth specific mental images.

        1) Abstractions thus serve as shorthand symbols that sum up large areas of experience.

    c. The danger with using abstract words is that they may not evoke in the listener's mind the specific items of experience the communicator intends.

    d. By using concrete words, the communicator narrows (and gains better control of) the image produced in the minds of the listeners and readers.

3.5 INSTRUCTOR RESPONSIBILITIES

1. Evaluation of demonstrated ability during flight instruction must be based upon established standards of performance, suitably modified to apply to the student's experience and stage of development as a pilot.

    a. In evaluating student demonstrations of piloting ability, it is important for the flight instructor to keep the student informed of his/her progress.

        1) This may be done as each procedure/maneuver is completed or summarized during postflight critiques.

2. Flight instructors have the responsibility and authority to make logbook endorsements for student pilots and other pilots.

    a. Examples of all common endorsements can be found in the current issue of AC 61-65, Appendix 1.

3. Flight instructors have a particular responsibility to provide guidance and restraint regarding the solo operations of their students.

    a. Before receiving an instructor endorsement for solo flight, a student should be required to demonstrate the consistent ability to perform all of the fundamental maneuvers.

    b. The student should also be capable of handling ordinary problems that might occur, such as traffic pattern congestion, a change in the active runway, or unexpected crosswinds.

3.6 INSTRUCTOR PROFESSIONALISM

1. Although the term professionalism is widely used, it is rarely defined. In fact, no single definition can encompass all of the qualifications and considerations of true professionalism. The following are some of the major considerations.

2. Professionals must be able to reason logically and accurately.

3. Professionalism requires good decision-making ability.

    a. Professionals cannot limit their actions and decisions to standard patterns and practice.

4. Professionalism demands a code of ethics.

5. The professional flight instructor should be straightforward and honest.

    a. Anything less than a sincere performance is quickly detected and immediately destroys instructor effectiveness.

    b. Student confidence tends to be destroyed if instructors bluff when in doubt about some point.

    c. The well-prepared instructor instills not only confidence but good habits, since preparing well for a flight is a basic requirement for safe flying. Students quickly become apathetic when they recognize that the flight instructor is inadequately prepared.

6. The attitude, movements, and general demeanor of the flight instructor contribute a great deal to his/her professional image.

    a. The instructor should avoid erratic movements, distracting speech habits, and capricious changes in mood. The professional image requires development of a calm, thoughtful, and disciplined, but not somber, demeanor.

7. The professional relationship between the instructor and the student should be based on a mutual acknowledgment that both the student and the instructor are important to each other and that both are working toward the same objective.

    a. Accepting lower-than-normal standards to please a student will **NOT** help the student/instructor relationship.

    b. Reasonable standards strictly enforced are not resented by an earnest student.

8. The professional flight instructor should accept students as they are with all of their faults and problems.

    a. However, (s)he should also build student self-confidence, set challenges, and generally create an atmosphere for learning.

9. A flight instructor who is not completely familiar with current pilot certification and rating requirements cannot do a competent job of flight instruction.

    a. For a professional performance as a flight instructor, it is essential that the instructor maintain current copies of

        1) The *Federal Aviation Regulations*, especially Parts 1, 61, and 91.
        2) An *Airman's Information Manual*,
        3) *Practical Test Standards*, and
        4) Appropriate pilot training manuals.

    b. True performance as a professional is based on study and research.

10. Flight instructors fail to provide competent instruction when they permit students to partially learn an important item of knowledge or skill.

    a. More importantly, such deficiencies may in themselves allow hazardous inadequacies to develop in the student's ongoing piloting performance.

11. Aviation instructors should be constantly alert for ways to improve the services they provide to their students, their effectiveness, and their qualifications.

QUESTIONS

3.1 Human Needs

1. Before a student can concentrate on learning, which human needs must be satisfied?

A. Safety.

B. Physical.

C. Security.

Answer (B) is correct. *(AIH Chap 1)*
DISCUSSION: Physical needs are the most basic of the human needs. Thus, they must be met before any learning can take place. Until the needs of food, water, rest, etc., are satisfied, the student cannot concentrate on learning.
Answer (A) is incorrect because physical, not safety, needs must be satisfied before a student can concentrate on learning. Safety needs are protection from danger, threat, and deprivation. Answer (C) is incorrect because physical, not security, needs must be satisfied before a student can concentrate on learning. Security (or safety) needs are protection from danger, threat, and deprivation.

2. After individuals are physically comfortable and have no fear for their safety, which human needs become the prime influence on their behavior?

A. Social.

B. Physical.

C. Egoistic.

Answer (A) is correct. *(AIH Chap 1)*
DISCUSSION: The order of human needs according to Abraham Maslow are (1) physical, (2) safety, (3) social, (4) egoistic, and (5) self-fulfillment. In this hierarchy, social needs come after physical and safety needs are satisfied.
Answer (B) is incorrect because the question states that the individuals are physically comfortable. Answer (C) is incorrect because egoistic needs have the fourth priority, not the third priority as the question asks.

3. Which of the student's human needs offer the greatest challenge to an instructor?

A. Social.

B. Egoistic.

C. Self-fulfillment.

Answer (C) is correct. *(AIH Chap 1)*
DISCUSSION: The greatest challenge for an instructor is to help the student realize his/her potentialities for continued development. This is helping the student meet the need for self-fulfillment.
Answer (A) is incorrect because social needs are not a challenge to the instructor. Social needs are those to belong and to give and receive friendship, which the student must satisfy on his/her own. Answer (B) is incorrect because although making a student feel self-confident and deserving of respect (egoism) is important and usually has a direct influence on the instructor-student relationship, it is not the instructor's greatest challenge.

3.2 Motivation

4. Which is generally the more effective way for an instructor to properly motivate students?

    A. Maintain pleasant personal relationships with students.

    B. Provide positive motivations by the promise or achievement of rewards.

    C. Reinforce their self-confidence by requiring no tasks beyond their ability to perform.

Answer (B) is correct. *(AIH Chap 2)*
    DISCUSSION: Providing positive motivation is generally considered the most effective way to properly motivate people. Positive motivations are provided by the promise or achievement of rewards.
    Answer (A) is incorrect because maintaining pleasant personal relationships with students (while desirable) is not the more effective way for an instructor to properly motivate students. Answer (C) is incorrect because a student who is not required to perform a task beyond present abilities will neither be motivated nor make any progress.

5. Motivations that cause a student to react with fear and anxiety are

    A. tangible.

    B. negative.

    C. difficult to identify.

Answer (B) is correct. *(AIH Chap 2)*
    DISCUSSION: Negative motivations may produce fears and may thus be seen by the student as threats. Negative motivation generally intimidates students and should be avoided.
    Answer (A) is incorrect because motivations, whether tangible or intangible, can be either positive or negative. Answer (C) is incorrect because motivations, whether very subtle or difficult to identify, can be either positive or negative.

6. Motivations in the form of reproof and threats should be avoided with all but the student who is

    A. overconfident and impulsive.

    B. avidly seeking group approval.

    C. experiencing a learning plateau.

Answer (A) is correct. *(AIH Chap 2)*
    DISCUSSION: Educational experts have shown that negative motivation is useful only for a student who is overconfident and impulsive. Otherwise, negative motivation in the form of reproof and threats tends to discourage student behavior.
    Answer (B) is incorrect because group approval is a strong motivating force. Use of reproofs and threats with a student seeking group approval would only alienate him/her from the group. Answer (C) is incorrect because one of the reasons a student has reached a learning plateau is due to a lack of motivation. Use of reproofs and threats would only cause a student to remain at the plateau longer.

7. When students are unable to see the benefits or purpose of a lesson, they will

    A. be less motivated.

    B. not learn as quickly.

    C. be expected to increase their efforts.

Answer (A) is correct. *(AIH Chap 2)*
    DISCUSSION: Students will be less motivated if they are unable to see the benefits or purpose of a lesson. It is important for the instructor to make the student aware that a particular lesson can help him/her reach an important goal.
    Answer (B) is incorrect because while a student may not learn as quickly when (s)he is unable to see the benefits or purpose of a lesson, (s)he will become less motivated. Answer (C) is incorrect because the frustration of working without a known goal will likely decrease, not increase, their efforts.

8. Confusion, disinterest, and uneasiness on the part of the student could happen as a result of not knowing the

    A. importance of each period of instruction.

    B. objective of each period of instruction.

    C. subject of each period of instruction.

Answer (B) is correct. *(AIH Chap 7)*
    DISCUSSION: Knowing the objective of each period of instruction gives meaning and interest to the student as well as the instructor. Not knowing the objective of the lesson often leads to confusion, disinterest, and uneasiness on the part of the student.
    Answer (A) is incorrect because confusion, disinterest, and uneasiness on the part of the student could happen as a result of not knowing the objective of each period of instruction, not its importance. Answer (C) is incorrect because confusion, disinterest, and uneasiness on the part of the student could happen as a result of not knowing the objective of each period of instruction, not its subject. The subject of the instructional period will be obvious if it has been planned appropriately.

9. Which statement is true concerning motivations?

A. Motivations must be tangible to be effective.

B. Motivations may be very subtle and difficult to identify.

C. Negative motivations often are as effective as positive motivations.

Answer (B) is correct. *(AIH Chap 2)*
DISCUSSION: Motivations may be subtle, subconscious, and difficult to identify. A student may be motivated without even being aware (s)he is being influenced.
Answer (A) is incorrect because intangible motivations can be as effective (or even more effective) than tangible motivations. Rewards such as accomplishment, fame, and peer acceptance are intangible, but they are among the best positive motivators. Answer (C) is incorrect because negative motivation tends to discourage the student.

10. For a motivation to be effective, students must believe their efforts will be rewarded in a definite manner. This type of motivation is

A. subtle.

B. negative.

C. tangible.

Answer (C) is correct. *(AIH Chap 2)*
DISCUSSION: Students, like any worker, need and want tangible returns for their efforts. These rewards must be constantly apparent to the student during instruction.
Answer (A) is incorrect because the student is often unaware of the application of subtle motivation and thus feels unrewarded for his/her effort. Answer (B) is incorrect because negative motivations are not as effective as positive motivations, as they tend to intimidate students and cause unpleasant experiences.

11. An instructor can most effectively maintain a high level of student motivation by

A. making each lesson a pleasurable experience.

B. relaxing the standards of performance required during the early phase of training.

C. continually challenging the student to meet the highest objectives of training that can be established.

Answer (A) is correct. *(AIH Chap 2)*
DISCUSSION: An instructor can most effectively maintain a high level of motivation by making each lesson a pleasant experience for a student. People avoid negative experiences, but they will seek out and want to repeat positive experiences.
Answer (B) is incorrect because relaxing the standards of performance required during the early phase of training may actually reduce a student's motivation. Reasonable standards strictly enforced are not resented by an earnest student. Answer (C) is incorrect because performance standards should be set to the student's potential and not his/her current ability or to unrealistically high objectives. Improvement must be fostered.

3.3 Effective Communication

12. The effectiveness of communication between instructor and student is measured by the

A. degree of dynamic, interrelated elements.

B. similarity between the idea transmitted and the idea received.

C. relationship between communicative and dynamic elements.

Answer (B) is correct. *(AIH Chap 3)*
DISCUSSION: Communication takes place when one person transmits ideas or feelings to another person or group of people. Its effectiveness is measured by the similarity between the idea transmitted and the idea received.
Answer (A) is incorrect because the process, not the effectiveness, of communication is composed of three dynamic, interrelated elements -- the source, the symbols, and the receiver. Answer (C) is incorrect because the relationship between the communicative elements (source, symbols, and receiver) is dynamic. There are no dynamic elements.

13. Effective communication has taken place when, and only when, the

A. information is transmitted and received.

B. receivers react with understanding and change their behavior accordingly.

C. receivers have the ability to question and comprehend ideas that have been transmitted.

Answer (B) is correct. *(AIH Chap 3)*
DISCUSSION: The rule of thumb among communicators is that communication succeeds only in relation to the reaction of the receiver. Effective communication has taken place only when the receivers react with understanding and change their behavior.
Answer (A) is incorrect because information may be transmitted and received without effective communication. Only when the receiver reacts to the information being transmitted and received with understanding, and changes his/her behavior accordingly, has effective communication taken place.
Answer (C) is incorrect because the ability to question and comprehend ideas that have been transmitted is only one characteristic of a receiver.

14. When has instruction taken place?

A. When a procedure has been explained, and the desired student response has occurred.

B. When the student hears what is presented.

C. When all the required material has been presented.

Answer (A) is correct. *(AIH Chap 3)*
DISCUSSION: Instruction has taken place when the instructor has explained a particular procedure and subsequently determined that the desired student response has occurred.
Answer (B) is incorrect because instruction has taken place when the instructor has explained a particular procedure and subsequently determined that the desired student response has occurred, not only when the student hears what is presented. Answer (C) is incorrect because instruction has taken place when the instructor has explained a particular procedure and subsequently determined that the desired student response has occurred, not only when all the required material has been presented.

15. To communicate effectively, instructors must

A. recognize the level of comprehension.

B. provide an atmosphere which encourages questioning.

C. reveal a positive attitude while delivering their message.

Answer (C) is correct. *(AIH Chap 3)*
DISCUSSION: Communicators consciously or unconsciously reveal attitudes toward themselves, the ideas they are trying to transmit, and their receivers. These attitudes must be positive if the communicators are to communicate effectively.
Answer (A) is incorrect because an instructor can recognize the level of a student's comprehension in the application step of the teaching process, not during the communication process. Answer (B) is incorrect because, while an instructor should provide an atmosphere that encourages questioning, the student must exercise his/her ability to ask questions to communicate effectively.

16. To be more likely to communicate effectively, an instructor should speak or write from a background of

A. technical expertise.

B. knowing the ideas presented.

C. up-to-date, stimulating material.

Answer (C) is correct. *(AIH Chap 3)*
DISCUSSION: A basic factor of a communicator's effectiveness is the ability to speak or write from a broad background of accurate, up-to-date, and stimulating material.
Answer (A) is incorrect because a speaker or writer with technical expertise may depend on technical jargon. Reliance on technical language can impede effective communication, especially when the receiver lacks a similar background. Answer (B) is incorrect because just knowing the ideas presented does not ensure that effective communication will take place. A communicator must be able to make the receiver react with understanding and change his/her behavior accordingly.

17. In the communication process, the communicator will be more successful in gaining and retaining the receiver's attention by

A. being friendly and informative.

B. using a varied communicative approach.

C. using a variety of audiovisual aids in class.

Answer (B) is correct. *(AIH Chap 3)*
DISCUSSION: The most successful communicator will use the variety of channels that best communicates the necessary ideas and techniques, i.e., a varied communicative approach.
Answer (A) is incorrect because effective, engaging communication is more complex than merely being friendly. The source, the symbols, and the receiver are all interrelated in the communication process. Answer (C) is incorrect because audio-visual aids can often further the learning, not the communication, process by supporting, supplementing, or reinforcing important ideas. By presenting the material in a new manner, instructional aids can even improve communication between instructor and student.

3.4 Barriers to Effective Communication

18. Probably the greatest single barrier to effective communication in the teaching process is a lack of

A. respect for the instructor.

B. personality harmony between instructor and student.

C. a common experience level between instructor and student.

Answer (C) is correct. *(AIH Chap 3)*
DISCUSSION: The greatest single barrier to effective communication is the lack of common experience between the communicator and the receiver. Those with the least in common usually find it difficult to communicate.
Answer (A) is incorrect because, while lack of respect for the instructor is a barrier to communication, it is not as great and as prevalent as a lack of common experience between the communicator and the receiver. Answer (B) is incorrect because, while lack of personality harmony is a barrier to communication, it is not as great and as prevalent as a lack of common experience between the communicator and the receiver.

19. A communicator's words cannot communicate the desired meaning to another person unless the

A. words have meaningful referents.

B. words give the meaning that is in the mind of the receiver.

C. listener or reader has had some experience with the objects or concepts to which these words refer.

Answer (C) is correct. *(AIH Chap 3)*
DISCUSSION: Since a common core of experience is basic to effective communication, a communicator's words cannot communicate the desired meaning to another person unless the listener or the reader has had some experience with the objects or concepts to which these words refer.
Answer (A) is incorrect because the words must have not only meaningful referents, but the exact same meaningful referents in order for the communicator and the receiver to share a desired meaning. Answer (B) is incorrect because words only arouse desired meanings if the communicator generates the desired response in the mind of the receiver. The nature of this response is determined by the receiver's past experiences with the words and the concepts to which they refer.

20. The danger in using abstract words is that they

A. sum up vast areas of experience.

B. call forth different mental images in the minds of the receivers.

C. will not evoke the specific items of experience in the listener's mind that the communicator intends.

Answer (C) is correct. *(AIH Chap 3)*
DISCUSSION: The purpose of abstract words is not to bring forth specific ideas in the mind of the receiver but to serve as shorthand symbols that sum up vast areas of experience. The danger in using abstract words is that they will not evoke the specific items in the listener's mind that the communicator intends.
Answer (A) is incorrect because the purpose, not the danger, of using abstract words is to use them as shorthand symbols that sum up vast areas of experience. Answer (B) is incorrect because abstract words do not call forth mental images; on the contrary, they stand for ideas that cannot be directly experienced.

21. By using abstractions in the communication process, the communicator will

A. bring forth specific items of experience in the minds of the receivers.

B. be using words which refer to objects or ideas that human beings can experience directly.

C. not evoke in the listener's or reader's mind the specific items of experience the communicator intends.

Answer (C) is correct. *(AIH Chap 3)*
DISCUSSION: Abstract words are necessary and useful. Their purpose is not to bring forth specific items of experience in the minds of receivers but to serve as shorthand symbols that refer to thoughts or ideas. The danger is that an abstract term might not evoke in the listener's mind the specific item of experience the communicator intended.
Answer (A) is incorrect because abstract words are not used to bring forth specific items of experience in the minds of the receivers. Answer (B) is incorrect because concrete, not abstract, words refer to objects or ideas that human beings can experience directly.

3.5 Instructor Responsibilities

22. Evaluation of demonstrated ability during flight instruction must be based upon

A. the progress of the student.

B. the instructor's opinion concerning the maneuver(s).

C. established standards of performance.

Answer (C) is correct. *(AIH Chap 7)*
DISCUSSION: Evaluation of demonstrated student ability during flight instruction must be based upon established standards of performance, suitably modified to apply to the student's experience and stage of development as a pilot.
Answer (A) is incorrect because evaluation must be based on established standards of performance, not the progress of the student. Answer (B) is incorrect because evaluation must be based upon established standards of performance, not on the instructor's opinion.

23. Evaluation of demonstrated ability during flight instruction must be based upon

A. the instructor's background and experience relating to student pilots at this stage of training.

B. the progress of the student, considering the time and experience attained since beginning training.

C. established standards of performance, suitably modified to apply to the student's experience.

Answer (C) is correct. *(AIH Chap 7)*
DISCUSSION: Evaluation of demonstrated student ability during flight instruction must be based upon established standards of performance, suitably modified to apply to the student's experience and stage of development as a pilot.
Answer (A) is incorrect because evaluation should be based on established standards of performance and modified based on the student's experience, not the instructor's experience. Answer (B) is incorrect because evaluation should be based on established standards of performance, not the student's progress since beginning training, modified based on the student's experience.

24. In evaluating student demonstrations of piloting ability, it is important for the flight instructor to

    A. remain silent and observe.

    B. keep the student informed of progress.

    C. explain errors in performance immediately.

Answer (B) is correct. *(AIH Chap 7)*
    DISCUSSION: In evaluating student demonstrations of piloting ability, it is important for the flight instructor to keep the student informed of his/her progress. This may be done as each procedure/maneuver is completed or summarized during post-flight critiques.
    Answer (A) is incorrect because, in evaluating student demonstrations of piloting ability, it is important for the flight instructor to keep the student informed of his/her progress, not remain silent and observe. Answer (C) is incorrect because students should be allowed to make mistakes and correct them on their own; errors should not be pointed out immediately because students learn by correcting their mistakes. The error can be explained at the completion of the procedure/maneuver or during a post-flight critique.

25. Examples of all common endorsements can be found in the current issue of

    A. AC 61-67, Appendix 1.

    B. AC 91-67, Appendix 1.

    C. AC 61-65, Appendix 1.

Answer (C) is correct. *(AIH Chap 7)*
    DISCUSSION: Examples of all common endorsements can be found in the current issue of AC 61-65, Appendix 1.
    Answer (A) is incorrect because examples of all common endorsements can be found in the current issue of AC 61-65, not AC 61-67, Appendix 1. Answer (B) is incorrect because examples of all common endorsements can be found in the current issue of AC 61-65, not AC 91-67, Appendix 1.

26. Before endorsing a student for solo flight, the instructor should require the student to demonstrate consistent ability to perform

    A. all maneuvers specified in the Student Pilot Guide.

    B. all of the fundamental maneuvers.

    C. slow flight, stalls, emergency landings, takeoffs and landings, and go-arounds.

Answer (B) is correct. *(AIH Chap 7)*
    DISCUSSION: Before endorsing a student for solo flight, the instructor should require the student to demonstrate the consistent ability to perform all of the fundamental maneuvers.
    Answer (A) is incorrect because, before endorsing a student for solo flight, the instructor should require the student to demonstrate the consistent ability to perform all of the fundamental maneuvers, not all maneuvers specified in the Student Pilot Guide (which contains no maneuvers). Answer (C) is incorrect because, before endorsing a student for solo flight, the instructor should require the student to demonstrate the consistent ability to perform all of the fundamental maneuvers, not just slow flight, stalls, emergency landings, takeoffs, landings, and go-arounds.

27. The student should be capable of handling problems that might occur, such as traffic pattern congestion, change in active runway, or unexpected crosswinds prior to

    A. the first solo cross-country flight.

    B. initial solo.

    C. being recommended for a Recreational or Private Pilot Certificate.

Answer (B) is correct. *(AIH Chap 7)*
    DISCUSSION: Flight instructors have a responsibility to provide guidance and restraint regarding the solo operations of their students. Before receiving an instructor endorsement for solo flight, a student should be required to demonstrate the consistent ability to perform all of the fundamental maneuvers and should be capable of handling ordinary problems that might occur, such as traffic pattern congestion, a change in the active runway, or unexpected crosswinds.
    Answer (A) is incorrect because the student should be capable of handling problems that might occur prior to initial solo, not the first solo cross-country flight. Answer (C) is incorrect because the student should be capable of handling problems that might occur prior to initial solo, not being recommended for a recreational or private pilot certificate.

3.6 Instructor Professionalism

28. Which statement is true regarding true professionalism as an instructor?

A. Anything less than sincere performance destroys the effectiveness of the professional instructor.

B. To achieve professionalism, actions and decisions must be limited to standard patterns and practices.

C. A single definition of professionalism would encompass all of the qualifications and considerations which must be present.

Answer (A) is correct. *(AIH Chap 7)*
DISCUSSION: Professionalism demands a code of ethics. Professionals must be true to themselves and to those they serve. Anything less than a sincere performance will be detected by students and immediately destroy instructor effectiveness.
Answer (B) is incorrect because professionalism requires good judgment. Professionals cannot limit their actions and decisions to standard patterns and practice. Answer (C) is incorrect because professionalism is so multi-dimensional that no single definition can encompass all of the qualifications and considerations.

29. Aviation instructors should be constantly alert for ways to improve the services they provide to their students, their effectiveness, and their

A. appearance.

B. qualifications.

C. demeanor.

Answer (B) is correct. *(AIH Chap 7)*
DISCUSSION: Professional aviation instructors must never become complacent or satisfied with their own qualifications and abilities. Aviation instructors should be constantly alert for ways to improve the services they provide to their students, their effectiveness, and their qualifications.
Answer (A) is incorrect because, while an instructor's personal appearance is important to maintaining a professional image, aviation instructors should be constantly alert for ways to improve the services they provide to their students, their effectiveness, and their qualifications. Answer (C) is incorrect because, while an instructor's demeanor is important to maintaining a professional image, aviation instructors should be constantly alert for ways to improve the services they provide to their students, their effectiveness, and their qualifications.

30. Student confidence tends to be destroyed if instructors

A. bluff whenever in doubt about some point.

B. continually identify student errors and failures.

C. direct and control the student's actions and behavior.

Answer (A) is correct. *(AIH Chap 7)*
DISCUSSION: No one, including students, expects an instructor to be perfect. An instructor can gain the respect of students by honestly acknowledging mistakes. If the instructor tries to cover up or bluff, students will be quick to sense it and lose their confidence in the instructor.
Answer (B) is incorrect because identifying the student's errors and failures helps the student to progress and gain confidence. Answer (C) is incorrect because directing the student's actions and behavior is a basic responsibility of the flight instructor.

31. Students quickly become apathetic when they

A. realize material is being withheld by the instructor.

B. understand the objectives toward which they are working.

C. recognize that the instructor is not adequately prepared.

Answer (C) is correct. *(AIH Chap 8)*
DISCUSSION: Students become apathetic when they recognize that the instructor has made inadequate preparations for the instruction being given or when the instruction appears to be deficient, contradictory, or insincere.
Answer (A) is incorrect because students will lose respect for the instructor (not become apathetic) when they realize material is being withheld by the instructor. Answer (B) is incorrect because it is optimal that both the student and instructor understand the objectives so that they may work cooperatively toward them.

32. Which is true regarding professionalism as an instructor?

A. Professionalism demands a code of ethics.

B. To achieve professionalism, actions and decisions must be limited to standard patterns and practices.

C. Professionalism does not require extended training and preparation.

Answer (A) is correct.   *(AIH Chap 7)*
  DISCUSSION: Professionalism demands a code of ethics. Professionals must be true to themselves and to those they serve. Anything less than a sincere performance will be detected by students and immediately destroy instructor effectiveness.
  Answer (B) is incorrect because professionalism requires good judgment. Professionals cannot limit their actions and decisions to standard patterns and practices. Answer (C) is incorrect because professionalism is achieved only after extended training and preparation.

33. Which statement is true regarding the achievement of an adequate standard of performance?

A. A flight instructor should devote major effort and attention to the continuous evaluation of student performance.

B. Flight instructors can affect a genuine improvement in the student/instructor relationship by not strictly enforcing standards.

C. Flight instructors fail to provide competent instruction when they permit students to partially learn an important item of knowledge or skill.

Answer (C) is correct.   *(AIH Chap 7)*
  DISCUSSION: Flight instructors fail to provide competent instruction when they permit their students to partially learn an important item of knowledge or skill. More importantly, such deficiencies may in themselves allow hazardous inadequacies in the student's later piloting performance.
  Answer (A) is incorrect because a flight instructor should devote major effort and attention to all areas of the teaching process, not only to the evaluation of student performance. Answer (B) is incorrect because it is a fallacy to believe that a flight instructor can affect a genuine improvement in the student/instructor relationship by not strictly enforcing standards. Reasonable standards strictly enforced are not resented by an earnest student.

34. True performance as a professional is based on study and

A. perseverance.

B. research.

C. attitude.

Answer (B) is correct.   *(AIH Chap 7)*
  DISCUSSION: True performance as a professional is based on study and research.
  Answer (A) is incorrect because true performance as a professional is based on study and research, not perseverance. Answer (C) is incorrect because true performance as a professional is based on study and research, not attitude.

END OF STUDY UNIT

STUDY UNIT FOUR
TEACHING METHODS

(5 pages of outline)

4.1 LECTURE METHOD

1. The lecture is used primarily for

    a. Introducing students to new subject material,
    b. Summarizing ideas,
    c. Showing relationships between theory and practice, and
    d. Reemphasizing main points.

2. There are four types of lectures:

    a. The illustrated talk in which the speaker relies heavily on visual aids to convey his ideas to the listeners;

    b. The briefing in which the speaker presents a concise array of facts to the listeners who do not expect elaboration or supporting material;

    c. The formal speech in which the speaker's purpose is to inform, persuade, or entertain; and

    d. The teaching lecture for which the instructor must plan and deliver an oral presentation in a manner that helps the students reach the desired learning outcomes.

3. One advantage of a teaching lecture is that the instructor can present many ideas in a relatively short time. Facts and ideas that have been logically organized can be concisely presented in rapid sequence.

    a. Thus, a teaching lecture is the most economical of all teaching methods in terms of the time required to present a given amount of material.

4. One disadvantage of a teaching lecture is that the instructor does not receive direct reaction (either words or actions) from the students when using the teaching lecture.

    a. Thus, the instructor must develop a keen perception for subtle response from the class and must be able to interpret the meaning of these reactions and adjust the lesson accordingly.

        1) These reactions could be in the form of facial expressions, manner of taking notes, and apparent interest or lack of interest in the lesson.

    b. The instructor must recognize that the lecture method is least useful for evaluating student performance.

5. The following four steps should be followed in preparing a lecture:

    a. Establish the objective and desired outcomes,
    b. Research the subject,
    c. Organize the material, and
    d. Plan productive classroom activities.

6. The teaching lecture is probably best delivered extemporaneously but from a written outline.

   a. Because the exact words used to express an idea are chosen at the moment of delivery, the lecture can be personalized or suited to the moment more easily than one that is read or spoken from memory.

7. In the teaching lecture, use simple rather than complex words whenever possible.

   a. Picturesque slang and free-and-easy colloquialisms, if they suit the subject, can add variety and vividness to a teaching lecture.

   b. Errors in grammar and use of vulgarisms detract from an instructor's dignity and reflect upon the intelligence of the students.

8. The lecture can be formal or informal.

   a. A formal lecture provides no active student participation.

   b. The distinguishing characteristic of an informal lecture is the active student participation.

      1) The instructor can inspire active student participation during informal lectures through the use of questions.

4.2 COOPERATIVE OR GROUP LEARNING METHOD

1. Cooperative group learning is an instructional strategy used to organize students into small groups so that they can work together to maximize their own and each other's learning.

   a. The most significant characteristic of group learning is that it continually requires active participation of the student.

   b. The main reason that students are put in cooperative learning groups is so they can individually achieve greater success than if they were to study alone.

2. Instructors should organize small heterogeneous groups of students who have different academic abilities, ethnic backgrounds, race, and gender.

   a. Heterogeneous groups lead students to learn to work together, to seek more support for opinions, and to tolerate each other's viewpoints.

      1) The main advantage of heterogeneous groups is that students tend to interact and achieve in ways and at levels that are rarely found with other instructional strategies.

4.3 GUIDED DISCUSSION METHOD

1. Fundamentally, the guided discussion method of teaching is the reverse of the lecture method. The instructor uses questions to guide and stimulate discussion among students. The instructor does not present new ideas.

2. In the guided discussion, learning is achieved through the skillful use of questions.

   a. Questions facilitate discussion, which in turn develops an understanding of the subject.

3. Questions used in a guided discussion can be broken into several types, each with its usefulness in the guided discussion:

   a. **Overhead** -- directed to the entire group to stimulate thought and response from each group member.

   b. **Rhetorical** -- also stimulates thought, but the instructor will answer it him/herself. This is normally used in a lecture, not a guided discussion.

   c. **Direct** -- question addressed to an individual for a response.

    d.   **Reverse** -- The instructor answers a student's question by redirecting the question for that student to provide the answer.

    e.   **Relay** -- The reverse question is addressed to the entire group, not the individual.

4.   In preparing questions, the instructor should remember that the purpose is to bring about discussion, not merely to get answers.

    a.   Leadoff questions should be open-ended, i.e., they should start with "how" or "why."

    b.   Avoid questions that begin with "what," "when," or "does" because they only require short, categorical answers such as "yes," "no," "green," "one," etc.

5.   Each question, in order to be effective, should

    a.   Have a specific purpose,
    b.   Be clear in meaning,
    c.   Contain a single idea,
    d.   Stimulate thought,
    e.   Require definite answers, and
    f.   Relate to previously taught information.

6.   When it appears the students have adequately discussed the ideas that support a particular part of the lesson, the instructor should summarize what they have accomplished.

    a.   This interim summary is one of the most effective tools available to the instructor.

        1)   This summary can be made immediately after the discussion of each learning outcome.

        2)   It consolidates what students learned, emphasizes how much they know already, and points out any aspects they missed.

7.   Unless the students have some knowledge to exchange with each other, they cannot reach the desired learning outcomes.

    a.   Students without some background in a subject should not be asked to discuss that subject.

4.4 DEMONSTRATION/PERFORMANCE METHOD

1.   The demonstration/performance method is based on the principle that we learn by doing.

    a.   It is the most commonly used teaching method of flight instructors.
    b.   This is the ideal method for teaching a skill, such as using a flight computer.

2.   The demonstration/performance method of instruction has five essential steps:

    a.   Explanation -- the instructor must explain the objectives of the particular lesson to the student.

    b.   Demonstration -- the instructor must show the student how to perform a skill.

    c.   Student performance -- the student must act and do, i.e., practice.

    d.   Instructor supervision -- this is done concurrently with student performance. The instructor coaches, as necessary, the student's practice.

    e.   Evaluation -- the instructor judges the student performance.

3.   The telling and doing technique of flight instruction is basically the demonstration/ performance method of instruction. This consists of performing several steps in proper order.

    a.   Instructor tells -- instructor does
    b.   Student tells -- instructor does
    c.   Student tells -- student does
    d.   Student does -- instructor evaluates

4.5 COMPUTER-BASED TRAINING (CBT) METHOD

1. The computer-based training (CBT) method takes advantage of the abilities of computers to organize and present information.

2. CBT can take different forms:

    a. An instructor can use software to present a lesson using graphics or text projected on a screen.

    b. Interactive software can be used by individuals or small groups to supplement traditional forms of instruction. The software can be used to learn, review, and practice new material.

        1) This type of CBT is directed by the instructor, who is available for questions and guides student activity.

        2) With interactive CBT software, the student is frequently able to control the pace of instruction, review previous material, jump forward, and receive instant feedback.

            a) One of the major advantages of interactive CBT is that students can progress at a rate that is comfortable for them.

        3) With interactive CBT, the presentation varies (i.e., the computer responds in different ways) based on the student's responses (input) to the interactive segments.

4.6 INTEGRATED METHOD OF FLIGHT INSTRUCTION

1. Integrated flight instruction is flight instruction during which students are taught to perform flight maneuvers, both by outside visual references and by reference to flight instruments, from the first time each maneuver is introduced.

    a. In a student's first instruction on the function of flight controls, you would include the instrument indication to be expected, as well as the outside references used in attitude control.

2. The primary objective of integrated flight instruction is to form the habit patterns for the observance of and reliance on flight instruments.

    a. Such habits have been proved to produce more capable and safer pilots.

    b. The ability to fly in instrument meteorological conditions (IMC) is not the objective of this type of primary training.

3. During the conduct of integrated flight instruction, you are responsible for collision avoidance while your student is flying by simulated instruments, i.e., under the hood.

    a. You must guard against diverting your attention to the student's performance for extended periods.

4. At the same time, you must be sure that your student develops, from the first lesson, the habit of looking for other traffic when (s)he is not operating under simulated instrument conditions.

    a. Any observed tendency of a student to enter a maneuver without clearing the area must be corrected immediately.

4.7 THE POSITIVE APPROACH IN FLIGHT INSTRUCTION

1. In flight instruction, an effective positive approach will point out the pleasurable features of flying before the unpleasant possibilities are discussed.

2. EXAMPLE: A positive first flight lesson:

   a. A preflight inspection familiarizing the student with the airplane and its components.
   b. A perfectly normal flight to a nearby airport and back.

      1) The instructor calls the student's attention to how easy the trip was in comparison with other ways to travel and the fact that no critical incidents were encountered or expected.

3. EXAMPLE: A negative first flight lesson:

   a. An exhaustive indoctrination on preflight procedures with emphasis on the potential for disastrous mechanical failures in flight.
   b. Instructions on the dangers of taxiing an airplane too fast.
   c. A series of stalls with emphasis on the difficulties in recovering from them. (The side effect of this performance is likely to be airsickness.)
   d. A series of simulated forced landings, stating that every pilot should always be prepared to cope with an engine failure.

QUESTIONS AND ANSWER EXPLANATIONS

All of the FAA questions from the Fundamentals of Instructing knowledge test relating to the teaching methods outlined above are reproduced on the following pages in the same subunits as the outlines. To the immediate right of each question are the correct answer and answer explanation. You should cover these answers and answer explanations while responding to the questions. Refer to the general discussion in the Introduction on how to take the FAA pilot knowledge test.

Remember that the questions from the FAA knowledge test bank have been reordered by topic, and the topics have been organized into a meaningful sequence. Also, the first line of the answer explanation gives the citation of the authoritative source for the answer.

QUESTIONS
4.1 Lecture Method

1. In the teaching process, which method of presentation is suitable for presenting new material, for summarizing ideas, and for showing relationships between theory and practice?

A. Lecture method.

B. Integrated instruction method.

C. Demonstration/performance method.

Answer (A) is correct. *(AIH Chap 4)*
   DISCUSSION: The lecture is used primarily to introduce students to new material. It is also valuable for summarizing ideas, showing relationships between theory and practice, and reemphasizing main points. The lecture is the most efficient teaching method in terms of time and student numbers, if not in other ways.
   Answer (B) is incorrect because the integrated method of flight instruction is designed to teach students to perform maneuvers both by outside visual references and by reference to flight instruments. Answer (C) is incorrect because the demonstration/performance method is better suited to teaching a skill (i.e., flight instruction).

2. What is one advantage of a lecture?

    A. Uses time economically.

    B. Excellent when additional research is required.

    C. Allows for maximum attainment of certain types of learning outcomes.

Answer (A) is correct. *(AIH Chap 4)*
    DISCUSSION: In a lecture, the instructor can present many ideas in a relatively short time. Facts and ideas that have been logically organized can be concisely presented in rapid sequence. Lecturing is unquestionably the most economical of all teaching methods in terms of time required to present a given amount of material.
    Answer (B) is incorrect because one advantage of the lecture is that it can be used to present information without requiring students to do additional research. Answer (C) is incorrect because a disadvantage, not an advantage, of a lecture is that the lecture does not enable the instructor to estimate the student's progress, thus learning may not be maximized.

3. Which teaching method is most economical in terms of the time required to present a given amount of material?

    A. Briefing.

    B. Teaching lecture.

    C. Demonstration/performance.

Answer (B) is correct. *(AIH Chap 4)*
    DISCUSSION: The teaching lecture is unquestionably the most economical of all teaching methods in terms of the time required to present a given amount of material. The instructor can concisely present many ideas that have been logically organized in rapid sequence.
    Answer (A) is incorrect because, although a briefing is a type of lecture, it is used to present a concise array of facts to the listeners who do not expect elaboration or supporting material. Answer (C) is incorrect because the demonstration/performance method is the least, not the most, economical in terms of time required to present a given amount of material.

4. Which is a true statement regarding the teaching lecture?

    A. Delivering the lecture in an extemporaneous manner is not recommended.

    B. Instructor receives direct feedback from students which is easy to interpret.

    C. Instructor must develop a keen perception for subtle responses and be able to interpret the meaning of these reactions.

Answer (C) is correct. *(AIH Chap 4)*
    DISCUSSION: In the teaching lecture, the instructor must develop a keen perception for subtle responses from the class (e.g., facial expressions, manner of taking notes, and apparent interest or lack of interest in the lesson), and must be able to interpret the meaning of these reactions and adjust the lesson accordingly.
    Answer (A) is incorrect because the lecture is best delivered extemporaneously but from a written outline. The lecture can thus be personalized to suit different audience moods.
Answer (B) is incorrect because, in the teaching lecture, the instructor's feedback is not as direct as other teaching methods and therefore is harder, not easier, to interpret.

5. The first step in preparing a lecture is to

    A. research the subject.

    B. develop the main ideas or key points.

    C. establish the objective and desired outcome.

Answer (C) is correct. *(AIH Chap 4)*
    DISCUSSION: The following four steps, in order, should be used in preparing a lecture.

1. Establish the objectives and desired outcomes
2. Research the subject
3. Organize the material
4. Plan productive classroom activities

    Answer (A) is incorrect because researching the subject is the second, not the first, step in preparing a lecture. Answer (B) is incorrect because developing the main ideas or key points is the third, not the first, step in preparing a lecture.

6. During a teaching lecture, what would detract from an instructor's dignity and reflect upon the student's intelligence?

    A. Use of figurative language.

    B. Errors in grammar and use of vulgarisms.

    C. Using picturesque slang and colloquialisms.

Answer (B) is correct. *(AIH Chap 4)*
    DISCUSSION: During a teaching lecture, errors in grammar and the use of vulgarisms detract from an instructor's dignity and reflect upon the student's intelligence.
    Answer (A) is incorrect because figurative language, when used properly, can add interest and color to a lecture.
Answer (C) is incorrect because picturesque slang and colloquialisms, if they suit the subject, can add variety and vividness to a lecture.

7. The distinguishing characteristic of an informal lecture is the

    A. use of visual aids.

    B. student's participation.

    C. requirement for informal notes.

Answer (B) is correct. *(AIH Chap 4)*
    DISCUSSION: The distinguishing characteristic of an informal lecture is the active student participation. A formal lecture does not include student participation.
    Answer (A) is incorrect because visual aids can be used in either the formal or informal lecture. Answer (C) is incorrect because the requirement for informal notes is not the distinguishing characteristic of an informal lecture. Notes may or may not be used in the formal or informal lecture.

8. An instructor can inspire active student participation during informal lectures through the use of

    A. questions.

    B. visual aids.

    C. encouragement.

Answer (A) is correct. *(AIH Chap 4)*
    DISCUSSION: An instructor can inspire student participation during informal lectures through the use of questions. In this way, the students are encouraged to make contributions that supplement the lecture.
    Answer (B) is incorrect because visual aids emphasize and enhance the lecture but do not help get the students actively involved. Answer (C) is incorrect because encouragement aids learning in all situations, not just participation during lectures.

4.2 Cooperative or Group Learning Method

9. An instructional strategy which organizes students into small groups so that they can work together to maximize their own and each other's learning is called

    A. workshop learning.

    B. heterogeneous group learning.

    C. cooperative or group learning.

Answer (C) is correct. *(AIH Chap 4)*
    DISCUSSION: Cooperative group learning is an instructional strategy which organizes students into small groups so that they can work together to maximize their own and each other's learning.
    Answer (A) is incorrect because workshop learning may take place individually; it does not necessarily involve groups. Answer (B) is incorrect because cooperative group learning is an instructional strategy which organizes students into small groups so that they can work together to maximize their own and each other's learning. Heterogeneous groups are recommended for effective cooperative group learning.

10. The most significant characteristic of group learning is that it

    A. continually requires active participation of the student.

    B. continually requires active participation of both the student and the instructor.

    C. usually requires passive participation of the student.

Answer (A) is correct. *(AIH Chap 4)*
    DISCUSSION: Many positive characteristics have been attributed to group learning, the most significant of which is that it continually requires active participation of the student.
    Answer (B) is incorrect because the most significant characteristic of group learning is that it continually requires active participation of the student, not the instructor. The instructor must allow groups to work by themselves if the students are to maximize each other's learning. Answer (C) is incorrect because group learning requires active, not passive, participation of the student.

11. The main reason that students are put in cooperative learning groups is so they

    A. learn and help each other.

    B. can individually achieve greater success than if they were to study alone.

    C. learn that teamwork is essential if all members are to learn equally well.

Answer (B) is correct. *(AIH Chap 4)*
    DISCUSSION: The main reason that students are put in cooperative learning groups is so they can individually achieve greater success than if they were to study alone.
    Answer (A) is incorrect because, while students do learn and help each other, the main reason that students are put in cooperative learning groups is so they can individually achieve greater success than if they were to study alone. Answer (C) is incorrect because, while teamwork is essential to group learning, it is unlikely that all members will learn equally well. Students are put in cooperative learning groups so they can individually achieve greater success than if they were to study alone.

12. The main advantage(s) with heterogeneous groups are that students tend to

    A. think for themselves since they are in a group of dissimilar students.

    B. interact and achieve in ways and at levels that are rarely found with other instructional strategies.

    C. interact and achieve since they are in a group of similar students.

Answer (B) is correct.   *(AIH Chap 4)*
    DISCUSSION: Instructors should organize small heterogeneous groups of students who have different academic abilities, ethnic backgrounds, race, and gender. The main advantage of heterogeneous groups is that students tend to interact and achieve in ways and at levels that are rarely found with other instructional strategies.
    Answer (A) is incorrect because heterogeneous groups lead students to learn to work together, to seek more support for opinions, and to tolerate each other's viewpoints, not to think for themselves. Answer (C) is incorrect because heterogeneous groups contain dissimilar, not similar, students.

4.3 Guided Discussion Method

13. In a guided discussion, learning is achieved through the

    A. skillful use of questions.

    B. use of questions, each of which contains several ideas.

    C. use of reverse questions directed to the class as a whole.

Answer (A) is correct.   *(AIH Chap 4)*
    DISCUSSION: The guided discussion method relies on the students to provide ideas, experiences, opinions, and information. The instructor guides the discussion by use of questions aimed at drawing out what the students know. Thus, learning is achieved through the skillful use of questions.
    Answer (B) is incorrect because, in a guided discussion, each question used should contain only one, not several, ideas. Answer (C) is incorrect because a relay, not reverse, question is redirected to the class as a whole.

14. A question directed to an entire group to stimulate thought and response from each group member is identified as

    A. Relay.

    B. Overhead.

    C. Rhetorical.

Answer (B) is correct.   *(AIH Chap 4)*
    DISCUSSION: In the guided discussion, learning is produced through skillful use of questions. To begin a guided discussion, the instructor should use an overhead question. This type of question is directed to the entire group to stimulate thought and response from each student.
    Answer (A) is incorrect because a relay question responds to a student's question by redirecting it back to the rest of the group. Answer (C) is incorrect because a rhetorical question is similar in nature to an overhead question, but the instructor answers the question. This is more commonly used in lecturing than in guided discussion.

15. In a guided discussion, leadoff questions should usually begin with

    A. why.

    B. what.

    C. when.

Answer (A) is correct.   *(AIH Chap 4)*
    DISCUSSION: In preparing questions, the instructor should remember that the purpose is to bring about discussion, not merely to get only short categorical answers (e.g., yes, no, one, etc.). Thus, lead-off questions should usually begin with "how" or "why."
    Answer (B) is incorrect because a question beginning with "what" usually requires only a short categorical answer and will not encourage a discussion. Answer (C) is incorrect because a question beginning with "when" usually requires a short answer and will not encourage a discussion.

16. Which question would be best as a leadoff question for a guided discussion on the subject of torque?

    A. Does torque affect an airplane?

    B. How does torque affect an airplane?

    C. What effect does torque have on an airplane in a turn?

Answer (B) is correct.   *(AIH Chap 4)*
    DISCUSSION: In preparing questions to lead off a guided discussion, the instructor should remember that the purpose is to bring about discussion, not merely answers. Avoid questions that require only short, categorical (i.e., yes or no) answers. Lead-off questions should usually begin with "how" or "why."
    Answer (A) is incorrect because a question beginning with "does" only requires a yes or no answer and will not encourage a discussion. Answer (C) is incorrect because a question beginning with "what" only requires a short, categorical answer and will not encourage a discussion.

17. When it appears students have adequately discussed the ideas presented during a guided discussion, one of the most valuable tools an instructor can use is

A. a session of verbal testing.

B. a written test on the subject discussed.

C. an interim summary of what the students accomplished.

Answer (C) is correct. *(AIH Chap 4)*
   DISCUSSION: When it appears the students have discussed the ideas that support a particular part of the lesson, the instructor should summarize what the students have accomplished. This interim summary is one of the most effective tools available to the instructor in a guided discussion. To bring ideas together and help in transition, an interim summary should be made after the discussion of each desired learning outcome.
   Answer (A) is incorrect because a session of verbal testing goes against the intention of the guided discussion, where the instructor aims to "draw out" what the students know in a structured but personable manner. Answer (B) is incorrect because a written test on the subject without an instructor summary would be testing student opinions and experiences rather than facts.

18. Which statement about the guided discussion method of teaching is true?

A. The lesson objective becomes apparent at the application level of learning.

B. Students without a background in the subject can also be included in the discussion.

C. Unless the students have some knowledge to exchange with each other, they cannot reach the desired learning outcomes.

Answer (C) is correct. *(AIH Chap 4)*
   DISCUSSION: Throughout the time the instructor prepares the students for their discussion (e.g., early lectures, homework assignments), the students should be made aware of the lesson objectives. This gives them the background for a fruitful guided discussion. Students without some background in a subject should not be asked to discuss that subject.
   Answer (A) is incorrect because the lesson objective should be known while the students are preparing for the guided discussion, or at least during the introduction, not afterward at the application level of learning. Answer (B) is incorrect because students with no background in the subject will not be able to contribute to an effective discussion.

4.4 Demonstration/Performance Method

19. Which method of presentation is desirable for teaching a skill such as ground school lesson on the flight computer?

A. Lecture/application.

B. Presentation/practice.

C. Demonstration/performance.

Answer (C) is correct. *(AIH Chap 4)*
   DISCUSSION: The demonstration/performance method of teaching is based on the principle that you learn by doing. Students learn physical or mental skills best by actually performing them under supervision. Learning to use a flight computer is an ideal application of this teaching method.
   Answer (A) is incorrect because the lecture method is not suitable to teach flight computer use because the lecture does not provide for student participation and, as a consequence, lets the instructor do all the work. Answer (B) is incorrect because presentation/practice is not a method of presentation.

20. What are the essential steps in the demonstration/performance method of teaching?

A. Demonstration, practice, and evaluation.

B. Demonstration, student performance, and evaluation.

C. Explanation, demonstration, student performance, instructor supervision, and evaluation.

Answer (C) is correct. *(AIH Chap 4)*
   DISCUSSION: The demonstration/performance method of teaching is based on the principle that we learn by doing. Thus, it is used by flight instructors in teaching procedures and maneuvers. The five essential steps are:

1. Explanation
2. Demonstration
3. Student performance
4. Instructor supervision
5. Evaluation

   Answer (A) is incorrect because the five, not three, essential steps in the demonstration/performance method of teaching are explanation, demonstration, student performance (not practice), instructor supervision, and evaluation. Answer (B) is incorrect because the five, not three, essential steps in the demonstration/performance method of teaching are explanation, demonstration, student performance, instructor supervision, and evaluation.

21. What is the last step in the demonstration/ performance method?

   A. Summary.

   B. Evaluation.

   C. Student performance.

Answer (B) is correct. *(AIH Chap 4)*
   DISCUSSION: The demonstration/performance method of teaching is based on the principle that we learn by doing. Thus, it is used by flight instructors in teaching procedures and maneuvers. The five essential steps are:

1. Explanation
2. Demonstration
3. Student performance
4. Instructor supervision
5. Evaluation

   Answer (A) is incorrect because summary is not a step in the demonstration/performance method. Answer (C) is incorrect because student performance is the third, not last, step in the demonstration/performance method.

22. In the demonstration/performance method of instruction, which two separate actions are performed concurrently?

   A. Instructor explanation and demonstration.

   B. Student performance and instructor supervision.

   C. Instructor explanation and student demonstration.

Answer (B) is correct. *(AIH Chap 4)*
   DISCUSSION: In the demonstration/performance method of instruction, student performance and instructor supervision are performed concurrently. As the student practices to learn, the instructor supervises and coaches as necessary.
   Answer (A) is incorrect because, during the explanation phase, the instructor explains to the student the actions they are to perform. This is accomplished during the preflight discussion. The demonstration is done in the airplane as the instructor shows the student how to perform a maneuver. Answer (C) is incorrect because instructor supervision, not explanation, and student performance, not demonstration, are performed concurrently.

23. The basic demonstration/performance method of instruction consists of several steps in proper order. They are

   A. instructor tells--student does; student tells-- student does; student does--instructor evaluates.

   B. instructor tells--instructor does; student tells-- instructor does; student does--instructor evaluates.

   C. instructor tells--instructor does; student tells-- instructor does; student tells--student does; student does--instructor evaluates.

Answer (C) is correct. *(AIH Chap 8)*
   DISCUSSION: The telling and doing technique of flight instruction (basically the demonstration/performance method) is very effective and valuable in teaching procedures and maneuvers. First, the instructor explains, then demonstrates. Then the student performs, first by explaining as the instructor does, then by explaining and doing it him/herself while the instructor supervises. Finally, the instructor evaluates how the student performs.
   Answer (A) is incorrect because it omits the first step, which is instructor tells--instructor does. The second step is student tells--instructor does, not vice versa. Answer (B) is incorrect because it omits the third step of student tells--student does.

4.5 Computer-Based Training (CBT) Method

24. Which statement is true concerning computer- based training (CBT)?

   A. The instructor need not be actively involved with the students when using instructional aids.

   B. CBT may be used by the instructor as stand-alone training.

   C. One of the major advantages of CBT is that students can progress at a rate which is comfortable for them.

Answer (C) is correct. *(AIH Chap 4)*
   DISCUSSION: With computer-based training software, the student is frequently able to control the pace of instruction, review previous material, jump forward, and receive instant feedback.
   Answer (A) is incorrect because the instructor does need to be involved with the students when using instructional aids. The instructor must either use those aids to present an idea to the class, or he/she must be available to assist students who are using instructional aids on their own. Answer (B) is incorrect because, while CBT can take a major role in some training programs, those programs must still be guided and enhanced by the instructor.

25. Some of the more advanced computer-based training (CBT) applications allow students to progress through a series of interactive segments where the presentation varies as a result of their

A. training.

B. responses.

C. needs.

Answer (B) is correct. *(AIH Chap 4)*
DISCUSSION: Interactive software varies the presentation based on the responses of the user to the interactive segments.
Answer (A) is incorrect because the presentation of more advanced CBT applications varies as a result of the student's responses to the interactive segments, not his/her training. The choice of CBT applications depends on the training that is being conducted. Answer (C) is incorrect because the presentation of more advanced CBT applications varies as a result of the student's responses to the interactive segments, not his/her needs. The choice of CBT applications may vary depending on an individual student's needs.

26. The major advantage of computer-based training (CBT) over other forms of instruction is that it is interactive - the computer responds in different ways, depending on the student's

A. background.

B. input.

C. training.

Answer (B) is correct. *(AIH Chap 4)*
DISCUSSION: The major advantage of CBT is that it is interactive. The software responds based on choices made by the user (input). This approach keeps the student involved in the learning process.
Answer (A) is incorrect because the computer responds based on the student's input, not background. The choice of CBT software may depend on the student's academic or experiential background. Answer (C) is incorrect because the computer responds based on the student's input, not training. The choice of CBT software depends on the type of training to be conducted.

4.6 Integrated Method of Flight Instruction

27. The primary objective of integrated flight instruction is the

A. formation of firm habit patterns for observing and relying on flight instruments.

B. difference in the pilot's operation of the flight controls during both VMC and IMC.

C. developing of the habit of occasionally monitoring their own and the aircraft's performance.

Answer (A) is correct. *(AIH Chap 8)*
DISCUSSION: The primary objective of the integrated flight training method is the formation of firm habit patterns for observing and relying on flight instruments from the student's first piloting experience. The goal is to teach proper use of flight instruments in VFR flight.
Answer (B) is incorrect because there should be no difference in the pilot's operation of the flight controls in either VMC or IMC. The manipulation of the flight controls is identical, regardless of which references are used to determine the attitude of the airplane. Answer (C) is incorrect because the pilot's habit of occasionally monitoring his/her own performance along with the aircraft's is an objective of basic flight instruction, not integrated flight instruction.

28. Integrated flight instruction has many benefits, but the main objective is to

A. develop the student's ability to fly the aircraft during inadvertent IMC.

B. ensure the student is not overly dependent on instruments during VFR flight.

C. help the student develop habit patterns for observance of and reference to flight instruments.

Answer (C) is correct. *(AIH Chap 8)*
DISCUSSION: The primary objective of the integrated method of flight training is to develop firm habit patterns for observance of and reliance on flight instruments as well as outside references from the student's first piloting experience. The goal is to teach proper use of flight instruments in VFR flight.
Answer (A) is incorrect because the ability to fly the aircraft in IMC is not an objective of integrated flight instruction. Answer (B) is incorrect because the objective of integrated flight instruction is to ensure that the student is not overly dependent on outside visual references, not flight instruments.

END OF STUDY UNIT

29. Which is an acceptable procedure when using the integrated method of flight instruction?

    A. Use alternate and distinct periods devoted entirely to instrument flight or to visual flight.

    B. Prior to the first flight, clearly explain the differences in the manipulation of flight controls for maintaining aircraft control when under simulated instrument conditions and when using references outside the aircraft.

    C. Include in the student's first instruction on the function of flight controls the instrument indication to be expected, as well as the outside references used in attitude control.

Answer (C) is correct. *(AIH Chap 8)*
    DISCUSSION: When using the integrated method of flight instruction, you should include in the student's first instruction on the function of flight controls the instrument indications to be expected, as well as the outside references used in attitude control.
    Answer (A) is incorrect because integrated flight instruction means simultaneous, not alternate, instruction in instrument and visual references. Answer (B) is incorrect because there is no distinction in the student's operation of the flight controls, regardless of whether outside references or instrument indications are used for the performance of a maneuver.

30. During integrated flight instruction, the instructor must be sure the student

    A. develops the habit of looking for other traffic.

    B. is able to control the aircraft for extended periods under IMC.

    C. can depend on the flight instruments when maneuvering by outside references.

Answer (A) is correct. *(AIH Chap 8)*
    DISCUSSION: If students are allowed to believe that the instructor assumes all responsibility for avoiding other traffic, they cannot develop the habit of keeping a constant watch, which is essential to safety. Any observed tendency of a student to enter flight maneuvers without first making a careful check for other possible air traffic must be corrected immediately.
    Answer (B) is incorrect because the ability to control the aircraft for extended periods under IMC is not the objective of integrated flight instruction. Answer (C) is incorrect because the instructor must be sure not to let the student focus his attention on the instruments at the expense of looking for other traffic.

4.7 The Positive Approach in Flight Instruction

31. Which is an example of a positive approach in the first flight lesson of a student with no previous aviation experience?

    A. Conducting a thorough preflight.

    B. A normal flight to a nearby airport and return.

    C. Instruction in the care which must be taken when taxiing an airplane.

Answer (B) is correct. *(AIH Chap 7)*
    DISCUSSION: A normal flight to a nearby airport and back shows the student some of the pleasant aspects of aviation. Such an introductory lesson leaves a positive impression in the new student's mind. Positive teaching results in positive learning.
    Answer (A) is incorrect because, in the first flight lesson of a student with no aviation experience, conducting a thorough, exhaustive preflight is an example of a negative, not a positive, approach. The student may question whether learning to fly is a good idea or not. Answer (C) is incorrect because, in the first flight lesson of a student with no aviation experience, instruction in the care that must be taken when taxiing an airplane is an example of a negative, not a positive, approach. The student may question whether learning to fly is a good idea or not.

32. Which statement is true regarding positive or negative approaches in aviation instructional techniques?

    A. A student with normal abilities should not be affected by an instructor who emphasizes emergency procedures early in training.

    B. A positive approach, to be effective, will point out the pleasurable features of aviation before the unpleasant possibilities are discussed.

    C. The introduction of emergency procedures before the student is acquainted with normal operations is likely to be neither discouraging nor affect learning.

Answer (B) is correct. *(AIH Chap 7)*
    DISCUSSION: Flight instructor success depends, in large measure, on the ability to frame instructions so that students develop a positive image of flying. A positive approach, to be effective, will point out the pleasurable features of aviation before the unpleasant possibilities are discussed. A negative approach generally results in negative learning because the student's perceptual process would be adversely affected by fear.
    Answer (A) is incorrect because an instructor who emphasizes emergency procedures early in training will most likely have a negative effect on the learning process regardless of a student's abilities. The student new to aviation is still quite impressionable. Answer (C) is incorrect because the introduction of emergency procedures before the student is acquainted with normal operations most likely will be discouraging or threatening and will adversely affect learning.

END OF STUDY UNIT

STUDY UNIT FIVE
PLANNING INSTRUCTIONAL ACTIVITY

(4 pages of outline)

5.1 COURSE DEVELOPMENT

1. Any instructional activity must be competently planned and organized if it is to achieve the desired learning outcomes.

    a. First, you must determine the overall objectives and standards of the course.

    b. Then, you must identify the blocks of learning which constitute the necessary parts of the total objective.

    1) You must ensure that each block of learning identified is truly an integral part of the overall objective.

    a) Extraneous blocks of instruction are expensive frills, especially in flight instruction, and detract from the completion of the final objective.

    2) The blocks of learning must be developed and arranged in their proper sequence.

    a) In this way, a student can master the segments of the overall pilot performance requirements individually and can progressively combine these with other related segments until their sum meets the final objective.

2. A training syllabus is an abstract or digest of the course of training. It consists of the blocks of learning to be completed in the most efficient order.

    a. The order of training can and should be altered when necessary to suit the progress of the student and the demands of special circumstances.

    1) However, it is often preferable to skip to a completely different part of the syllabus when the conduct of a scheduled lesson is impossible, rather than proceeding to the next lesson, which may be predicated completely on skills to be developed during the lesson being postponed.

5.2 ORGANIZATION OF MATERIAL

1. The teaching process can be divided into four basic steps: preparation, presentation, application, and review/evaluation.

    a. Every lesson, when developed adequately, falls logically into these four steps.

2. Regardless of the teaching method used (lecture, guided discussion, or demonstration-performance), an instructor must properly organize the material. One effective way to organize a lesson is -- introduction, development, and conclusion.

    a. The **introduction** sets the stage for everything to come. The introduction can be divided into three subparts:

    1) **Attention** -- The instructor must gain the students' attention and focus it on the subject.

    2) **Motivation** -- The instructor should offer specific reasons why they need to learn the material. This motivation should appeal to each student personally and accentuate the desire to learn.

    3) **Overview** -- Each lesson introduction should contain an overview that tells the group what is to be covered during the period.

  b. The **development** is the main part of the lesson during which the instructor organizes the explanations and demonstrations in a manner that helps the students achieve the desired learning outcomes.

    1) The instructor must logically organize the material to show the relationships of the main points to each other. This is done by developing the main points in one of the following ways:

        a) From past to present

        b) From simple to complex

        c) From known to unknown (i.e., using a student's previous experiences and knowledge to acquire new concepts)

        d) From most frequently used (most familiar) to least frequently used

  c. The **conclusion** retraces the important elements of the lesson and relates them to the objective.

    1) This reinforces the student's learning and improves retention of what has been learned.

    2) New ideas should not be introduced in the conclusion because doing so at this point in the lesson will only confuse the student.

5.3 LESSON PLAN

1. Each lesson of the training syllabus includes an objective, content, and completion standards.

2. A lesson plan is an organized outline that is developed for a single instructional period.

  a. A properly constructed lesson plan will provide an outline that tells the instructor what to do, in what order to do it, and what teaching procedure to use.

  b. The lesson plan must be appropriate for the particular student.

    1) Standard lesson plans may not be effective for students requiring a different approach.

    2) Therefore, the main concern in developing a lesson plan is the student.

3. A lesson plan should be prepared in writing for each instructional period, regardless of the instructor's experience.

  a. A so-called mental outline is not a lesson plan.

  b. Another instructor should be able to take the lesson plan and know what to do in conducting the same period of instruction.

4. Lesson plans help instructors keep a constant check on their own activity, as well as that of their students.

5. A characteristic of a well-planned lesson is that it should contain new material that is related to the lesson previously presented.

  a. In flight training, a short review of earlier lessons is usually necessary.

6. Each lesson plan should contain the following items: lesson objective, content, schedule, equipment, instructor's actions, student's actions, and completion standards. See the illustration below.

LESSON GROUND REFERENCE MANEUVERS   STUDENT _____   DATE _____

OBJECTIVE
- TO DEVELOP THE STUDENT'S SKILL IN PLANNING AND FOLLOWING A PATTERN OVER THE GROUND COMPENSATING FOR WIND DRIFT AT VARYING ANGLES.

CONTENT
- USE OF GROUND REFERENCES TO CONTROL PATH.
- OBSERVATION AND CONTROL OF WIND EFFECT.
- CONTROL OF AIRPLANE ATTITUDE, ALTITUDE, AND HEADING.

SCHEDULE
- PREFLIGHT DISCUSSON.   : 10
- INSTRUCTOR DEMONSTRATIONS.   : 25
- STUDENT PRACTICE.   : 45
- POSTFLIGHT CRITIQUE.   : 10

EQUIPMENT
- CHALKBOARD FOR PREFLIGHT DISCUSSION.
- IFR VISOR FOR MANEUVERS REVIEWED.

INSTRUCTOR'S ACTIONS
- PREFLIGHT - DISCUSS LESSON OBJECTIVE. DIAGRAM "S" TURNS, EIGHTS ALONG A ROAD, AND RECTANGULAR COURSE ON A CHALKBOARD.

- INFLIGHT - DEMONSTRATE ELEMENTS. DEMONSTRATE FOLLOWING A ROAD, "S" TURNS, EIGHTS ALONG A ROAD, AND RECTANGULAR COURSE. COACH STUDENT PRACTICE.

- POSTFLIGHT - CRITIQUE STUDENT PERFORMANCE AND MAKE STUDY ASSIGNMENT.

STUDENT'S ACTIONS
- PREFLIGHT - DISCUSS LESSON OBJECTIVE AND RESOLVE QUESTIONS.

- INFLIGHT - REVIEW PREVIOUS MANEUVERS INCLUDING POWER-OFF STALLS AND FLIGHT AT MINIMUM CONTROLLABLE AIRSPEED. PERFORM EACH NEW MANEUVER AS DIRECTED.

- POSTFLIGHT - ASK PERTINENT QUESTIONS.

COMPLETION STANDARDS
- STUDENT SHOULD DEMONSTRATE COMPETENCY IN MAINTAINING ORIENTATION, AIRSPEED WITHIN 10 KNOTS, ALTITUDE WITHIN 100 FEET, AND HEADINGS WITHIN 10 DEGREES, AND IN MAKING PROPER CORRECTION FOR WIND DRIFT.

---

7. Also see Figure 1A on page 75 for an example of a ground lesson plan.

8.   The objectives of each lesson should be clearly stated.

   a.   The objective is the reason for the lesson -- what the student is expected to know or be able to do at the end of the lesson.

   b.   Keeping the student informed of lesson objectives and completion standards minimizes the student's insecurity.

9.   Fatigue is the primary consideration in determining the length and frequency of flight instruction periods.

   a.   Fatigue resulting from excessive or lengthy instruction reduces a student's learning ability.

10.   When planning time for student performance, a primary consideration is the length of the practice session.

   a.   A beginning student reaches a point where additional practice is not only unproductive but may be harmful.

   b.   As a student gains experience, longer periods of practice are profitable.

11.   A blank lesson plan is provided on page 155 so you may make copies for your use.

5.4 INSTRUCTIONAL AIDS

1.   Instructional aids are useful tools to emphasize, support, and supplement the key points in a lesson.

   a.   Instructional aids include models, chalkboards, charts, and projected material (e.g., videotapes, movies, slides, etc.).

2.   The following four-step procedure should be used to determine if and when instructional aids are necessary:

   a.   Clearly establish the lesson objective, being certain what must be communicated.

   b.   Gather the necessary data by researching for support material.

   c.   Organize the material into an outline or lesson plan. The outline should include all key points to be presented.

   d.   Finally, determine what ideas should be supported with instructional aids.

      1)   They should be compatible with the learning outcomes to be achieved.
      2)   They should be designed to cover the key points in a lesson.

3.   Instructional aids used in the teaching/learning process should not be used as a crutch by the instructor.

QUESTIONS AND ANSWER EXPLANATIONS

   All of the FAA questions from the Fundamentals of Instructing knowledge test relating to planning instructional activity outlined above are reproduced on the following pages in the same subunits as the outlines. To the immediate right of each question are the correct answer and answer explanation. You should cover these answers and answer explanations while responding to the questions. Refer to the general discussion in the Introduction on how to take the FAA pilot knowledge test.

   Remember that the questions from the FAA knowledge test bank have been reordered by topic, and the topics have been organized into a meaningful sequence. Also, the first line of the answer explanation gives the citation of the authoritative source for the answer.

QUESTIONS

5.1 Course Development

1. In planning any instructional activity, the first consideration should be to

- A. determine the overall objectives and standards.
- B. establish common ground between the instructor and student.
- C. identify the blocks of learning which make up the overall objective.

Answer (A) is correct. *(AIH Chap 6)*
   DISCUSSION: The first step in planning any instructional activity is to determine the overall objectives and standards. If the instructor does not have a logical view of what is to be achieved, then the students will not.
   Answer (B) is incorrect because establishing a common ground between the instructor and student is the purpose of a lesson introduction, not the first step in planning instructional activity. Answer (C) is incorrect because the second, not the first, consideration in planning for any instructional activity is to identify the blocks of learning that make up the overall objective.

2. In planning instructional activity, the second step is to

- A. develop lesson plans for each period or unit of instruction.
- B. identify blocks of learning which constitute the necessary parts of the total objective.
- C. develop a training syllabus that will serve as a guide for conducting training at each level of learning.

Answer (B) is correct. *(AIH Chap 6)*
   DISCUSSION: In planning instructional activity, the second step (after the overall training objectives have been established) is the identification of the blocks of learning that constitute the necessary parts of the total objective.
   Answer (A) is incorrect because, to develop lesson plans for each period or unit of instruction, an instructor must first determine the overall objectives, then identify the blocks of learning necessary to meet those objectives. Answer (C) is incorrect because a training syllabus is an abstract of the course of training. It consists of the blocks of learning to be completed in the most efficient order and thus must be developed after the blocks have been identified.

3. Development and assembly of blocks of learning in their proper relationship will provide a means for

- A. both the instructor and student to easily correct faulty habit patterns.
- B. challenging the student by progressively increasing the units of learning.
- C. allowing the student to master the segments of the overall pilot performance requirements individually and combining these with other related segments.

Answer (C) is correct. *(AIH Chap 6)*
   DISCUSSION: Training for a skill as complicated and involved as piloting an aircraft requires the development and assembly, in their appropriate sequence, of many segments or blocks of learning. In this way, a student can master the segments of the overall pilot performance requirements individually and can progressively combine these with other related segments until (s)he learns to fly, which is the final objective.
   Answer (A) is incorrect because organizing the appropriate blocks of learning in their proper relationship should prevent the formation of bad habits. This is the basic reason for the building block technique of instruction. Answer (B) is incorrect because the challenge presented to the student is one way to test for a useful size of a minimum block of learning, but progressively increasing the blocks of learning may deter the student's progress.

4. Which statement is true concerning extraneous blocks of instruction during a course of training?

- A. They are usually necessary parts of the total objective.
- B. They detract from the completion of the final objective.
- C. They assist in the attainment of the lesson's objective.

Answer (B) is correct. *(AIH Chap 6)*
   DISCUSSION: While identifying the blocks of learning to be used in the course, the instructor must examine each carefully to see that it is truly an integral part of the structure. Extraneous blocks of instruction can detract from, rather than assist, in the completion of the final objective.
   Answer (A) is incorrect because extraneous blocks of instruction are unnecessary parts of the total objective.
Answer (C) is incorrect because extraneous blocks of instruction detract, not assist, in the attainment of the lesson's objective.

5. When it is impossible to conduct a scheduled lesson, it is preferable for the instructor to

- A. review and possibly revise the training syllabus.
- B. proceed to the next scheduled lesson, or if this is not practical, cancel the lesson.
- C. conduct a lesson that is not predicated completely on skills to be developed during the lesson which was postponed.

Answer (C) is correct. *(AIH Chap 6)*
DISCUSSION: It is preferable for the instructor to skip to a completely different part of the syllabus when it is impossible to conduct a scheduled lesson, rather than proceeding to the next lesson, which may be predicated completely on skills to be developed during the lesson that was postponed.
Answer (A) is incorrect because an instructor should review and possibly revise the training syllabus when there is an applicable change to the FARs or PTSs, not because a lesson had to be postponed. Answer (B) is incorrect because the next lesson may need skills that were to be learned in the postponed lesson.

5.2 Organization of Material

6. When teaching new material, the teaching process can be divided into which steps?

- A. Preparation, presentation, application, and review and evaluation.
- B. Preparation, demonstration, practice, and review.
- C. Explanation, demonstration, practice, and evaluation.

Answer (A) is correct. *(AIH Chap 4)*
DISCUSSION: The four basic steps in the teaching process are preparation, presentation, application, and review and evaluation.
Answer (B) is incorrect because demonstration and practice are examples of teaching methods, not basic steps in the teaching process. Answer (C) is incorrect because explanation, demonstration, and practice are examples of teaching methods, not basic steps in the teaching process.

7. Every lesson, when adequately developed, falls logically into the four steps of the teaching process -

- A. preparation, introduction, presentation, and review and evaluation.
- B. preparation, introduction, presentation, and review and application.
- C. preparation, presentation, application, and review and evaluation.

Answer (C) is correct. *(AIH Chap 6)*
DISCUSSION: Every lesson, when developed adequately, falls logically into the four steps of the teaching process: preparation, presentation, application, and review/evaluation.
Answer (A) is incorrect because the second basic step in the teaching process is presentation, not introduction, and the third basic step is application, not presentation. Answer (B) is incorrect because the second basic step in the teaching process is presentation, not introduction, the third basic step is application, not presentation, and the fourth basic step is review and evaluation, not review and application.

8. The method of arranging lesson material from the simple to complex, past to present, and known to unknown, is one that

- A. creates student thought pattern departures.
- B. shows the relationships of the main points of the lesson.
- C. requires students to actively participate in the lesson.

Answer (B) is correct. *(AIH Chap 4)*
DISCUSSION: An instructor must logically organize the lesson material to show the relationships of the main points. This can be done by arranging the material from the simple to the complex, past to present, known to unknown, and from the most frequently used to the least frequently used.
Answer (A) is incorrect because, by arranging lesson material from the simple to complex, past to present, and known to unknown, the instructor will make meaningful transitions from one point to another and thus keep the students oriented, not creating thought pattern departures. Answer (C) is incorrect because the objective of each lesson, not the method of arranging material, should require students to actively participate (either directly or indirectly) in the lesson in order to achieve the desired learning outcomes.

9. In organizing lesson material, which step sets the stage for everything to come?

- A. Overview.
- B. Conclusion.
- C. Introduction.

Answer (C) is correct. *(AIH Chap 4)*
DISCUSSION: The introduction to a lesson should set the stage for everything to come. The introduction is made up of three elements: attention, motivation, and overview.
Answer (A) is incorrect because the overview is included in the introduction and tells the group what is to be covered during the period of instruction, not how it relates to the entire course. Answer (B) is incorrect because the conclusion retraces the important elements of the lesson and relates them to the lesson objective. It does not set the stage for everything to come because it is at the end of a lesson.

10. The proper sequence for the subparts of an introduction is

   A. attention, motivation, and overview.

   B. attention, development, and overview.

   C. overview, motivation, and conclusion.

Answer (A) is correct.   *(AIH Chap 4)*
   DISCUSSION: The proper sequence for the subparts of an introduction is attention, motivation, and overview. First, the instructor must gain the student's attention and focus it on the subject at hand. Second, the introduction should offer the students specific reasons for needing to be familiar with, to know, to understand, to apply, or to be able to perform whatever they are about to learn. This motivation should appeal to each student personally and accentuate the desire to learn. Third, every lesson introduction should contain an overview that tells the group what is to be covered during the period.
   Answer (B) is incorrect because development is the main part of the lesson, not a subpart of the introduction. Answer (C) is incorrect because conclusion is the review portion of the lesson, not a subpart of the introduction.

11. In developing a lesson, the instructor should organize explanations and demonstrations to help the student

   A. achieve the desired learning outcome.

   B. acquire a thorough understanding of the material presented.

   C. acquire new concepts, generally progressing from the known to the unknown.

Answer (A) is correct.   *(AIH Chap 4)*
   DISCUSSION: In developing a lesson, the instructor should organize the subject matter (explanations and demonstrations) in a manner that helps the student achieve the desired learning outcome.
   Answer (B) is incorrect because the student's ability to acquire a thorough understanding of the material is dependent on more than an instructor's organized presentation, e.g., motivation, needs, etc. Answer (C) is incorrect because progressing from the known to the unknown is a way of logically organizing the lesson material to show the relationships of the main points, not the intent of developing a lesson, which is to help the student achieve the desired learning outcome.

12. When teaching from the known to the unknown, an instructor is using the student's

   A. current knowledge of the subject.

   B. previous experiences and knowledge.

   C. previously held opinions, both valid and invalid.

Answer (B) is correct.   *(AIH Chap 4)*
   DISCUSSION: Teaching from the known to the unknown allows the instructor to use the student's previous experience and knowledge as the point of departure from which to lead into new ideas and concepts.
   Answer (A) is incorrect because, when teaching from the known to the unknown, an instructor is using a student's knowledge of related subjects, not the subject at hand. Answer (C) is incorrect because organizing lessons using the known to the unknown pattern requires students' previous knowledge, not their previously held opinions.

13. The KNOWN to UNKNOWN pattern helps the instructor lead the student into new ideas and concepts by

   A. anxieties and insecurities.

   B. using something the student already knows.

   C. previously held opinions, both valid and invalid.

Answer (B) is correct.   *(AIH Chap 4)*
   DISCUSSION: By using something the student already knows as the point of departure, the instructor can lead into new ideas and concepts. For example, in developing a lesson on heading indicators, the instructor could begin with a discussion of the vacuum-driven heading indicator before proceeding to a description of the radio magnetic indicator (RMI).
   Answer (A) is incorrect because the KNOWN to UNKNOWN pattern helps the instructor lead the student into new ideas and concepts by using something the student already knows, not through anxieties and insecurities. Answer (C) is incorrect because, by using something the student already knows as the point of departure, the instructor can lead into new ideas and concepts, not through previously held opinions.

5.3 Lesson Plan

14. (Refer to Figure 1 on page 71.) Section A is titled:

- A. Overview.
- B. Objective.
- C. Introduction.

Answer (B) is correct.   *(AIH Chap 6)*
    DISCUSSION: Section A of Fig. 1 is titled: Objective. The objective of the lesson is the reason for the lesson and should clearly state what the instructor expects the student to know or do at the completion of the lesson.
    Answer (A) is incorrect because overview is a subpart of an introduction to a lesson, not a titled section of a lesson plan. Answer (C) is incorrect because an introduction is part of an effective way to organize a lesson, not a titled section of a lesson plan.

15. (Refer to Figure 1 on page 71.) Section B is titled:

- A. Content.
- B. Elements.
- C. Course of Training.

Answer (A) is correct.   *(AIH Chap 6)*
    DISCUSSION: Section B of Fig. 1 is titled: Content. This is a statement of the knowledge and skill necessary for the fulfillment of the lesson objective. This may include both elements previously learned and those to be introduced during this lesson.
    Answer (B) is incorrect because "elements" is not a titled section of a lesson plan. Answer (C) is incorrect because the course of training is the overall objective of the instruction and is comprised of many different lesson plans, not a titled section of a lesson plan.

16. (Refer to Figure 1 on page 71.) Section C is titled:

- A. Schedule.
- B. Overview.
- C. Training Schedule.

Answer (A) is correct.   *(AIH Chap 6)*
    DISCUSSION: Section C of Fig. 1 is titled: Schedule. The instructor should estimate the amount of time to be devoted to the presentation of the elements of that lesson.
    Answer (B) is incorrect because overview is a subpart of an introduction to a lesson, not a titled section of a lesson plan. Answer (C) is incorrect because the correct title is schedule, not training schedule.

17. (Refer to Figure 1 on page 71.) Section D is titled:

- A. Instructor's Actions.
- B. Equipment.
- C. Content.

Answer (B) is correct.   *(AIH Chap 6)*
    DISCUSSION: Section D of Fig. 1 is titled: Equipment. This includes all instructional materials and training aids required to teach the lesson.
    Answer (A) is incorrect because "instructor's actions" is the title of the section of a lesson plan that contains a statement of the instructor's proposed procedures for presenting the elements of knowledge and performance involved in the lesson (Section E). Answer (C) is incorrect because "content" is a statement of the knowledge and skill necessary for fulfillment of the lesson objective, not a list of instructional materials to be used in the lesson.

18. (Refer to Figure 1 on page 71.) Section E is titled:

- A. Content.
- B. Discussion.
- C. Instructor's Actions.

Answer (C) is correct.   *(AIH Chap 6)*
    DISCUSSION: Section E of Fig. 1 is titled: Instructor's Actions. This is a statement of the instructor's proposed procedures for presenting the elements of knowledge and performance involved in the lesson.
    Answer (A) is incorrect because "content" is a statement of the knowledge and skill necessary for fulfillment of the lesson objective, not a list of the instructor's actions. Answer (B) is incorrect because, while this section states that a discussion will take place, it is specifically those actions taken by the instructor and not the student.

19. (Refer to Figure 1 on page 71.) Section F is titled:

- A. Application.
- B. Understanding.
- C. Student's Actions.

Answer (C) is correct.   *(AIH Chap 6)*
    DISCUSSION: Section F of Fig. 1 is titled: Student's Actions. This is a statement of desired student responses to instruction.
    Answer (A) is incorrect because, while this involves application of what the instructor has presented to the student, this section is the instructor's desired student's action during the lesson. Answer (B) is incorrect because understanding is a level of learning, not a titled section of a lesson plan.

20. (Refer to Figure 1 below.) Section G is titled:

A. Summary.

B. Evaluation.

C. Completion Standards.

Answer (C) is correct. *(AIH Chap 6)*

DISCUSSION: Section G of Fig. 1 is titled: Completion Standards. This is the evaluation basis for determining how well the student has met the objective of the lesson in terms of knowledge and skill.

Answer (A) is incorrect because a summary of a lesson would take place during the postflight discussion. Answer (B) is incorrect because evaluation is part of the teaching process and would be used by the instructor to compare the student's performance to the completion standards.

LESSON   <u>GROUND REFERENCE MANEUVERS</u>   **STUDENT** _____   **DATE** _____

A _____   TO DEVELOP THE STUDENT'S SKILL IN PLANNING AND FOLLOWING A PATTERN OVER THE GROUND COMPENSATING FOR WIND DRIFT AT VARYING ANGLES.

B _____   USE OF GROUND REFERENCES TO CONTROL PATH. OBSERVATION AND CONTROL OF WIND EFFECT. CONTROL OF AIRPLANE ATTITUDE, ALTITUDE, AND HEADING.

C _____   PREFLIGHT DISCUSSON.   : 10
INSTRUCTOR DEMONSTRATIONS.   : 25
STUDENT PRACTICE.   : 45
POSTFLIGHT CRITIQUE.   : 10

D _____   CHALKBOARD FOR PREFLIGHT DISCUSSION. IFR VISOR FOR MANEUVERS REVIEWED.

E _____   PREFLIGHT - DISCUSS LESSON OBJECTIVE. DIAGRAM "S" TURNS, EIGHTS ALONG A ROAD, AND RECTANGULAR COURSE ON A CHALKBOARD.

INFLIGHT - DEMONSTRATE ELEMENTS. DEMONSTRATE FOLLOWING A ROAD, "S" TURNS, EIGHTS ALONG A ROAD, AND RECTANGULAR COURSE. COACH STUDENT PRACTICE.

POSTFLIGHT - CRITIQUE STUDENT PERFORMANCE AND MAKE STUDY ASSIGNMENT.

F _____   PREFLIGHT - DISCUSS LESSON OBJECTIVE AND RESOLVE QUESTIONS.

INFLIGHT - REVIEW PREVIOUS MANEUVERS INCLUDING POWER-OFF STALLS AND FLIGHT AT MINIMUM CONTROLLABLE AIRSPEED. PERFORM EACH NEW MANEUVER AS DIRECTED.

POSTFLIGHT - ASK PERTINENT QUESTIONS.

G _____   STUDENT SHOULD DEMONSTRATE COMPETENCY IN MAINTAINING ORIENTATION, AIRSPEED WITHIN 10 KNOTS, ALTITUDE WITHIN 100 FEET, AND HEADINGS WITHIN 10 DEGREES, AND IN MAKING PROPER CORRECTION FOR WIND DRIFT.

Figure 1. – Lesson Plan.

21. Which statement is true regarding lesson plans?

   A. Lesson plans should not be directed toward the course objective; only to the lesson objective.

   B. A well-thought-out mental outline of a lesson may be used any time as long as the instructor is well prepared.

   C. Lesson plans help instructors keep a constant check on their own activity as well as that of their students.

Answer (C) is correct. *(AIH Chap 6)*
   DISCUSSION: Lesson plans help instructors keep a constant check on their own activity, as well as that of their students. The development of lesson plans by instructors signifies, in effect, that they have taught the lesson to themselves prior to attempting to teach the lesson to students.
   Answer (A) is incorrect because a lesson plan should serve as a means of relating the lesson to the objectives of the course, as well as the lesson. Answer (B) is incorrect because a mental outline of a lesson is not a lesson plan. A lesson plan should be in written form regardless of an instructor's preparation.

22. When the instructor keeps the student informed of lesson objectives and completion standards, it minimizes the student's feelings of

   A. insecurity.

   B. resignation.

   C. aggressiveness.

Answer (A) is correct. *(AIH Chap 7)*
   DISCUSSION: Students feel insecure when they do not know the lesson objectives and the completion standards to which they will be held. Instructors can minimize such feelings of insecurity by telling students what is expected of them and what to anticipate.
   Answer (B) is incorrect because resignation occurs when a student completes the early phase of training without understanding the fundamentals, not the objectives or completion standards, and becomes lost in the advanced phase. Answer (C) is incorrect because aggression occurs when a student becomes angry at something or someone. Aggression (or any other defense mechanism) may be used to defend a feeling of insecurity when a student is not kept informed.

23. Which statement is true about lesson plans?

   A. Lesson plans should follow a prescribed format.

   B. Standard prepared lesson plans are effective for teaching all students.

   C. The use of standard lesson plans may not be effective for students requiring a different approach.

Answer (C) is correct. *(AIH Chap 6)*
   DISCUSSION: A lesson plan for an instructional period should be appropriate to the background, experience, and ability of the particular student(s). If the procedures outlined in the lesson plan are not leading to the desired results, the instructor should change the approach. Thus, the use of standard lesson plans may not be effective for students requiring a different approach.
   Answer (A) is incorrect because, although lesson plans should all contain certain items, the format to be followed should be tailored to the particular student(s). Answer (B) is incorrect because lesson plans are only an outline of the lesson. An instructor may have to adapt the procedures in a standard prepared lesson plan so it will be effective with different students.

24. The main concern in developing a lesson plan is the

   A. format.

   B. content.

   C. student.

Answer (C) is correct. *(AIH Chap 6)*
   DISCUSSION: The lesson plan must be appropriate for the particular student. Because standard lesson plans may not be effective for students who require a different approach, the main concern in developing a lesson plan is the student.
   Answer (A) is incorrect because the format of the lesson plan will be developed based on the needs of the student and the subject being taught. One lesson plan format does not work well for all students; therefore, the format of a lesson plan is an ending point, not a starting point, in lesson plan development. Answer (B) is incorrect because, while the content of a lesson plan is a concern in its development (e.g., how much time should be devoted to which subjects), the main concern in developing a lesson plan is the student.

25. With regard to the characteristics of a well-planned lesson, each lesson should contain

A. new material that is related to the lesson previously presented.

B. one basic element of the principle, procedure, or skill appropriate to that lesson.

C. every bit of information needed to reach the objective of the training syllabus.

Answer (A) is correct. *(AIH Chap 6)*
DISCUSSION: One characteristic of a well-planned lesson is content, which means each lesson should contain new material. However, the new facts, principles, or skills should be related to the lesson previously presented. A short review of earlier lessons is usually necessary, especially in flight training.
Answer (B) is incorrect because all of the elements, not only one, necessary to learn a simple procedure, principle, or skill should be presented. Answer (C) is incorrect because each lesson should include all of the information needed to reach the objective of a particular lesson but not everything needed for the entire syllabus.

26. What is the primary consideration in determining the length and frequency of flight instruction periods?

A. Fatigue.

B. Mental acuity.

C. Instructor preparation.

Answer (A) is correct. *(AIH Chap 8)*
DISCUSSION: Fatigue is the primary consideration in determining the length and frequency of flight instruction periods. Flight instruction should be continued only so long as the student is alert, receptive to instruction, and performing at a level consistent with experience.
Answer (B) is incorrect because fatigue, not mental acuity, is the primary consideration in determining the length and frequency of flight instruction periods. Fatigue may be either physical or mental, or both. Answer (C) is incorrect because fatigue, not instructor preparation, is the primary consideration in determining the length and frequency of flight instruction periods. Poor instructor preparation will make students become apathetic, not fatigued.

27. A primary consideration in planning for student performance is the

A. student's motivational level.

B. student's intellectual level.

C. length of the practice session.

Answer (C) is correct. *(AIH Chap 2)*
DISCUSSION: In planning for student performance, a primary consideration is the length of time devoted to practice. A beginning student reaches a point where additional practice is not only unproductive but may even be harmful. When that point is reached, errors increase and motivation declines. As a student gains experience, longer periods of practice are profitable.
Answer (A) is incorrect because a student's motivational level is important to an instructor since it directly relates to the student's progress and ability to learn, not as a primary consideration in planning for student performance. Answer (B) is incorrect because a primary consideration in student performance is the length of time devoted to practice, not the student's intellectual level.

28. A lesson plan, if constructed properly, will provide an outline for

A. proceeding from the unknown to the known.

B. the teaching procedure to be used in a single instructional period.

C. establishing blocks of learning that become progressively larger in scope.

Answer (B) is correct. *(AIH Chap 6)*
DISCUSSION: A properly constructed lesson plan is an organized outline or blueprint for a single instructional period. It is a necessary guide for the instructor in that it tells what to do, in what order to do it, and what procedure to use in teaching the material of the lesson.
Answer (A) is incorrect because the lesson plan will usually proceed from the known to the unknown, not unknown to known. Answer (C) is incorrect because a syllabus, not a lesson plan, will provide an outline for establishing blocks of learning that become progressively larger in scope.

29. Each lesson of a training syllabus includes

A. attention, motivation, and overview.

B. introduction, development, and conclusion.

C. objective, content, and completion standards.

Answer (C) is correct. *(AIH Chap 6)*
DISCUSSION: Each lesson of a written training syllabus includes an objective, content, and completion standards.
Answer (A) is incorrect because attention, motivation, and overview are the parts of an introduction to a lesson. Answer (B) is incorrect because the structure of every lesson as it is being presented to a student, not as found in a written syllabus, should be based on an introduction, a development, and a conclusion.

5.4 Instructional Aids

30.   Which is a true statement concerning the use of instructional aids?

A.   Instructional aids ensure getting and holding the student's attention.

B.   Instructional aids should be designed to cover the key points in a lesson.

C.   Instructional aids should not be used simply to cover a subject in less time.

Answer (B) is correct.   *(AIH Chap 4)*
DISCUSSION: Instructional aids are a good way to improve communication between the instructor and the students. Instructional aids should be designed to cover the key points in a lesson.
Answer (A) is incorrect because appropriate instructional aids will help get the student's attention, but they cannot ensure that it will hold the student's attention. Answer (C) is incorrect because instructional aids can help get a point across quickly and clearly, thus reducing the time spent on some subjects.

31.   The use of instructional aids should be based on their ability to support a specific point in the lesson. What is the first step in determining if and where instructional aids are necessary?

A.   Organize subject material into an outline or a lesson plan.

B.   Determine what ideas should be supported with instructional aids.

C.   Clearly establish the lesson objective, being certain what must be communicated.

Answer (C) is correct.   *(AIH Chap 4)*
DISCUSSION: The first step in developing a lesson plan using instructional aids is, as in any lesson plan, to establish the lesson objective. Visual or other aids must help achieve the overall lesson objective. They should be strategically placed to recapture interest, shift to a new topic, or provide emphasis.
Answer (A) is incorrect because organizing the outline or lesson plan is the third, not first, step in the process. Answer (B) is incorrect because the final, not first, step in determining if and where instructional aids are necessary is to determine what ideas in the lesson should be supported with instructional aids.

32.   Instructional aids used in the teaching/learning process should be

A.   self-supporting and require no explanation.

B.   compatible with the learning outcomes to be achieved.

C.   selected prior to developing and organizing the lesson plan.

Answer (B) is correct.   *(AIH Chap 4)*
DISCUSSION: After establishing lesson objectives, researching the subject, and organizing the material into a lesson plan, the instructor should determine what needs to be supported by visual or other instructional aids. The aids should be compatible with the learning outcomes to be achieved.
Answer (A) is incorrect because instructional aids are not self-supporting and will require explanation. Answer (C) is incorrect because instructional aids should be compatible with the desired learning outcomes, which can best be done after, not prior to, developing and organizing the lesson plan.

33.   Instructional aids used in the teaching/learning process should not be used

A.   as a crutch by the instructor.

B.   for teaching more in less time.

C.   to visualize relationships between abstracts.

Answer (A) is correct.   *(AIH Chap 4)*
DISCUSSION: Aids used in conjunction with oral presentation should emphasize, not distract from, the oral message. Also, the instructor should realize that such aids do not take the place of a sound lesson plan or instructor's input.
Answer (B) is incorrect because aids do help teach more in less time because they clarify and emphasize the lecture. The class can move to new material sooner. Answer (C) is incorrect because instructional aids should be used to help students to visualize relationships between abstracts.

LESSON PLAN

Introduction (3 minutes)

A _____ Relates aircraft accident in which a multi-engine ran off the end of the runway. This could have been avoided by correctly computing the landing distance. Relate similar personal experience of the same type of mishap.

B _____ Tell students how landing distance can affect then (any aircraft, plus future application).

C _____ Explain what will be learned. Explain how the lesson will proceed. Define landing distance and explain the normal landing distance chart. Then, demonstrate how to solve for landing distance. The students will practice the procedure: at least once with supervision and at least once with as little help as possible. Next, the students will be evaluated according to the standards. Finally, the lesson will conclude with questions and answers, followed by a brief summary.

Body (29 minutes)

D _____ Define landing distance. Explain the normal landing distance chart to include the scale and interpolation. Ensure students can see demonstrations and encourage questions. Demonstrate the procedure using °C with a headwind and °F with a tailwind. Show the normal landing distance chart with given data in the following order:
1. temperature
2. pressure altitude
3. gross weight
4. headwind-tailwind component
5. read ground roll distance from graph

E _____ Review standards. Hand out chart and practice problems. Remind students to use a pencil, to make small tick marks, and to work as accurately as possible. Explain that they should follow the procedure on the chart to work the practice problems. Encourage students to ask questions. Check progress of each student continually so they develop skill proficiency within acceptable standards. Reteach any area(s) of difficulty to the class as they go along.

F _____ Review procedure again from the chart. Reemphasize standards of acceptable performance including time available. Prepare area for evaluation by removing the task step chart and practice problem sheets, and by handing out the evaluation problems. Ask students to work the three problems according to conditions and standards specified. Terminate evaluation after 6 minutes. Evaluate each student's performance and tactfully reveal results. Record results for use in reteaching any area(s) of difficulty in the summary.

Conclusion (3 minutes)

G _____ Review lessons with emphasis on any weak area(s).

H _____ Remind students that landing distance will be an important consideration in any aircraft they fly.

I _____ Advise students that this lesson will be used as a starting point for the next lesson. Assign study materials for the next lesson.

Figure 1A. – Lesson Plan.

Figure 1A is a sample ground lesson plan in contrast to the sample flight lesson plan illustrated in Figure 1 (on page 71). Lesson plans are discussed on pages 103 through 107. The FAA also provides various sample lesson plans in a digital document located online at www.faa.gov/library/manuals/aviation/aviation_instructors_handbook/media/sample_lesson_plans.pdf. Use the lesson plan on the first page of that digital document to write in the section titles in Figure 1A above, so you will be able to answer any FAA questions about Figure 1A. Reference the other lesson plans contained in that document as well as the pages referenced above to better understand this important instructional topic.

END OF STUDY UNIT

STUDY UNIT SIX
CRITIQUE AND EVALUATION

(5 pages of outline)

6.1 THE INSTRUCTOR'S CRITIQUE

1. No instructor skill is more important than the ability to analyze, appraise, and judge student performance.

   a. A student looks to the instructor for guidance, suggestions for improvement, and encouragement.

   b. To enhance a student's acceptance of further instruction, the instructor should keep the student informed of the progress made.

      1) This will help to minimize student frustrations, which will keep the student motivated to learn.

2. A critique should always be conducted immediately after the student's performance, while the details are easy to recall.

   a. The instructor may critique any activity that a student performs or practices to improve skill, proficiency, and learning.

3. A critique is a step in the learning process, not the grading process.

4. A critique is not necessarily negative in content. It considers the good along with the bad, the whole in terms of its parts, and the parts in relation to each other.

5. The purpose of a critique is to improve the student's performance and to provide him/her with something constructive with which to work and on which to build.

   a. The critique should provide direction and guidance to improve performance.

6. A critique should be **objective**.

   a. The effective critique is focused on student performance and should not reflect the personal opinions, likes, dislikes, and biases of the instructor.

   b. The critique must be based on the performance as it was, not as it could have been.

7. A critique should be **flexible**.

   a. The instructor must fit the tone, technique, and content of the critique to the occasion and the student.

   b. An effective critique is flexible enough to satisfy the requirements of the moment.

8. A critique should be **acceptable**.

   a. Before students willingly accept their instructor's criticism, they must first accept the instructor.

   b. The students must have confidence in the instructor's qualifications, teaching ability, sincerity, competence, and authority.

   c. Instructors cannot rely solely on their position to make a critique acceptable to their students.

9. A critique should be **comprehensive**.

   a. A comprehensive critique is not necessarily long, nor must it treat every aspect of the performance in detail.

   b. The instructor must decide whether the greater benefit will come from a discussion of a few major points or a number of minor points.

   c. An effective critique covers strengths as well as weaknesses.

10. A critique should be **constructive**.

    a. A critique is pointless unless a student profits from it.

    b. Praise for praise's sake is of no value if a student is not taught how to capitalize on things that are done well and to use them to compensate for lesser accomplishments.

    c. Also, it is not enough to identify a fault or weakness.

       1) To tell students that their work is unsatisfactory with no explanation will most likely result in the students becoming frustrated.

       2) The students must be briefed on the errors made and told how to correct them, so progress and accomplishment can be made.

11. A critique should be **thoughtful**.

    a. An effective critique reflects an instructor's thoughtfulness toward the student's need for self-esteem, recognition, and approval from others.

       1) The critique should never minimize the inherent dignity and importance of the individual.

    b. Ridicule, anger, or fun at the expense of the student has no place in the critique.

12. A critique should be **specific**.

    a. The instructor's comments and recommendations should be specific, not so general that the student can find nothing to hold onto.

    b. Express ideas with firmness and authority in terms that cannot be misunderstood.

       1) Students should have no doubt what they did well and what they did poorly, and specifically how they can improve.

6.2 TYPES OF TESTING

1. **Norm-referenced testing** measures a student's performance against the performance of other students.

2. **Criterion-referenced testing** measures a student's performance against a carefully written, measurable standard or criterion.

   a. Practical tests for pilot certification are an example of criterion-referenced testing.

      1) The objective of the Practical Test Standards (PTS) is to ensure the certification of pilots at a high level of performance and proficiency, consistent with safety.

   b. A pretest constructed to measure knowledge and skills necessary to begin a course is a criterion-referenced test.

6.3 ORAL QUIZZING

1. The most practical means of evaluation is oral quizzing of students by the instructor. Questions may be loosely classified as fact and thought questions.

    a. The answer to a fact question is based on memory or recall.

    b. Thought questions require the student to combine a knowledge of facts with an ability to analyze situations, solve problems, and arrive at conclusions.

2. Proper quizzing by the instructor can have a number of desirable results. It can

    a. Reveal the effectiveness of training procedures,
    b. Check student retention and comprehension of what has been learned,
    c. Review material already covered,
    d. Help retain student interest and stimulate thinking,
    e. Emphasize the important points of training,
    f. Identify points that need more emphasis, and
    g. Promote active student participation.

3. Characteristics of effective questions:

    a. Each question must have only one correct answer.

        1) This is a characteristic of good objective-type (fact) questions and generally true of all good questions.

        2) Each question should call for a specific answer that can be readily evaluated by the instructor.

    b. Each question must apply to the subject being taught.

    c. Each question should be brief and concise but must be clear and definite.

    d. Each question should center on only one idea limited to who, what, where, when, how, or why, not a combination.

    e. Each question should present a challenge.

        1) A question must be of suitable difficulty for the students at that particular stage of training.

4. When answering student questions, the instructor needs to clearly understand the question before attempting an answer.

    a. The instructor should display interest in the student's questions and give as direct and accurate an answer as possible.

    b. If a student's question is too advanced for the particular lesson and confusion may result from a complete answer, the instructor may

        1) Carefully explain that the question was good and pertinent;

        2) Explain that to answer would unnecessarily complicate the learning task at hand; and

        3) Advise the student to reintroduce the question later at the appropriate point in training or meet outside class for a more complete discussion.

5. Occasionally, a student will ask a question the instructor cannot answer. The best course is to freely admit not knowing the answer.

    a. The instructor should then promise to find out or offer to help the student look it up in appropriate references.

6.4 TYPES OF WRITTEN TEST QUESTIONS

1. Written test questions fall into two general categories:

    a. Supply-type and
    b. Selection-type.

2. Supply-type questions require the student to furnish a response in the form of a word, sentence, or paragraph.

    a. Supply-type test items

        1) Require students to organize their thoughts and ideas,
        2) Demand the ability to express ideas, and
        3) Are subjective.

            a) Thus, their main disadvantage is that they cannot be graded uniformly.

            b) The same test graded by different instructors probably would be assigned different scores.

        4) Take longer for students to answer and for instructors to grade, which is another disadvantage.

3. Selection-type questions include items for which two or more alternative responses are provided.

    a. Selection-type test items

        1) Are highly objective.

            a) Thus, they are graded uniformly regardless of the student or grader.

        2) Allow direct comparison of students' accomplishments. For example, it is possible to compare student performance

            a) Within the same class,
            b) Between classes, and
            c) Under different instructors.

    b. True-false, multiple-choice, and matching type questions are prime examples of selection-type questions.

4. The true-false test item is well adapted to the testing of knowledge of facts and detail, especially when there are only two possible answers.

    a. The chief disadvantage of the true-false test item is that it creates the greatest probability of guessing since the student always has a 50% chance of guessing correctly.

5. Multiple-choice test items may be used to determine student achievement, ranging from acquisition of facts to understanding, reasoning, and ability to apply what has been learned.

    a. One of the major difficulties encountered in the construction of multiple test items is inventing plausible sounding incorrect choices (distractors) that will be attractive to students lacking knowledge or understanding.

    b. When multiple-choice items are intended to measure achievement at a higher level of learning, some or all of the alternatives should be acceptable, but one should be clearly better than the others.

    c. Multiple-choice test items should have all alternatives of approximately equal length.

        1) The common error made by instructors is to make the correct alternative longer than the incorrect ones.

6. Matching test items are particularly good for measuring the student's ability to recognize relationships and to make associations between terms, parts, words, phrases, or symbols listed in one column with related items in another column.

    a. Matching reduces the probability of guessing correct responses compared to a series of multiple-choice items covering the same material.

6.5 CHARACTERISTICS OF A GOOD TEST

1. Reliability

    a. A written test that has reliability yields consistent results.

2. Validity

    a. A written test has validity when it measures what it is supposed to measure and nothing else.

3. Usability

    a. A written test is usable when it is easy to give, easy to read, the wording is clear and concise, figures are appropriate to the test items and clearly drawn, and is easily graded.

4. Comprehensiveness

    a. A written test is said to be comprehensive when it samples liberally whatever is being measured.

5. Discrimination

    a. A written test having the characteristic of discrimination will measure small differences in achievement between students.

        1) It will also distinguish between students both low and high in achievement of the course objectives.

6.6 REVIEW AND EVALUATION

1. Review and evaluation of the student's learning should be an integral part of each lesson.

    a. Evaluation of student performance and accomplishment should be based on the objectives and goals established in the lesson plan.

2. Performance testing is desirable for evaluating training that involves an operation, procedure, or process.

    a. This method of evaluation is particularly suited to the measurement of a student's ability in performing a task, either mental or physical.

QUESTIONS AND ANSWER EXPLANATIONS

All of the FAA questions from the Fundamentals of Instructing knowledge test relating to critique and evaluation and the material previously outlined are reproduced on the following pages in the same subunits as the outlines. To the immediate right of each question are the correct answer and answer explanation. You should cover these answers and answer explanations while responding to the questions. Refer to the general discussion in the Introduction on how to take the FAA pilot knowledge test.

Remember that the questions from the FAA knowledge test bank have been reordered by topic, and the topics have been organized into a meaningful sequence. Also, the first line of the answer explanation gives the citation of the authoritative source for the answer.

QUESTIONS

6.1 The Instructor's Critique

1. To enhance a student's acceptance of further instruction, the instructor should

   A. keep the student informed of the progress made.

   B. continually prod the student to maintain motivational levels.

   C. establish performance standards a little above the student's actual ability.

Answer (A) is correct. *(AIH Chap 7)*
DISCUSSION: Keeping the student informed of progress will tend to enhance a student's acceptance of further instruction. A student who is unaware of progress may lose interest, which decreases motivation and hinders learning.
   Answer (B) is incorrect because, if an instructor continually prods a student, the student's motivational level will decrease, not remain the same, due to his/her becoming frustrated. This will then lead to a decrease, not increase, in the student's desire to learn. Answer (C) is incorrect because the student will become frustrated by his/her inability to reach standards above his/her actual level of skill. This will lead to a decrease, not increase, in the desire to learn.

2. When an instructor critiques a student, it should always be

   A. done in private.

   B. subjective rather than objective.

   C. conducted immediately after the student's performance.

Answer (C) is correct. *(AIH Chap 5)*
DISCUSSION: The critique should always be conducted immediately after the student's performance, while the performance is still fresh in the student's mind. Specific comments on "your third turn," for instance, would have little value a week after the maneuver was performed.
   Answer (A) is incorrect because a critique may be conducted in private or before the entire class. A critique presented before the entire class can be beneficial to every student in the classroom as well as to the student who performed the exercise. Answer (B) is incorrect because the critique should be objective rather than subjective.

3. Which statement is true about an instructor's critique of a student's performance?

   A. The critique should always be conducted in private.

   B. It is a step in the learning process, not in the grading process.

   C. Instructor comments and recommendations should be based on the performance the way it should have been.

Answer (B) is correct. *(AIH Chap 5)*
DISCUSSION: A critique is a step in the learning process, not the grading process. A critique should be used to guide students to better performance.
   Answer (A) is incorrect because a critique may be conducted in private or before the entire class. A critique presented before the entire class can be beneficial to every student in the classroom as well as to the student who performed the exercise. Answer (C) is incorrect because a critique must be based on the performance as it was, not as it should have been.

4. An instructor's critique of a student's performance should

    A. treat every aspect of the performance in detail.

    B. be private so that the student is not embarrassed.

    C. provide direction and guidance to improve performance.

Answer (C) is correct. *(AIH Chap 5)*
    DISCUSSION: A critique should improve a student's performance and provide something constructive with which (s)he can work and build on. It should provide direction and guidance to improve performance.
    Answer (A) is incorrect because a comprehensive critique is not necessarily a long one nor must it treat every aspect of the performance in detail. The instructor must decide whether the greater benefit will come from discussing a few major points or a number of minor points. Answer (B) is incorrect because a critique may be conducted in private or before the entire class. A critique presented before the entire class can be beneficial to every student in the classroom as well as to the student who performed the exercise.

5. Which is true about an instructor's critique of a student's performance?

    A. Praise for praise's sake is of value.

    B. It should be constructive and objective.

    C. It should treat every aspect of the performance in detail.

Answer (B) is correct. *(AIH Chap 5)*
    DISCUSSION: A critique must be constructive by explaining to the student how to capitalize on things that are done well and to use them to compensate for lesser accomplishments. A critique must also be objective by basing it on the performance as it was, not as it could have been.
    Answer (A) is incorrect because praise for praise's sake is of no value if a student is not taught how to capitalize on things that are done well and to use them to compensate for lesser accomplishments. Answer (C) is incorrect because a comprehensive critique is not necessarily a long one nor must it treat every aspect of the performance in detail. The instructor must decide whether the greater benefit will come from discussing a few major points or a number of minor points.

6. To be effective, a critique should

    A. not contain negative remarks.

    B. treat every aspect of the performance in detail.

    C. be flexible enough to satisfy the requirements of the moment.

Answer (C) is correct. *(AIH Chap 5)*
    DISCUSSION: An effective critique is one that is flexible enough to satisfy the requirements of the moment. The instructor must fit the tone, technique, and content of the critique to the occasion and the student. Thus, the instructor is faced with the problem of what to say, what to omit, and what to minimize. The challenge of the critique is that the instructor must determine what to say at the proper moment.
    Answer (A) is incorrect because a critique may contain negative remarks as long as they point toward improvement or a higher level of performance. Answer (B) is incorrect because a comprehensive critique is not necessarily a long one, nor must it treat every aspect of the performance in detail. The instructor must decide whether the greater benefit will come from discussing a few major points or a number of minor points.

7. Which statement is true about instructors' critiques?

    A. Instructors should rely on their personality to make a critique more acceptable.

    B. A comprehensive critique should emphasize positive aspects of student performance.

    C. Before students willingly accept their instructor's critique, they must first accept the instructor.

Answer (C) is correct. *(AIH Chap 5)*
    DISCUSSION: Students must have confidence in the instructor's qualifications, teaching ability, sincerity, competence, and authority before they will willingly accept their instructor's criticism. A critique holds little weight if the student has no respect for the instructor.
    Answer (A) is incorrect because the effective critique is focused on student performance and should not reflect the personal opinions, likes, dislikes, and biases (i.e., personality) of the instructor. Answer (B) is incorrect because a comprehensive critique means that good and bad points are covered adequately but not necessarily in exhaustive detail.

8. Which would more likely result in students becoming frustrated?

    A. Giving the students meaningless praise.

    B. Telling students their work is unsatisfactory with no explanation.

    C. Covering up instructor mistakes or bluffing when the instructor is in doubt.

Answer (B) is correct. *(AIH Chap 7)*
    DISCUSSION: If a student has made an earnest effort but is told that the work is not satisfactory, with no other explanation, frustration occurs. On the other hand, if the student is briefed on the errors made and is told how to correct them, progress and accomplishment can be made.
    Answer (A) is incorrect because giving meaningless praise is valueless, not frustrating, to a student. Answer (C) is incorrect because covering up instructor mistakes or bluffing when the instructor is in doubt results in destroying student confidence, not creating frustration.

6.2 Types of Testing

9. Practical tests for pilot certification are

    A. evaluation-referenced.

    B. norm-referenced.

    C. criterion-referenced.

Answer (C) is correct. *(AIH Chap 5)*
    DISCUSSION: Criterion-referenced tests measure an applicant's performance against carefully written, measurable standards or criteria. Practical tests for pilot certification are criterion-referenced. The Practical Test Standards are the criteria.
    Answer (A) is incorrect because practical tests are a form of evaluation, not evaluation-referenced. Evaluation-referenced is not a type of testing. Answer (B) is incorrect because norm-referenced testing measures a student's performance against that of other students; a practical test for pilot certification measures the applicant's performance against carefully written, measurable standards (the Practical Test Standards).

10. The objective of the Practical Test Standards (PTS) is to ensure the certification of pilots at a high level of performance and proficiency, consistent with

    A. the time available.

    B. safety.

    C. their abilities.

Answer (B) is correct. *(AIH Chap 5)*
    DISCUSSION: The objective of the Practical Test Standards is to ensure the certification of pilots at a high level of performance and proficiency, consistent with safety.
    Answer (A) is incorrect because the objective of the Practical Test Standards (PTS) is to ensure the certification of pilots at a high level of performance and proficiency, consistent with safety, not the time available. Answer (C) is incorrect because the objective of the Practical Test Standards (PTS) is to ensure the certification of pilots at a high level of performance and proficiency, consistent with safety, not their abilities.

11. A pretest constructed to measure knowledge and skills necessary to begin a course is referred to as a

    A. virtual-reality test.

    B. norm-referenced test.

    C. criterion-referenced test.

Answer (C) is correct. *(AIH Chap 7)*
    DISCUSSION: A pretest is a criterion-referenced test constructed to measure the knowledge and skills that are necessary to begin a course. Criterion-referenced tests measure a student's performance against carefully written, measurable standards or criteria.
    Answer (A) is incorrect because virtual reality is a potential future method of computer-based training (CBT) that can simulate environments very realistically. It is not a type of test. Answer (B) is incorrect because a pretest is a criterion-referenced test, not a norm-referenced test. Norm-referenced tests measure a student's performance against that of other students.

6.3 Oral Quizzing

12. One desirable result of proper oral quizzing by the instructor is to

A. reveal the effectiveness of the instructor's training procedures.

B. fulfill the requirements set forth in the overall objectives of the course.

C. reveal the essential information from which the student can determine progress.

Answer (A) is correct. *(AIH Chap 5)*
DISCUSSION: One desirable result of proper oral quizzing by the instructor is that it reveals the effectiveness of the instructor's training procedures.
Answer (B) is incorrect because quizzing can only measure achievement, not fulfill the requirements, of the overall objectives of the course. Answer (C) is incorrect because an instructor should use the critique, not a quiz, to reveal the essential information from which the student can determine progress.

13. Which is a valid reason for the use of proper oral quizzing during a lesson?

A. Promotes active student participation.

B. Identifies points that need less emphasis.

C. Helps the instructor determine the general intelligence level of the students.

Answer (A) is correct. *(AIH Chap 5)*
DISCUSSION: A valid reason for the use of proper oral quizzing during a lesson is to promote active student participation, which is important to effective teaching.
Answer (B) is incorrect because a valid reason for the use of proper oral quizzing during a lesson is that it identifies points that need more, not less, emphasis. Answer (C) is incorrect because a valid reason for the use of proper oral quizzing during a lesson is to check the students' comprehension of what has been learned, not their general intelligence level.

14. Proper oral quizzing by the instructor during a lesson can have which result?

A. Promotes effective use of available time.

B. Identifies points which need more emphasis.

C. Permits the introduction of new material not covered previously.

Answer (B) is correct. *(AIH Chap 5)*
DISCUSSION: One desirable result of oral quizzing is that it helps the instructor identify points that need more emphasis. By noting students' answers, the instructor can quickly spot weak points in understanding and give these extra attention.
Answer (A) is incorrect because the use of a lesson plan, not oral quizzing, by the instructor will promote effective use of available time. Answer (C) is incorrect because the introduction of new material is accomplished during the presentation, not evaluation, step of the teaching process.

15. To be effective in oral quizzing during the conduct of a lesson, a question should

A. be of suitable difficulty for that stage of training.

B. include a combination of where, how, and why.

C. divert the student's thoughts to subjects covered in other lessons.

Answer (A) is correct. *(AIH Chap 5)*
DISCUSSION: During oral quizzing, an effective question must present a challenge to the student. A question must be of suitable difficulty for the student at that particular stage of training. These types of questions stimulate learning.
Answer (B) is incorrect because an effective question should be limited to who, what, when, where, how, or why, not a combination. Answer (C) is incorrect because an effective question must apply to the subject of instruction, not divert the student's thoughts to subjects covered in other lessons.

16. During oral quizzing in a given lesson, effective questions should

A. be brief and concise.

B. provide answers that can be expressed in a variety of ways.

C. divert the student's thoughts to subjects covered in previous lessons.

Answer (A) is correct. *(AIH Chap 5)*
DISCUSSION: During oral quizzing, an effective question should be brief and concise but must also be clear and definite. Enough words must be used to establish the conditions or situations exactly so that instructor and students will have the same mental picture.
Answer (B) is incorrect because all effective questions will have only one correct answer. Answer (C) is incorrect because an effective question must apply to the subject of instruction, not divert the student's thoughts to subjects covered in previous lessons.

17. In all quizzing as a portion of the instruction process, the questions should

  A. include catch questions to develop the student's perceptive power.

  B. call for specific answers and be readily evaluated by the instructor.

  C. include questions with more than one central idea to evaluate how completely a student understands the subject.

Answer (B) is correct. *(AIH Chap 5)*
  DISCUSSION: In any kind of testing, questions should have one specific answer so that the instructor can readily evaluate the student's response. General questions tend to confuse rather than help, and unanswered questions serve no useful purpose at all.
  Answer (A) is incorrect because catch questions should be avoided at all times. The students will feel they are engaged in a battle of wits with the instructor, and the whole significance of the subject of instruction will be lost. Answer (C) is incorrect because effective questions used in quizzing should center on only one central idea.

18. To answer a student's question, it is most important that the instructor

  A. clearly understand the question.

  B. have complete knowledge of the subject.

  C. introduce more complicated information to partially answer the question, if necessary.

Answer (A) is correct. *(AIH Chap 5)*
  DISCUSSION: The answering of students' questions can be an effective teaching method. To answer a student's question, it is most important that the instructor clearly understands the question.
  Answer (B) is incorrect because, while an instructor may have knowledge of a subject, occasionally a student will ask a question the instructor cannot answer. The instructor should admit not knowing the answer and should promise to get the answer or help the student to find it. Answer (C) is incorrect because introducing more complicated information to partially answer the question is normally unwise. Doing so would confuse the student and complicate the learning task at hand.

19. With regards to oral quizzing, which type of question would be answered by memory or recall?

  A. A fact question.

  B. A thought question.

  C. A provocative question.

Answer (A) is correct. *(AIH Chap 5)*
  DISCUSSION: Fact questions involve answers that are based on memory or recall. This type of question usually concerns who, what, when, and where.
  Answer (B) is incorrect because thought questions usually involve why or how and require the student to combine knowledge of facts with the ability to analyze situations, solve problems, and arrive at conclusions. Answer (C) is incorrect because controversial questions are a type that should be avoided in oral quizzing.

20. With regards to oral quizzing, which type of question requires the student to combine knowledge with the ability to analyze, solve problems, and arrive at conclusions?

  A. A fact question.

  B. A thought question.

  C. A provocative question.

Answer (B) is correct. *(AIH Chap 5)*
  DISCUSSION: Thought questions usually involve why or how and require the student to combine knowledge of facts with the ability to analyze situations, solve problems, and arrive at conclusions.
  Answer (A) is incorrect because fact questions involves answers that are based on memory or recall. This type of question usually concerns who, what, when, and where. Answer (C) is incorrect because controversial questions are a type that should be avoided in oral quizzing.

21. For oral quizzing to be effective during a lesson, a question should

  A. center on only one idea.

  B. include a combination of where, how, and why.

  C. be easy for the student at that particular stage of training.

Answer (A) is correct. *(AIH Chap 5)*
  DISCUSSION: To be effective in oral quizzing, each question should center on only one idea, which is limited to who, what, where, when, how, or why, not a combination.
  Answer (B) is incorrect because a single question should be limited to who, what, when, where, how, or why, not a combination. Answer (C) is incorrect because questions of suitable difficulty serve to stimulate learning. To be effective, questions must be adapted to the ability, experience, and stage of training of the students and be of suitable difficulty.

6.4 Types of Written Test Questions

22. What is a characteristic of supply-type test items?

A. They are easily adapted to testing knowledge of facts and details.

B. Test results would be graded the same regardless of the student or the grader.

C. The same test graded by different instructors would probably be given different scores.

Answer (C) is correct. *(AIH Chap 5)*
DISCUSSION: A characteristic of supply-type test items is that they cannot be graded with uniformity. The same test graded by different instructors would probably be assigned different scores. The same test graded by the same instructor on consecutive days might be assigned two different scores. There is no assurance that the grade assigned is the grade deserved.
Answer (A) is incorrect because true-false, not supply-type, test items are easily adapted to testing knowledge of facts and details. Answer (B) is incorrect because selection-type, not supply-type, test items would be graded the same regardless of the student or the grader.

23. Which is the main disadvantage of supply-type test items?

A. They cannot be graded with uniformity.

B. They are readily answered by guessing.

C. They are easily adapted to statistical analysis.

Answer (A) is correct. *(AIH Chap 5)*
DISCUSSION: The main disadvantage of supply-type test items is that they cannot be graded with uniformity. The same test graded by different instructors would probably be assigned different scores. The same test graded by the same instructor on consecutive days might be assigned two different scores. There is no assurance that the grade assigned is the grade deserved.
Answer (B) is incorrect because the main disadvantage of true-false, not supply-type, test items is they are readily answered by guessing. Answer (C) is incorrect because an advantage, not disadvantage, of selection-type, not supply-type, test items is that they are easily adapted to statistical analysis.

24. One of the main advantages of selection-type test items over supply-type test items is that the selection-type

A. decreases discrimination between responses.

B. would be graded objectively regardless of the student or the grader.

C. precludes comparison of students under one instructor with those under another instructor.

Answer (B) is correct. *(AIH Chap 5)*
DISCUSSION: One of the main advantages of selection-type test items over supply-type test items is that the selection-type are graded objectively regardless of the student or grader.
Answer (A) is incorrect because an advantage of the selection-type test item over the supply-type test item is that more areas of knowledge can be tested in a given time, thus increasing, not decreasing, comprehensiveness, validity, and discrimination. Answer (C) is incorrect because an advantage of the selection-type test item over supply-type test item is the ability to compare, not to preclude comparison of, student performance under one instructor with those of another instructor.

25. Which statement is true about multiple-choice test items that are intended to measure achievement at a higher level of learning?

A. It is unethical to mislead students into selecting an incorrect alternative.

B. Some or all of the alternatives should be acceptable, but only one should be clearly better than the others.

C. The use of common errors as distracting alternatives to divert the student from the correct response is ineffective and invalid.

Answer (B) is correct. *(AIH Chap 5)*
DISCUSSION: When multiple-choice test items are intended to measure achievement at a higher level of learning, some or all of the alternatives should be acceptable, but only one should be clearly better than the others. The instructions given should direct the student to select the best alternative.
Answer (A) is incorrect because, when using multiple-choice test items, the students are not supposed to guess the correct answer; they should select it only if they know it is correct. Thus, it is ethical, not unethical, to mislead students into selecting an incorrect alternative. Answer (C) is incorrect because, when using multiple-choice test items, the use of common errors as distracting alternatives to divert the student from the correct response is effective, not ineffective, and valid, not invalid.

26. Which statement is true relative to effective multiple-choice test items?

A. Negative words or phrases need not be emphasized.

B. Items should call for abstract background knowledge.

C. Keep all alternatives of approximately equal length.

Answer (C) is correct. *(AIH Chap 5)*
DISCUSSION: In preparing and reviewing the alternatives to a multiple-choice item, it is advisable to keep all alternatives approximately the same length. Research of instructor-made tests reveals that, in general, correct alternatives are longer than incorrect ones.
Answer (A) is incorrect because, when negative words or phrases are used, they should be emphasized in order to be effective. Answer (B) is incorrect because items should call for essential knowledge rather than for abstract background knowledge or unimportant facts.

27. Which type of test item creates the greatest probability of guessing?

A. True-false.

B. Supply-type.

C. Multiple-choice.

Answer (A) is correct.   *(AIH Chap 5)*
DISCUSSION: The true-false test item creates the greatest probability of guessing since the student always has a 50% chance of guessing correctly.
Answer (B) is incorrect because the true-false, not the supply-type, test item creates the greatest probability of guessing. Answer (C) is incorrect because the true-false, not the multiple-choice, test item creates the greatest probability of guessing.

28. Which is one of the major difficulties encountered in the construction of multiple-choice test items?

A. Adapting the items to statistical item analysis.

B. Keeping all responses approximately equal in length.

C. Inventing distractors which will be attractive to students lacking knowledge or understanding.

Answer (C) is correct.   *(AIH Chap 5)*
DISCUSSION: Three major difficulties are encountered in the construction of multiple-choice test items:

1. Development of a question or an item stem that can be expressed clearly without ambiguity.
2. Statement of an answer that cannot be refuted.
3. The invention of lures or distractors attractive to those students who do not possess the knowledge or understanding necessary to recognize the correct answer.

Answer (A) is incorrect because it is a major advantage, not difficulty, for a multiple-choice test item to be well adapted to statistical item analysis. Answer (B) is incorrect because a principle, not difficulty, of constructing a multiple-choice test item is to keep all responses approximately equal in length.

29. In a written test, which type of selection-type test items reduces the probability of guessing correct responses?

A. Essay.

B. Matching.

C. Multiple-choice.

Answer (B) is correct.   *(AIH Chap 5)*
DISCUSSION: In a written test, matching test items reduces the probability of guessing correct responses compared to a series of multiple-choice items covering the same material, especially if alternatives are used more than once.
Answer (A) is incorrect because an essay question is a supply-type, not selection-type, test item. Answer (C) is incorrect because matching, not multiple-choice, test items reduce the probability of guessing correct responses.

6.5 Characteristics of a Good Test

30. A written test that has reliability

A. yields consistent results.

B. measures small differences in the achievement of students.

C. actually measures what it is supposed to measure and nothing else.

Answer (A) is correct.   *(AIH Chap 5)*
DISCUSSION: A written test that has reliability is one that yields consistent results.
Answer (B) is incorrect because a written test that shows discrimination, not reliability, measures small differences in the achievement of students. Answer (C) is incorrect because a written test that has validity, not reliability, actually measures what it is supposed to measure and nothing else.

31. A written test has validity when it

A. yields consistent results.

B. samples liberally whatever is being measured.

C. measures what it is supposed to measure and nothing else.

Answer (C) is correct.   *(AIH Chap 5)*
DISCUSSION: A written test has validity when it measures what it is supposed to measure and nothing else.
Answer (A) is incorrect because a written test has reliability, not validity, when it yields consistent results. Answer (B) is incorrect because a written test has comprehensiveness, not validity, when it samples liberally whatever is being measured.

32. A written test is said to be comprehensive when it

A. includes all levels of difficulty.

B. samples liberally whatever is being measured.

C. measures knowledge of the same topic in many different ways.

Answer (B) is correct.   *(AIH Chap 5)*
DISCUSSION: A written test is said to be comprehensive when it samples liberally whatever is being measured.
Answer (A) is incorrect because a written test shows discrimination, not comprehensiveness, when it includes all levels of difficulty. Answer (C) is incorrect because a written test shows discrimination, not comprehensiveness, when it measures knowledge of the same topic in many different ways.

33. The characteristic of a written test, which measures small differences in achievement between students, is its

   A. validity.

   B. reliability.

   C. discrimination.

Answer (C) is correct. *(AIH Chap 5)*
   DISCUSSION: The characteristic of a written test that measures small differences in achievement between students is its discrimination.
   Answer (A) is incorrect because a written test has validity when it measures what it is supposed to and nothing else, not when it measures small differences in achievement between students. Answer (B) is incorrect because a written test that has reliability is one which yields consistent results, not which measures small differences in achievement between students.

34. A written test having the characteristic of discrimination will

   A. be easy to give and be easily graded.

   B. distinguish between students both low and high in achievement.

   C. include a representative and comprehensive sampling of the course objectives.

Answer (B) is correct. *(AIH Chap 5)*
   DISCUSSION: When a written test has the characteristic of discrimination, each item will distinguish between students who are low and students who are high in achievement of the course objectives.
   Answer (A) is incorrect because a written test having the characteristic of usability, not discrimination, will be easy to give and be easily graded. Answer (C) is incorrect because a written test having the characteristic of comprehensiveness, not discrimination, will include a representative and comprehensive sampling of the course objectives.

6.6 Review and Evaluation

35. Evaluation of student performance and accomplishment during a lesson should be based on

   A. objectives and goals established in the lesson plan.

   B. performance of each student compared to an objective standard.

   C. each student's ability to make an objective evaluation of their own progress.

Answer (A) is correct. *(AIH Chap 4)*
   DISCUSSION: The evaluation of student performance and accomplishment during a lesson should be based on the objectives and goals that were established in the instructor's lesson plan.
   Answer (B) is incorrect because a critique, not an evaluation, is based on comparing a student's performance to an objective standard. Answer (C) is incorrect because a student's own evaluation can only be subjective, not objective. Only the instructor can provide a realistic evaluation of performance and progress.

36. Which statement is true regarding student evaluation?

   A. The student's own evaluations can only be objective.

   B. Evaluation of the student's learning should be an integral part of each lesson.

   C. If deficiencies or faults not associated with the present lesson are revealed, they should be corrected immediately.

Answer (B) is correct. *(AIH Chap 4)*
   DISCUSSION: Review and evaluation should be an integral part of each classroom or flight lesson. At the end of each class period, the instructor should review what has been covered during the lesson and require the students to demonstrate the extent to which the lesson objectives have been met. Evaluation can be formal (performance, written tests) or informal (oral quiz or guided discussion).
   Answer (A) is incorrect because the student's own evaluations can only be subjective, not objective. Answer (C) is incorrect because, if deficiencies or faults not associated with the present lesson are revealed, they should be noted and pointed out. Corrective measures that are practicable at the time should be taken immediately, but more thorough remedial actions must be included in future lesson plans.

37. Which type test is desirable for evaluating training that involves an operation, procedure, or process?

   A. Oral.

   B. Performance.

   C. Proficiency.

Answer (B) is correct. *(AIH Chap 5)*
   DISCUSSION: Performance testing is desirable for evaluating training that involves an operation, procedure, or process. This method of evaluation is particularly suited to the measurement of a student's ability in performing a task, either mental or physical.
   Answer (A) is incorrect because performance, not oral, testing is desirable for evaluating training that involves an operation, procedure, or process. Answer (C) is incorrect because there is no proficiency-type test in evaluation, only oral, written, or performance.

END OF STUDY UNIT

APPENDIX A
FUNDAMENTALS OF INSTRUCTING PRACTICE TEST

The following 50 questions have been randomly selected from the fundamentals of instructing questions in the FAA's flight and ground instructor test bank. Topical coverage in this practice test is similar to that of the FAA pilot knowledge test. Use the correct answer listing on page 96 to grade your practice test.

1. A change in behavior as a result of experience can be defined as

A — learning.
B — knowledge.
C — understanding.

2. Individuals make more progress learning if they have a clear objective. This is one feature of the principle of

A — primacy.
B — readiness.
C — willingness.

3. Things most often repeated are best remembered because of which principle of learning?

A — Principle of effect.
B — Principle of recency.
C — Principle of exercise.

4. Which principle of learning often creates a strong impression?

A — Principle of primacy.
B — Principle of intensity.
C — Principle of readiness.

5. Instruction, as opposed to the trial and error method of learning, is desirable because competent instruction speeds the learning process by

A — motivating the student to a better performance.
B — emphasizing only the important points of training.
C — teaching the relationship of perceptions as they occur.

6. The factor which contributes most to a student's failure to remain receptive to new experiences and which creates a tendency to reject additional training is

A — basic needs.
B — element of threat.
C — negative self-concept.

7. In the learning process, fear or the element of threat will

A — narrow the student's perceptual field.
B — decrease the rate of associative reactions.
C — cause a student to focus on several areas of perception.

8. Which statement is true concerning motivations?

A — Motivations must be tangible to be effective.
B — Motivations may be very subtle and difficult to identify.
C — Negative motivations often are as effective as positive motivations.

9. Which is generally the more effective way for an instructor to properly motivate students?

A — Maintain pleasant personal relationships with students.
B — Provide positive motivations by the promise or achievement of rewards.
C — Reinforce their self-confidence by requiring no tasks beyond their ability to perform.

10. During the flight portion of a practical test, the examiner simulates complete loss of engine power by closing the throttle and announcing "simulated engine failure." What level of learning is being tested?

A — Application.
B — Correlation.
C — Understanding.

11. The best way to prepare a student to perform a task is to

A — explain the purpose of the task.
B — provide a clear, step-by-step example.
C — give the student an outline of the task.

12. According to one theory, some forgetting is due to the practice of submerging an unpleasant experience into the subconscious. This is called

A — blanking.
B — immersion.
C — repression.

13. Responses that produce a pleasurable return are called

A — reward.
B — praise.
C — positive feedback.

14. To ensure proper habits and correct techniques during training, an instructor should

A — use the building block technique of instruction.
B — repeat subject matter the student has already learned.
C — introduce challenging material to continually motivate the student.

15. Which of the student's human needs offer the greatest challenge to an instructor?

A — Social.
B — Egoistic.
C — Self-fulfillment.

16. When a student asks irrelevant questions or refuses to participate in class activities, it usually is an indication of the defense mechanism known as

A — flight.
B — aggression.
C — resignation.

17. When students display the defense mechanism called aggression, they

A — become visibly angry, upset, and childish.
B — may refuse to participate in class activities.
C — attempt to justify actions by asking numerous questions.

18. Which would more likely result in students becoming frustrated?

A — Giving the students meaningless praise.
B — Telling students their work is unsatisfactory with no explanation.
C — Covering up instructor mistakes or bluffing when the instructor is in doubt.

19. Student confidence tends to be destroyed if instructors

A — bluff whenever in doubt about some point.
B — continually identify student errors and failures.
C — direct and control the student's actions and behavior.

20. To communicate effectively, instructors must

A — recognize the level of comprehension.
B — provide an atmosphere which encourages questioning.
C — reveal a positive attitude while delivering their message.

21. By using abstractions in the communication process, the communicator will

A — bring forth specific items of experience in the minds of the receivers.
B — be using words which refer to objects or ideas that human beings can experience directly.
C — not evoke in the listener's or reader's mind the specific items of experience the communicator intends.

22. A communicator's words cannot communicate the desired meaning to another person unless the

A — words have meaningful referents.
B — words give the meaning that is in the mind of the receiver.
C — listener or reader has had some experience with the objects or concepts to which these words refer.

23. Which statement is true regarding student evaluation?

A — The student's own evaluations can only be objective.
B — Evaluation of the student's learning should be an integral part of each lesson.
C — If deficiencies or faults not associated with the present lesson are revealed, they should be corrected immediately.

24. To enhance a student's acceptance of further instruction, the instructor should

A — keep the student informed of the progress made.
B — continually prod the student to maintain motivational levels.
C — establish performance standards a little above the student's actual ability.

25. The method of arranging lesson material from the simple to complex, past to present, and known to unknown, is one that

A — creates student thought pattern departures.
B — shows the relationships of the main points of the lesson.
C — requires students to actively participate in the lesson.

26. The first step in preparing a lecture is to

A — research the subject.
B — develop the main ideas or key points.
C — establish the objective and desired outcome.

27. What is one advantage of a lecture?

A — Uses time economically.
B — Excellent when additional research is required.
C — Allows for maximum attainment of certain types of learning outcomes.

28. Which teaching method is most economical in terms of the time required to present a given amount of material?

A — Briefing.
B — Teaching lecture.
C — Demonstration/performance.

29. In a guided discussion, learning is achieved through the

A — skillful use of questions.
B — use of questions, each of which contains several ideas.
C — use of reverse questions directed to the class as a whole.

30. When it appears students have adequately discussed the ideas presented during a guided discussion, one of the most valuable tools an instructor can use is

A — a session of verbal testing.
B — a written test on the subject discussed.
C — an interim summary of what the students accomplished.

31. What is the last step in the demonstration/performance method?

A — Summary.
B — Evaluation.
C — Student performance.

32. When an instructor critiques a student, it should always be

A — done in private.
B — subjective rather than objective.
C — conducted immediately after the student's performance.

33. To be effective, a critique should

A — not contain negative remarks.
B — treat every aspect of the performance in detail.
C — be flexible enough to satisfy the requirements of the moment.

34. One desirable result of proper oral quizzing by the instructor is to

A — reveal the effectiveness of the instructor's training procedures.
B — fulfill the requirements set forth in the overall objectives of the course.
C — reveal the essential information from which the student can determine progress.

35. To be effective in oral quizzing during the conduct of a lesson, a question should

A — be of suitable difficulty for that stage of training.
B — include a combination of where, how, and why.
C — divert the student's thoughts to subjects covered in other lessons.

36. A written test that has reliability

A — yields consistent results.
B — measures small differences in the achievement of students.
C — actually measures what it is supposed to measure and nothing else.

37. A written test is said to be comprehensive when it

A — includes all levels of difficulty.
B — samples liberally whatever is being measured.
C — measures knowledge of the same topic in many different ways.

38. One of the main advantages of selection-type test items over supply-type test items is that the selection-type

A — decreases discrimination between responses.
B — would be graded objectively regardless of the student or the grader.
C — precludes comparison of students under one instructor with those under another instructor.

39. In a written test, which type of selection-type test items reduces the probability of guessing correct responses?

A — Essay.
B — Matching.
C — Multiple-choice.

40. Instructional aids used in the teaching/learning process should not be used

A — as a crutch by the instructor.
B — for teaching more in less time.
C — to visualize relationships between abstracts.

41.   Which statement is true regarding true professionalism as an instructor?

A — Anything less than sincere performance destroys the effectiveness of the professional instructor.
B — To achieve professionalism, actions and decisions must be limited to standard patterns and practices.
C — A single definition of professionalism would encompass all of the qualifications and considerations which must be present.

42.   What should an instructor do with a student who assumes that correction of errors is unimportant?

A — Divide complex flight maneuvers into elements.
B — Try to reduce the student's overconfidence to reduce the chance of an accident.
C — Raise the standard of performance for each lesson, demanding greater effort.

43.   When under stress, normal individuals usually react

A — by showing excellent morale followed by deep depression.
B — by responding rapidly and exactly, often automatically, within the limits of their experience and training.
C — inappropriately such as extreme overcooperation, painstaking self-control, and inappropriate laughing or singing.

44.   The basic demonstration/performance method of instruction consists of several steps in proper order. They are

A — instructor tells--student does; student tells--student does; student does--instructor evaluates.
B — instructor tells--instructor does; student tells--instructor does; student does--instructor evaluates.
C — instructor tells--instructor does; student tells--instructor does; student tells--student does; student does--instructor evaluates.

45.   During integrated flight instruction, the instructor must be sure the student

A — develops the habit of looking for other traffic.
B — is able to control the aircraft for extended periods under IMC.
C — can depend on the flight instruments when maneuvering by outside references.

46.   Students quickly become apathetic when they

A — realize material is being withheld by the instructor.
B — understand the objectives toward which they are working.
C — recognize that the instructor is not adequately prepared.

47.   Development and assembly of blocks of learning in their proper relationship will provide a means for

A — both the instructor and student to easily correct faulty habit patterns.
B — challenging the student by progressively increasing the units of learning.
C — allowing the student to master the segments of the overall pilot performance requirements individually and combining these with other related segments.

48.   Which statement is true regarding lesson plans?

A — Lesson plans should not be directed toward the course objective; only to the lesson objective.
B — A well-thought-out mental outline of a lesson may be used any time as long as the instructor is well prepared.
C — Lesson plans help instructors keep a constant check on their own activity as well as that of their students.

49.   (Refer to Figure 1 on page 71.) Section A is titled:

A — Overview.
B — Objective.
C — Introduction.

50.   (Refer to Figure 1 on page 71.) Section C is titled:

A — Schedule.
B — Overview.
C — Training Schedule.

Page Intentionally Left Blank

PRACTICE TEST LIST OF ANSWERS

The listing below gives the correct answers for your fundamentals of instructing practice knowledge test and the page number in this book on which you will find each question with the complete Gleim answer explanation.

Q. #	Answer	Page	Q. #	Answer	Page	Q. #	Answer	Page	Q. #	Answer	Page
1.	A	23	14.	A	29	27.	A	56	40.	A	74
2.	B	24	15.	C	43	28.	B	56	41.	A	49
3.	C	24	16.	B	36	29.	A	58	42.	C	38
4.	A	24	17.	B	36	30.	C	59	43.	B	37
5.	C	27	18.	B	84	31.	B	60	44.	C	60
6.	C	35	19.	A	49	32.	C	82	45.	A	62
7.	A	26	20.	C	46	33.	C	83	46.	C	49
8.	B	45	21.	C	47	34.	A	85	47.	C	67
9.	B	44	22.	C	47	35.	A	85	48.	C	72
10.	B	30	23.	B	89	36.	A	88	49.	B	70
11.	B	32	24.	A	82	37.	B	88	50.	A	70
12.	C	29	25.	B	68	38.	B	87			
13.	B	29	26.	C	56	39.	B	88			

APPENDIX B
REPRINTS FROM THE FAA'S
AVIATION INSTRUCTOR'S HANDBOOK

The FAA's *Aviation Instructor's Handbook* (FAA-H-8083-9A) consists of nine chapters, which are briefly outlined in Study Units 1 through 6 of this book. Chapters 6, 7, and 8 are reprinted for your reference as you prepare for your FAA knowledge test and your FAA practical test. These chapters may also be useful to you whether you are an active flight instructor or are becoming a flight instructor.

Chapter 6: Planning Instructional Activity
Chapter 7: Instructor Responsibilities and Professionalism
Chapter 8: Techniques of Flight Instruction

They are reprinted beginning on the next page and continue through page 141.

Chapter 6

Planning Instructional Activity

Introduction

Susan (student) and Bill (Certificated Flight Instructor (CFI)) are flying a lesson scenario which consists of a short cross-country leg to a local airport for some practice landings followed by a return to the home airport located in Class C airspace. While practicing landings at the nontowered airport, the student notes that the ceiling is lowering and the crosswind is beginning to increase. In his own mind, Bill is convinced that they can practice landings for another 30 minutes to an hour and still return to home base. However, instead of telling Susan this, while taxiing back after a full stop landing, he first asks her several questions.

- Has the flight situation changed since they left the home field?

- What does she think of the weather situation?

- How can we gain more information?

  - Check with Automated Flight Service Station (AFSS) on the radio?

  - Stop at the Fixed Based Operator (FBO) and call back to the FBO to check on weather and the schedule?

- Are there other issues?

  - Fuel?

  - Schedule?

- Aircraft equipment (instrument flight rules (IFR)/visual flight rules (VFR)) and pilot capability?

Susan decides that she would be more comfortable returning to the home airport and practicing landings there to stay out of the weather. Although not his plan, it is a good plan based on accurate situational awareness and good risk management skills, so Bill agrees. Susan is now beginning to gain confidence by practicing her judgment and decision-making skills. In the postflight critique, Susan leads a discussion of this and other decisions she has made in order to learn more about the process.

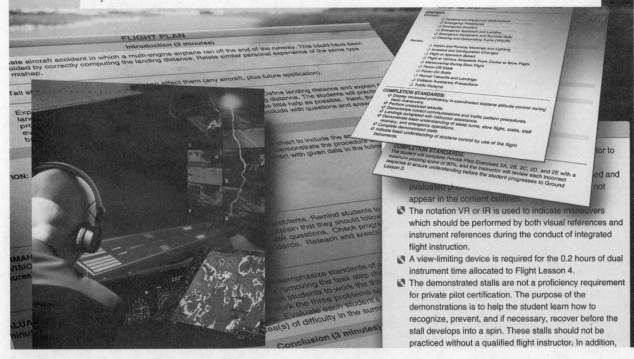

In the past, the aviation instructor was a capable pilot or aviation technician with a rather general understanding of basic teaching methods and techniques. More recently, the Federal Aviation Administration (FAA) has paid more attention to the instructor's role as teacher and mentor, and has provided a much better grounding in instructional techniques. The instructor is now required to master the teaching methods, write lesson objectives, outline and write lesson plans, and motivate students by example. The instructor is responsible for what is taught in the aircraft and classroom. The amount of learning that takes place is a direct result of how well the lesson is prepared and the teaching skill of the instructor.

Historically, aviation instruction focused on the performance of specific procedures and/or maneuvers, and learning was measured with objective standards. Changing technology and innovations in learning provide today's aviation instructors with the opportunity to use new methods and teach to new standards. One of these methods, introduced in Chapter 4, The Teaching Process, is scenario-based training (SBT). While SBT is an integral component of today's aviation training, the instructor is crucial to its implementation. By emphasizing SBT, the instructor functions in the learning environment as an advisor and guide for the learner.

Whatever the method of teaching, the key to developing well-planned and organized aviation instruction includes using lesson plans and a training syllabus that meet all regulatory certification requirements. Much of the basic planning necessary for the flight instructor and maintenance instructor is provided by the knowledge and proficiency requirements published in Title 14 of the Code of Federal Regulations (14 CFR) parts 61 and 65, approved school syllabi, and the various texts, manuals, and training courses available. This chapter reviews the planning required by the professional aviation instructor as it relates to four key topics—course of training, blocks of learning, training syllabus, and lesson plans. It also explains how to integrate SBT, aeronautical decision-making (ADM), and risk management into the aviation training lesson.

Course of Training

As discussed in chapter 4, a course of training is a series of studies leading to attainment of a specific goal such as a certificate of completion, graduation, or an academic degree. An instructor plans instructional content around the course of training by determining the objectives and standards, which in turn determine individual lesson plans, test items, and levels of learning. For a complete discussion of determining these items, see chapter 4.

Blocks of Learning

After the overall training objectives have been established, the next step is the identification of the blocks of learning which constitute the necessary parts of the total objective. Just as in building a pyramid, some blocks are submerged in the structure and never appear on the surface, but each is an integral and necessary part of the structure. Thus, the various blocks are not isolated subjects, but essential parts of the whole. During the process of identifying the blocks of learning to be assembled for the proposed training activity, the instructor must also examine each block to ensure it is an integral part of the structure. Extraneous blocks of instruction are expensive frills, especially in flight instruction, and detract from, rather than assist in, the completion of the final objective.

While determining the overall training objectives is a necessary first step in the planning process, early identification of the foundation blocks of learning is also essential. Training for any such complicated and involved task as piloting or maintaining an aircraft requires the development and assembly of many segments or blocks of learning in their proper relationships. In this way, a student can master the segments or blocks individually and can progressively combine these with other related segments until their sum meets the overall training objectives.

The blocks of learning identified during the planning and management of a training activity should be fairly consistent in scope. They should represent units of learning which can be measured and evaluated—not a sequence of periods of instruction. For example, the flight training of a private pilot might be divided into the following major blocks: achievement of the knowledge and skills necessary for solo, the knowledge and skills necessary for solo cross-country flight, and the knowledge and skills appropriate for obtaining a private pilot certificate. *[Figure 6-1]*

Use of the building block approach provides the student with a boost in self-confidence. This normally occurs each time a block is completed. Otherwise, an overall goal, such as earning a mechanic's certificate, may seem unobtainable. If the larger blocks are broken down into smaller blocks of instruction, each on its own is more manageable. Humans learn from the simple to the complex. For example, an student airplane pilot should understand and master the technique of a normal landing prior to being introduced to short and soft field landings. A helicopter pilot must be proficient in running landings before the instructor introduces a no hydraulics approach and landing.

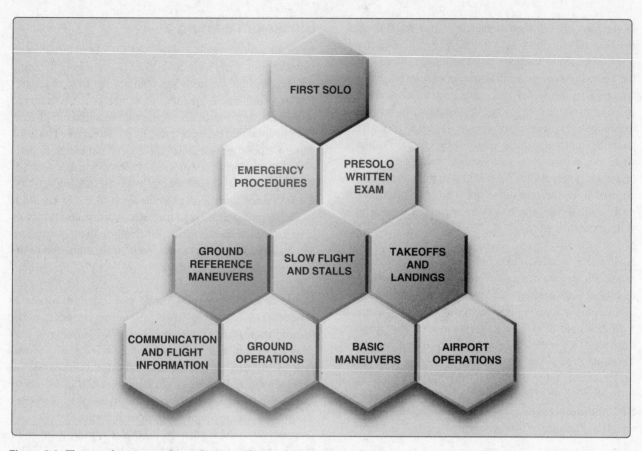

Figure 6-1. *The presolo stage or phase of private pilot training is comprised of several basic building blocks. These blocks of learning, which should include coordinated ground and flight training, lead up to the first solo.*

By becoming familiar with the student's aviation background, an instructor can plan the sequence of instruction blocks. Does the applicant have previous aeronautical experience or posses a pilot certificate in another category? This information will help the instructor design appropriate training blocks. For example, if the student is a helicopter pilot who is transitioning to an airplane, he or she will understand speed control, but not necessarily know how to achieve it in an airplane. The instructor can plan blocks of instruction that build on what the student already knows.

Training Syllabus

Aviation instructors use a training syllabus because as technology advances, training requirements become more demanding. At the same time, new, and often more complicated, rules continue to be proposed and implemented. In addition, the rules for instruction in other than an approved aviation school are still quite specific about the type and duration of training. These factors, along with the continuing growth of aviation, add to the complexity of aviation training and certification. Instructors need a practical guide to help them make sure the training is accomplished in a logical sequence and that all of the requirements are completed and properly documented. A well organized, comprehensive syllabus can fulfill these needs.

Syllabus Format and Content

The format and organization of the syllabus may vary, but it always should be in the form of an abstract or digest of the course of training. It should contain blocks of learning to be completed in the most efficient order. Since a syllabus is intended to be a summary of a course of training, it should be fairly brief, yet comprehensive enough to cover essential information. This information is usually presented in an outline format with lesson-by-lesson coverage. Some syllabi include tables to show recommended training time for each lesson, as well as the overall minimum time requirements. *[Figure 6-2]*

While many instructors may develop their own training syllabi, there are many well-designed commercial products that may be used. These are found in various training manuals, approved school syllabi, and other publications available from industry.

Syllabi developed for approved flight schools contain specific information that is outlined in 14 CFR parts 141 and 142. In contrast, syllabi designed for training in other than approved schools may not provide certain details such as enrollment

STAGE 1 | GROUND LESSON 2

LESSON OBJECTIVES
- Learn important safety of flight considerations.
- Become thoroughly familiar with airports, including marking and lighting aids.
- Learn the significance of airspace divisions and how to use the radio for communications.
- Understand the capabilities and use of radar and other ATC services.

CONTENT
Introduce:

Section A—Safety of Flight
- ❏ Visual Scanning
- ❏ Collision Avoidance Precautions
- ❏ Blind Spots and Aircraft Design
- ❏ Right-of-Way Rules
- ❏ Minimum Safe Altitudes
- ❏ VFR Cruising Altitudes
- ❏ Special Safety Considerations

Section B—Airports
- ❏ Towered and Nontowered Airports
- ❏ Runway and Taxiway Markings
- ❏ Airport Signs
- ❏ Wind Direction Indicators
- ❏ Segmented Circle
- ❏ Noise Abatement Procedures
- ❏ Airport Lighting

Section C—Airspace
- ❏ Cloud Clearance and Visibility
- ❏ Special Use and Other Airspace Areas

Section D—Radio Communications
- ❏ VHF Communications Equipment
- ❏ Coordinated Universal Time
- ❏ Radio Procedures
- ❏ Common Traffic Advisory Frequency
- ❏ Flight Service Stations

Section E—Radar and ATC Services
- ❏ Radar
- ❏ Transponder
- ❏ FAA Radar Systems

COMPLETION STANDARDS
The student will complete Private Pilot Exercises 2A, 2B, 2C, 2D, and 2E with a minimum passing score of 80%. The instructor will review each incorrect response to ensure understanding before the student progresses to Ground Lesson 3.

Figure 6-2. *This excerpt of a ground lesson shows a unit of ground instruction. In this example, neither the time nor the number of ground training periods to be devoted to the lesson is specified. The lesson should include three parts—objective, content, and completion standards.*

prerequisites, planned completion times, and descriptions of checks and tests to measure student accomplishments for each stage of training.

Since effective training relies on organized blocks of learning, all syllabi should stress well-defined objectives and standards for each lesson. Appropriate objectives and standards should be established for the overall course, the separate ground and flight segments, and for each stage of training. Other details may be added to a syllabus in order to explain how to use it and describe the pertinent training and reference materials. Examples of the training and reference materials include textbooks, video, compact disks, exams, briefings, and instructional guides.

How To Use a Training Syllabus

Any practical training syllabus must be flexible and should be used primarily as a guide. *[Figure 6-3]* When necessary, the order of training can and should be altered to suit the progress of the student and the demands of special circumstances. For example, previous experience or different rates of learning often require some alteration or repetition to fit individual students. The syllabus should also be flexible enough so it can be adapted to weather variations, aircraft availability, and scheduling changes without disrupting the teaching process or completely suspending training.

Figure 6-3. *The curriculum and training syllabus provide teaching guidelines.*

In departing from the order prescribed by the syllabus, however, it is the responsibility of the instructor to consider how the relationships of the blocks of learning are affected. For example, if the student is having a difficult time with normal approaches and landings, the instructor might decide to delay adding short field landings, which were originally to be the next step in his block of instruction. To prevent the student from becoming frustrated with his or her poor landing technique, the instructor may choose to review the block on slow flight, which offers the student a chance to do well and regain confidence. This exercise also builds the skills necessary for the student to master approaches and normal landings.

Each approved training course provided by a certificated aviation school should be conducted in accordance with a training syllabus specifically approved by the FAA. At certificated schools, the syllabus is a key part of the training course outline. The instructional facilities, airport, aircraft, and instructor personnel must be able to support the course of training specified in the syllabus. Compliance with the appropriate, approved syllabus is a condition for graduation from such courses. Therefore, effective use of a syllabus requires that it be referred to throughout the entire course of training. Both the instructor and the student should have a copy of the approved syllabus. However, as previously mentioned, adherence to a syllabus should not be so stringent that it becomes inflexible or unchangeable. It must be flexible enough to adapt to the special needs of individual students.

Ground training lessons and classroom lectures concentrate on the cognitive domain of learning. A typical lesson might include defining, labeling, or listing what the student has learned so far. Many of the knowledge areas are directly or indirectly concerned with safety, ADM, and judgment. Since these subjects are associated with the affective domain of learning (emotion), instructors who find a way to stress safety, ADM, and judgment, along with the traditional aviation subjects, can favorably influence a student's attitude, beliefs, and values.

Flight training lessons or aviation technical lab sessions also include knowledge areas, but they generally emphasize the psychomotor domain of learning because the student is "doing" something. The lesson plan shown in *Figure 6-4* shows the main elements of a ground lesson for a flight student. The affective domain of learning is also important in this type of training; a student's attitude toward safety, ADM, and judgment, should be a major concern of the instructor.

The flight training syllabus should include special emphasis items that have been determined to be cause factors in aircraft accidents or incidents. For example, the instructor should emphasize collision and wake turbulence avoidance procedures throughout a student's flight training. The aviation technician syllabus should also emphasize what constitutes unsafe practices, such the ease of introducing foreign object damage (FOD) to an aircraft when the location of tools is not monitored.

A syllabus may include several other items that add to or clarify the objective, content, or standards. A lesson may specify the recommended class time, reference or study materials, recommended sequence of training, and study assignment for the next lesson. Both ground and flight lessons may have explanatory information notes added to specific lessons. *[Figure 6-5]*

While a syllabus is designed to provide a road map showing how to accomplish the overall objective of a course of training, it may be useful for other purposes. As already mentioned, it can be used as a checklist to ensure that required training has successfully been completed. Thus, a syllabus can be an effective tool for recordkeeping. Enhanced syllabi,

---

STAGE 1   FLIGHT LESSON 4

Dual—Local (1.0)

Note: A view-limiting device is required for 0.2 hours of dual instrument time allocated to Flight Lesson 4.

LESSON OBJECTIVES

- Practice the maneuvers listed for review to gain additional proficiency and demonstrate the ability to recognize and recover from stalls.
- The student will also receive instruction and practice in the maneuvers and procedures listed for introduction, including emergency operations and additional practice of airplane control by instrument reference (IR).
- Instructor may demonstrate secondary, accelerated maneuver, crossed-control, and elevator trim stalls.
- Emphasis will be on procedures related to airport operations, steep turns, slow flight, stalls, and stall recovery.

CONTENT

Introduce:

- ❏ Systems and Equipment Malfunctions
- ❏ Emergency Procedures
- ❏ Emergency Descent
- ❏ Emergency Approach and Landing
- ❏ Emergency Equipment and Survival Gear
- ❏ Climbing and Descending Turns (VR)(IR)

Review:

- ❏ Airport and Runway Markings and Lighting
- ❏ Airspeed and Configuration Changes
- ❏ Flight at Approach Speed
- ❏ Flight at Various Airspeeds From Cruise to Slow Flight
- ❏ Maneuvering During Slow Flight
- ❏ Power-Off Stalls
- ❏ Power-On Stalls
- ❏ Normal Takeoffs and Landings
- ❏ Collision Avoidance Precautions
- ❏ Traffic Patterns

COMPLETION STANDARDS

- Displays increased proficiency in coordinated airplane attitude control during basic maneuvers.
- Performs unassisted takeoffs.
- Demonstrates correct communications and traffic pattern procedures.
- Completes landings with instructor assistance.
- Demonstrates basic understanding of steep turns, slow flight, stalls, stall recovery, and emergency operations.
- Completes demonstrated stalls.
- Indicates basic understanding of airplane control by use of the flight instruments.

Figure 6-4. *A flight training lesson, like a ground training lesson, should include an objective, content, and completion standards. More than one objective could, and often does, apply to a single flight lesson.*

which also are designed for recordkeeping, can be very beneficial to the independent instructor.

This recordkeeping function is usually facilitated by boxes or blank spaces adjacent to the knowledge areas, procedures, or maneuvers in a lesson. Most syllabi introduce each procedure or maneuver in one lesson and review them in subsequent lessons. Some syllabi also include provisions for grading student performance and recording both ground and flight training time. Accurate recordkeeping is necessary to keep both the student and the instructor informed on the status of training. These records also serve as a basis for endorsements and recommendations for knowledge and practical tests. Some training syllabi or records may include

Typical syllabus notes

- Students should read Chapter 1 of the textbook prior to Ground Lesson 1.
- All preflight duties and procedures will be performed and evaluated prior to each flight. Therefore, they will not appear in the content outlines.
- The notation "VR" or "IR" is used to indicate maneuvers which should be performed by both visual references and instrument references during the conduct of integrated flight instruction.
- A view-limiting device is required for the 0.2 hours of dual instrument time allocated to Flight Lesson 4.
- The demonstrated stalls are not a proficiency requirement for private pilot certification. The purpose of the demonstrations is to help the student learn how to recognize, prevent, and if necessary, recover before the stall develops into a spin. These stalls should not be practiced without a qualified flight instructor. In addition, some stalls may be prohibited in some airplanes.

Figure 6-5. *Information in the form of notes may be added to individual ground or flight lessons in a syllabus when they are necessary.*

coded numbers or letters for other instructors to record their evaluation of a student's progress and knowledge or skill level. *[Figure 6-6]*

Another benefit of using a syllabus is that it helps in the development of lesson plans. A well constructed syllabus already contains much of the essential information that is required in a lesson plan, including objectives, content, and completion standards.

Lesson Plans

A lesson plan is an organized outline for a single instructional period. It is a necessary guide for the instructor because it tells what to do, in what order to do it, and what procedure to use in teaching the material of a lesson. Lesson plans should be prepared for each training period and be developed to show specific knowledge and/or skills to be taught.

A mental outline of a lesson is not a lesson plan. A lesson plan should be put into writing. Another instructor should be able to take the lesson plan and know what to do in conducting the same period of instruction. Written out, the lesson plan can be analyzed for adequacy and completeness.

Lesson plans make excellent recordkeeping forms that can become a permanent part of a pilot's training record. They can be formatted for the instructor to carry in the aircraft and include a checklist for indicating what portions of the lesson were completed, date of completion, the flight instructor's signature, and time flown. The lesson plan can also have a notation section for flight instructor comments.

A training folder for each student helps an instructor keep all pertinent data in one place. The folder should include items such as lesson plans, training requirements, flight or ground instruction received, 14 CFR part 61 requirements met, solo endorsements, and any other training information. These records should be kept in a safe area for at least 3 years. Good recordkeeping also provides each instructor with the number of students he or she has trained, which is helpful information for an instructor who needs to renew his or her certificate. For sample lesson plans, please refer to Appendix A.

Purpose of the Lesson Plan

Lesson plans are designed to assure that each student receives the best possible instruction under the existing conditions. Lesson plans help instructors keep a constant check on their own activity, as well as that of their students. The development of lesson plans by instructors signifies, in effect, that they have taught the lessons to themselves prior to attempting to teach the lessons to students. An adequate lesson plan, when properly used, should:

- Assure a wise selection of material and the elimination of unimportant details.
- Make certain that due consideration is given to each part of the lesson.
- Aid the instructor in presenting the material in a suitable sequence for efficient learning.
- Provide an outline of the teaching procedure to be used.
- Serve as a means of relating the lesson to the objectives of the course of training.
- Give the inexperienced instructor confidence.
- Promote uniformity of instruction regardless of the instructor or the date on which the lesson is given.

Characteristics of a Well-Planned Lesson

The quality of planning affects the quality of results. Successful professionals understand that the price of excellence is hard work and thorough preparation. The effective instructor realizes that the time and energy spent in planning and preparing each lesson is well worth the effort in the long run.

A complete cycle of planning usually includes several steps. After the objective is determined, the instructor must research the subject as it is defined by the objective. Once the research is complete, the instructor determines the method of

FLIGHT INSTRUCTION LOG (GLIDER)

Student: _____   Instructor: _____

	Flight Number	1	2	3	4	5	6	7	8	9	10	11	12	13	14	15	16
	Lesson Number																
Glider Assembly																	
Preflight Inspection																	
Ground Handling																	
Takeoff (Normal)																	
Crosswind Takeoff																	
Tow (High-Tow & Low-Tow)																	
Boxing the Wake																	
Slack Line Recovery																	
Straight Glides																	
Turns (Shallow & Medium)																	
Steep Turns (50 to 60 Degrees of Bank)																	
Slow Flight & Minimum Controllable Airspeed																	
Straight-Ahead Stalls																	
Turning Stalls																	
Accelerated Stalls																	
Spin Recovery																	
Traffic Pattern																	
Use of Spoilers																	
Forward Slips (With & Without Spoilers)																	
Landings (Normal)																	
Crosswind Landings (Simulated)																	
Off-Airport Landings (Simulated)																	
Airspeed Control																	
Vigilance & Collision Avoidance																	
Judgment																	
Use of Checklists																	
Flight Time (This flight)																	
Total Flight Time																	

Figure 6-6. *Glider training log.*

instruction and identifies a useful lesson planning format. The decision of how to organize the lesson and the selection of suitable support material come next. The final steps include assembling training aids and writing the lesson plan outline. One technique for writing the lesson plan outline is to prepare the beginning and ending first. Then, complete the outline and revise as required. A lesson plan should be a working document that can and should be revised as changes occur or are needed.

The following are some of the important characteristics that should be reflected in all well-planned lessons.

Unity—each lesson should be a unified segment of instruction. A lesson is concerned with certain limited objectives, which are stated in terms of desired student learning outcomes. All teaching procedures and materials should be selected to attain these objectives.

Content—each lesson should contain new material. However, the new facts, principles, procedures, or skills should be related to the lesson previously presented. A short review of earlier lessons is usually necessary, particularly in flight training.

Scope—each lesson should be reasonable in scope. A person can master only a few principles or skills at a time, the number depending on complexity. Presenting too much material in a lesson results in confusion; presenting too little material results in inefficiency.

Practicality—each lesson should be planned in terms of the conditions under which the training is to be conducted. Lesson plans conducted in an airplane or ground trainer will differ from those conducted in a classroom. Also, the kinds and quantities of instructional aids available have a great influence on lesson planning and instructional procedures.

Flexibility—although the lesson plan provides an outline and sequence for the training to be conducted, a degree of flexibility should be incorporated. For example, the outline of content may include blank spaces for add-on material, if required.

Relation to course of training—each lesson should be planned and taught so that its relation to the course objectives is clear to each student. For example, a lesson on short field takeoffs and landings should be related to both the certification and safety objectives of the course of training.

Instructional steps—every lesson, when adequately developed, falls logically into the four steps of the teaching process: preparation, presentation, application, and review and evaluation.

How To Use a Lesson Plan Properly

Be familiar with the lesson plan. The instructor should study each step of the plan and should be thoroughly familiar with as much information related to the subject as possible.

Use the lesson plan as a guide. The lesson plan is an outline for conducting an instructional period. It assures that pertinent materials are at hand and that the presentation is accomplished with order and unity. Having a plan prevents the instructor from getting off track, omitting essential points, and introducing irrelevant material. Students have a right to expect an instructor to give the same attention to teaching that they give to learning. The most certain means of achieving teaching success is to have a carefully reviewed lesson plan.

Adapt the lesson plan to the class or student. In teaching a class, the instructor may find that the procedures outlined in the lesson plan are not leading to the desired results. In this situation, the instructor should change the approach. There is no certain way of predicting the reactions of different groups of students. An approach that has been successful with one group may not be equally successful with another.

A lesson plan for an instructional flight period should be appropriate to the background, flight experience, and ability of the particular student. A lesson plan may have to be modified considerably during flight, due to deficiencies in the student's knowledge or poor mastery of elements essential to the effective completion of the lesson. In some cases, the entire lesson plan may have to be abandoned in favor of review.

Revise the lesson plan periodically. After a lesson plan has been prepared for a training period, a continuous revision may be necessary. This is true for a number of reasons such as availability or non-availability of instructional aids, changes in regulations, or new manuals and textbooks.

Lesson Plan Formats

The format and style of a lesson plan depends on several factors. Certainly the subject matter helps determine how a lesson is presented and what teaching method is used. Individual lesson plans may be quite simple for one-on-one training, or they may be elaborate and complicated for large, structured classroom lessons. Preferably, each lesson should have somewhat limited objectives that are achievable within a reasonable period of time. This principle should apply to both ground and flight training. However, as previously noted, aviation training is not simple. It involves all three domains of learning, and the objectives usually include the higher levels of learning, at least at the application level.

In spite of need for varied subject coverage, diverse teaching methods, and relatively high level learning objectives, most aviation lesson plans have the common characteristics already discussed. All should include objectives, content to support the objectives, and completion standards. Various authorities often divide the main headings into several subheadings; terminology, even for the main headings, varies extensively. For example, completion standards may be called assessment, review and feedback, performance evaluation, or some other related term.

Commercially developed lesson plans are acceptable for most training situations, including use by flight instructor applicants during their practical tests. However, all instructors should recognize that even well-designed preprinted lesson plans may need to be modified. Therefore, instructors are encouraged to use creativity when adapting preprinted lesson plans or when developing their own lesson plans for specific students or training circumstances.

In the traditional lesson plan illustrated by *Figure 6-7,* the objective is "The student will learn to control for wind drift." The content has the instructor pilot giving a thorough

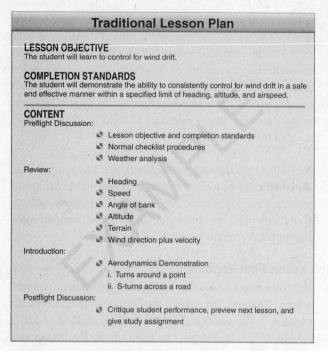

Figure 6-7. *Example of a traditional training lesson plan.*

coverage of heading, speed, angle of bank, altitude, terrain, and wind direction plus velocity. This explanation is followed by a demonstration and repeated practice of a specific flight maneuver, such as turns around a point or S-turns across the road until the maneuver can be consistently accomplished in a safe and effective manner within a specified limit of heading, altitude, and airspeed. At the end of this lesson, the student is only capable of practicing the maneuver with assistance from the instructor.

The traditional type of training lesson plan with its focus on the task and maneuver or procedure continues to meet many aviation learning requirements, but as discussed earlier in the chapter, it is being augmented by more realistic and fluid forms of problem-based learning such as SBT. For the CFI, this type of training does not preclude traditional maneuver-based training. Rather, flight maneuvers are integrated into the flight scenarios and conducted as they would occur in the real world. Those maneuvers requiring repetition are still taught during concentrated settings; once learned, they are then integrated into realistic flight situations.

For the aviation technician instructor, SBT enhances traditional classroom instruction. By integrating SBT into the lesson, students are required to deal with problems they will encounter in the real world.

Scenario-Based Training (SBT)

Improper pilot decisions cause a significant percentage of all accidents and the majority of fatal accidents in light single- and twin-engine aircraft. The goal of SBT is to challenge the student or transitioning pilot with a variety of flight scenarios to improve decision-making skills. These scenarios require the pilot to manage the resources available in the flight deck, exercise sound judgment, and make timely decisions.

As defined in chapter 4, SBT is a training method that uses a highly structured script of real world experiences to address aviation training objectives in an operational environment. Such training can include initial training, transition training, upgrade training, recurrent training, and special training. Since humans develop cognitive skills through active interaction with the world, an effective aviation instructor uses the maneuver- or procedure-based approach of the PTS but presents the objectives in a scenario situation.

Although some CFIs have used the SBT approach as a teaching method for many years, the recent emphasis on SBT in aviation training reflects education research that shows students learn more effectively when actively involved in the learning process. The introduction of advanced avionics is also a factor. Advanced avionics have changed the role of general aviation (GA) from an industry dominated by pleasure flying to a viable alternative to the scheduled airlines. With glass displays, GPS, and autopilot, advanced avionics may allow easier and safer operation, but are more complex.

Advanced avionics have contributed to a shift in the focus of aviation training to include aeronautical decision-making (ADM) and risk management. For the pilot, this is called Single-Pilot Resource Management (SRM). Since SRM training requires the student or transitioning pilot to practice the decision-making process in real-world situations, it combines traditional task and maneuver-based training with SBT to enhance ADM, risk management, and SRM skills without compromising basic stick and rudder skills. Instead of training pilots to pass practical tests, this program focuses on expertly managed real-world challenges.

Duties, Responsibilities, and Authority of the Aviation Instructor

The duties, responsibilities, and authority of the aviation instructor include the following:

1. Orient new learners to the SBT approach.

2. Help the learner become a confident planner and a critical evaluator of his or her own performance.

3. Help the learner understand the knowledge requirements present in real world applications.

4. Diagnose learning difficulties and help the individual overcome them.

5. Evaluate student progress and maintain appropriate records.

6. Provide continuous review of student learning.

The aviation instructor is the key to the success of SBT. Remember, the overall learning objective is for the student to be ready to exercise sound judgment and make good decisions. For example, the flight instructor must be ready to turn the responsibility for planning and execution of the flight over to the student as soon as possible. The flight instructor continues to demonstrate and instruct skill maneuvers in the traditional manner; but, when the student begins to make decisions, the flight instructor should revert to the role of mentor and/or learning facilitator.

A situation a student faces may not have one right or one wrong answer. Instead, a student encounters situations in training that may have several "good" outcomes and few "poor" ones. Rather than requiring the student to make a decision that matches the instructor's personal preference, he or she should understand in advance which outcomes are positive and/or negative and give the student the freedom to make both good and poor decisions. This does not mean that the student should be allowed to make an unsafe decision or commit an unsafe act. However, it does allow the student to make decisions that fit his or her experience level and result in positive outcomes.

SBT Lesson Plan

The SBT lesson plan differs from the traditional lesson plan. *[Figure 6-8]* In this example, the instructor pilot tells the student to plan for arrival at a specific nontowered airport. The planning should take into consideration the possible wind conditions, arrival paths, airport information and communication procedures, available runways, recommended traffic patterns, courses of action, and preparation for unexpected situations. Upon arrival at the airport, the student makes decisions (with guidance and feedback, as necessary) to safely enter and fly the traffic pattern. This is followed by a discussion of what was done, why it was done, the consequences, other possible courses of action, and how it applies to other airports. In contrast to the student who trained under the traditional lesson plan, the student who trains under the SBT format is not only capable of a specific flight maneuver, he or she is now capable of detailing the safe arrival at any nontowered airport in any wind condition.

Scenario-Based Training Lesson Plan

TYPE OF TRAINING
Initial

MANEUVER OR TRAINING OBJECTIVE
Plan for arrival at a specific nontowered airport.

SCENARIO
Prepare to fly to the Enterprise Municipal Airport (EDN) in order to visit the Army Aviation Museum at Fort Rucker.

COMPLETION STANDARDS
The student is capable of explaining the safe arrival at any nontowered airport in any wind condition.

POSSIBLE HAZARDS OR CONSIDERATIONS
- Ground-based obstructions/hazards
- Winds conditions
- Visibility/ceiling
- Engine-out procedures
- Airport traffic

MITIGATION STRATEGIES AND RESOURCES (Every hazard or consideration should be addressed through the use of some mitigating strategy or resource. Those provided below serve only as an example to illustrate the system safety methodology.)

Ground-based obstructions/hazards:
The instructor and student will review all available resources, including sectional/terminal area charts, A/FD, and Notices To Airmen (NOTAMs). Using aircraft performance data found in the POH/FM, the potential impact of any obstructions or hazards during departure, en route, and arrival will be assessed and a strategy developed to address any concerns.

Wind conditions:
The instructor and student will use the aircraft POH/FM and assess the runway environment prior to making a determination. This would also be an excellent catalyst for a discussion of personal minimums and any additional training requirements.

Visibility/ceiling:
The instructor and student will discuss the impact of visibility/ceiling as it relates to departure, en route, and landing at an nontowered airport in various wind conditions. For example, if circumstances demand the conduct of a circling approach under marginal VFR conditions, does the student have the confidence and proficiency to fly a tight pattern while managing airspeed, aircraft coordination, etc? Under such circumstances, would it be more desirable to conduct a straight-in approach with a slight tailwind (if that is even an option)? How much wind would be too much? What other variables/options should be considered (perhaps a diversion to a more suitable airport)?

Engine-out procedures:
Should an engine fail or partial loss of power occur, the student and instructor should discuss and simulate in a manner consistent with safety, engine-out procedures as part of a comprehensive training program.

Airport traffic:
Traffic at both towered and nontowered airports often necessitates wide variations in landing patterns. While issues stemming from airport traffic may largely be addressed through sound flying technique, the instructor can take an otherwise routine lesson and introduce other risk elements, thus promoting the student's development of critical decision-making skills.

FLY THE SCENARIO

POSTFLIGHT REVIEW
This review should include a dialogue between the instructor pilot and the student or transitioning pilot encompassing the flight scenario. Generally, the instructor pilot should lead the discussion with questions that generate reflective thinking on how the overall flight went. The instructor pilot should use this to assist in evaluating the student or transitioning pilot's assessment skills, judgment, and decision-making skills. Typically, the discussion should begin with student self-critique; the instructor pilot enables the student to solve the problems and draw conclusions. Based on this analysis, the student and instructor pilot should discuss methods for improvement, even on those items that were considered successful.

Figure 6-8. *SBT lesson plan.*

Prescenario Planning

For SBT instruction to be effective, it is vital that the aviation instructor and student establish the following information:

Flight scenario:

- Scenario destination(s)
- Desired student learning outcomes
- Desired level of student performance
- Possible inflight scenario changes

Nonflight scenario:

- Narrative of the task goal
- Desired student learning outcomes
- Desired level of student performance
- Possible scenario changes

The aviation industry is moving from traditional knowledge-related learning outcomes to an emphasis on increased internalized learning in which learners assess situations and react appropriately. Knowledge components are becoming an important side effect of a dynamic learning experience.

Reality is the ultimate learning situation and SBT attempts to get as close as possible to this ideal. It addresses learning that occurs in a context or situation. It is based on the concept of situated cognition, which is the idea that knowledge cannot be known and fully understood independent of its context. In other words, humans learn better, the more realistic the situation is and the more they are counted on to perform.

For example, realistic cross-country flight scenarios planned and executed by the pilot in training with assistance from the flight instructor begin the early development of flight deck management skills, situational awareness, and ADM. Continued engagement by the student in the planning, executing, and assessment of each scenario reinforces it throughout the training. It is important to remember the student is responsible for planning the flight scenario from a menu of short cross-country flights developed by the training provider. While the flight instructor will certainly assist the student in aircraft performance data, weight and balance, and general aircraft layout prior to the first lesson, the sooner the student assumes these responsibilities, the better the learning environment. The scenario descriptions offered in the FAA generic syllabi are a starting point for the training provider. Scenarios can be tailored for the local weather and terrain conditions and are most effective when they replicate the environment most likely encountered by the students.

SBT is a compilation of basic learning theory, adult learning concepts, and the best of the traditional aviation training procedures. Above all, it is about learning complex tasks in a realistic environment at a pace and in a structure the individual student can comprehend and process. *[Figure 6-9]* Good teaching techniques are still important, but only if they aid in student learning. More detailed information about SBT can be found at www.faa.gov/education_research/training/fits/.

**The Main Points To Remember
About Scenario-Based Training**

- SBT is situated in a real context and is based on the idea that knowledge cannot be gained and fully integrated independent of its context.

- SBT accords with a performance improvement and behavior change philosophy of the learning function.

- SBT is different from traditional instructional design; one must be aware of the differences to successfully employ SBT.

- Most learning solutions should employ both traditional training and SBT.

- Traditional learning elements should enhance the SBT elements.

- It is essential to place boundaries around scenarios to make the transitions between scenarios and traditional learning as efficient as possible.

- Open-ended qualitative learner feedback is key to successful scenario revision, but revisions should not further complicate the scenario unless highly justified.

Figure 6-9. *Points to remember about scenario-based training.*

Single-Pilot Resource Management

SRM is the art and science of managing all the resources (both on-board the aircraft and from outside sources) available to a single pilot (prior and during flight) to ensure that the successful outcome of the flight is never in doubt.

The emergence of very light jet (VLJ) aircraft will revolutionize the way America travels. *[Figure 6-10]* Central to their economic success is the concept of single-pilot operations. Since the aircraft is heavily automated, the pilot's workload may actually be less than the current workload in a high performance single-engine aircraft of today. This allows more time for the pilot to gather and analyze information about weather, winds, landing conditions, fuel state, pilot physical condition, and passenger desires.

Figure 6-10. *Very light jet aircraft in flight.*

However, unless the pilot is trained to manage all of these factors and to let the aircraft automation assist, the workload may be very high. SRM training helps the pilot maintain situational awareness by managing the automation and associated aircraft control and navigation tasks. This enables the pilot to accurately assess, manage risk, and make accurate and timely decisions. SBT enhances SRM because SBT helps pilots learn how to gather information, analyze it, and make decisions.

Chapter Summary

As indicated by this chapter, it is possible to develop well-planned and organized instruction by using a training syllabus and lesson plans that meet all regulatory certification requirements. By identifying and incorporating "blocks of learning" into the teaching of objectives, the instructor can plan lessons that build on prior knowledge. Maneuver and/or procedure training coupled with SBT will help the aviation instructor train professional aviators and technicians who are able to gather and analyze information to aid in making good aeronautical decisions and decrease risk factors, leading to a successful flight or maintenance outcome.

As this training program evolves and new resources are introduced, aviation instructors will have immediate, web-based access to documents such as the generic transition syllabus through http://www.faa.gov/.

Another helpful website for SBT is:
www.faa.gov/education_research/training/fits/training/flight_instructor/media/Volume1.pdf

Chapter 7

Instructor Responsibilities and Professionalism

Introduction

Since students look to aviation instructors as authorities in their respective areas, it is important that instructors not only know how to teach, but that they project a knowledgeable and professional image. This chapter addresses the responsibilities of aviation instructors in the training process and role as safety advocates, discusses how aviation instructors can enhance their professional image, and offers suggestions and sources of information to assist in professional development.

Responsibilities of All Aviation Instructors

- Helping Students Learn
- Providing Adequate Instruction
- Demanding Adequate Standards of Performance
- Emphasizing the Positive
- Ensuring Safety of Flight

Additional Responsibilities of Flight Instr

- Evaluation of Student Piloting Ability
- Pilot Supervision
- Practical Test Recommendations
- Flight Instructor Endorsements
- Additional Training and Endorsements
- Pilot Proficiency
- See and Avoid Responsibility
- Student's Pre-solo Flight Thought Process

Special Emphasis Areas

- Positive aircraft control
- Procedures for positive exchange of flight
- Stall and spin awareness (if appropriate)
- Collision avoidance
- Wake turbulence and low level wind shear avoidance
- Runway incursion avoidance
- Controlled flight into terrain (CFIT)
- ADM/risk management
- Checklist usage
- Spatial disorientation
- Temporary flight restrictions (TFR)
- Special use airspace (SUA)
- Aviation security
- Wire strike avoidance
- Other areas deemed appropriate to any phase of the practical test or proficiency check

Aviation Instructor Responsibilities

The job of an aviation instructor is to teach. Previous chapters have discussed how people learn, the teaching process, and teaching methods. As indicated, the learning process can be made easier by helping students learn, providing adequate instruction to meet established standards, measuring student performance against those standards, and emphasizing the positive. *[Figure 7-1]*

Responsibilities of All Aviation Instructors

- Helping students learn
- Providing adequate instruction
- Demanding adequate standards of performance
- Emphasizing the positive
- Ensuring aviation safety

Figure 7-1. *There are five main responsibilities of aviation instructors.*

Helping Students Learn

Learning should be an enjoyable experience. By making each lesson a pleasurable experience for the student, the instructor can maintain a high level of student motivation. This does not mean the instructor makes things easy for the student or sacrifices standards of performance to please the student. The student experiences satisfaction from doing a good job or from successfully meeting the challenge of a difficult task.

The idea that people must be led to learning by making it easy is a fallacy. Though students might initially be drawn to less difficult tasks, they ultimately devote more effort to activities that bring rewards. The use of standards, and measurement against standards, is key to helping students learn. Meeting standards holds its own satisfaction for students. People want to feel capable; they are proud of the successful achievement of difficult goals.

Learning should be interesting. Knowing the objective of each period of instruction gives meaning and interest to the student as well as the instructor. Not knowing the objective of the lesson often leads to confusion, disinterest, and uneasiness on the part of the student.

Providing Adequate Instruction

To tailor his or her teaching technique to the student, the flight instructor analyzes the student's personality, thinking, and ability. No two students are alike, and a particular method of instruction cannot be equally effective for all students. The instructor talks with a student at some length to learn about the student's background, interests, temperament, and way of thinking, and is prepared to change his or her methods of instruction as the student advances through successive stages of training.

An instructor who incorrectly analyzes a student may find the instruction does not produce the desired results. For example, the instructor at first thinks the student is not a quick learner because that student is quiet and reserved. Such a student may fail to act at the proper time due to lack of self-confidence, even though the situation is correctly understood. In this case, instruction is directed toward developing student self-confidence, rather than drill on flight fundamentals. In another case, too much criticism may discourage a timid person, whereas brisk instruction may force a more diligent application to the learning task. A student requiring more time to learn also requires instructional methods that combine tact, keen perception, and delicate handling. If such a student receives too much help and encouragement, a feeling of incompetence may develop.

A student whose slow progress is due to discouragement and a lack of confidence should be assigned subgoals that can be attained more easily than the usual learning goals. For this purpose, complex lessons can be separated into elements, and each element practiced until an acceptable performance is achieved before the whole maneuver or operation is attempted. For example, instruction in S-turns may begin with consideration for headings only. Elements of altitude control, drift correction, and coordination can be introduced one at a time. As the student gains confidence and ability, goals are increased in difficulty until progress is normal.

Conversely, students who are fast learners can also create challenges for the instructor. Because these students make few mistakes, they may assume that the correction of errors is unimportant. Such overconfidence can result in faulty performance. For these students, the instructor constantly raises the standard of performance for each lesson, demanding greater effort. Individuals learn when they are aware of their errors. Students who are permitted to complete every flight lesson without corrections and guidance will not retain what they have practiced as well as those students who have their attention constantly directed to an analysis of their performance. On the other hand, deficiencies should not be invented solely for the students' benefit because unfair criticism immediately destroys their confidence in the instructor.

In some ways, an aviation instructor serves as a practical psychologist. As discussed in chapters 1 and 2, an instructor can meet this responsibility through a careful analysis of and continuing interest in students.

Most new instructors tend to adopt the teaching methods used by their own instructors. The fact that one has learned under a certain system of instruction does not mean that the instructor, though well respected by the former student, used the best method. The new instructor needs to continue to grow in his or her role of instructor, seeking other resources and information to enhance his or her own teaching skills.

Standards of Performance

An aviation instructor is responsible for training an applicant to acceptable standards in all subject matter areas, procedures, and maneuvers included in the tasks within each area of operation in the appropriate Practical Test Standard (PTS). It must be emphasized that the PTS book is a testing document, not a teaching document. *[Figure 7-2]*

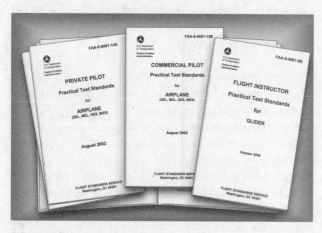

Figure 7-2. *Acceptable standards in all subject matter areas, procedures, and maneuvers are included in the appropriate Practical Test Standards.*

When teaching a particular procedure, an instructor might be tempted to point out the consequences of doing it differently, perhaps telling the student that failure to perform the procedure as taught will court disaster. The instructor may believe this "consequence approach" is necessary to ensure the student commits the procedure to memory, but the stated reasons for performing the procedure a certain way must contribute to the learning situation to be effective.

Emphasizing the Positive

Aviation instructors have a tremendous influence on a student's perception of aviation. The way instructors conduct themselves, the attitudes they display, and the manner in which they develop instruction all contribute to the formation of either positive or negative impressions by students. The success of an aviation instructor depends greatly on his or her ability to present instruction in a manner that gives students a positive image of aviation. *[Figure 7-3]*

Figure 7-3. *Students learn more when instruction is presented in a positive and professional manner.*

Chapter 1, Human Behavior, emphasized that a negative self-concept inhibits the perceptual process, that fear adversely affects student perceptions, that the feeling of being threatened limits the ability to perceive, and that negative motivation is not as effective as positive motivation. Merely knowing about these factors is not enough. Instructors must be able to detect these factors in their students and strive to prevent negative feelings from undermining the instructional process.

Consider how the following scenarios conducted during the first lesson might influence and impress a new student pilot who has limited or no aviation experience:

- An indoctrination in preflight procedures with emphasis on the critical precautions which must be taken before every flight because "… emergencies in flight can be caused by an improper preflight and are often disastrous."

- Instruction and hands-on training in the care that must be taken in taxiing an airplane because "… if you go too fast, you may lose directional control of the aircraft."

- Introduction and demonstration of stalls, because "… this is how so many people lose their lives in airplanes."

- Illustrating and demonstrating forced landings during the first lesson, because "… one should always be prepared to cope with a rope break in a glider."

These new experiences might make the new student wonder if learning to fly is a good idea.

In contrast, consider a first flight lesson in which the preflight inspection is presented to familiarize the student with the aircraft and its components, and the flight is a perfectly normal one to a nearby airport, with return. Following the flight, the instructor can call the student's attention to the ease with which the trip was made in comparison with other modes of transportation, and the fact that no critical incidents were encountered or expected.

This does not mean stalls and emergency procedures should be omitted from training. It only illustrates the positive approach in which the student is not overwhelmed with information that he or she may not be prepared to digest. Again, this reinforces the need for the instructor to employ a syllabus that makes sense and consider student ability to comprehend new information. The introduction of emergency procedures after the student has developed an acquaintance with normal operations is not as likely to be discouraging and frightening, or to inhibit learning by the imposition of fear.

There is nothing in aviation that demands that students must suffer as part of their instruction. Every effort should be made to ensure instruction is given under positive conditions that reinforce training conducted to standard and modification of the method of instruction when students have difficulty grasping a task. In essence, a student's failure to perform is viewed as an instructor's inability to transfer the information. Otherwise, the instructor fails to consider himself or herself as part of a broken learning chain. Emphasize the positive because positive instruction results in positive learning.

Minimizing Student Frustrations

Minimizing student frustrations in the classroom, shop, or during flight training is an instructor's responsibility. By following basic rules, instructors can reduce student frustrations and create a learning environment that encourages rather than discourages learning.

For example, lesson plans used as part of an organized curriculum help the student pilot measure training progress. Since most pilots don't want to be students, the ability to measure their progress or "see an end in sight" reduces frustration and increases pilot motivation. *[Figure 7-4]*

Motivate students—more can be gained from wanting to learn than from being forced to learn. Too often, students do not realize how a particular lesson or course can help them reach an important goal. When students can see the benefits and purpose of the lesson or course, their enjoyment and their efforts increase.

Keep students informed—students feel insecure when they do not know what is expected of them or what is going to happen to them. Instructors can minimize feelings of insecurity by

Minimizing Student Frustration
Motivate students
Keep students informed
Approach students as individuals
Give credit when due
Criticize constructively
Be consistent
Admit errors

Figure 7-4. *These are practical ways to minimize student frustration.*

telling students what is expected of them and what they can expect in return. Instructors keep students informed in various ways, including giving them an overview of the course, keeping them posted on their progress, and giving them adequate notice of examinations, assignments, or other requirements.

Approach students as individuals—when instructors limit their thinking to the whole group without considering the individuals who make up that group, their efforts are directed at an average personality that really fits no one. Each group has its own personality that stems from the characteristics and interactions of its members. However, each individual within the group has a unique personality to constantly be considered.

Give credit when due—when students do something extremely well, they normally expect their abilities and efforts to be noticed. Otherwise, they may become frustrated. Praise or credit from the instructor is usually ample reward and provides an incentive to do even better. Praise pays dividends in student effort and achievement when deserved, but when given too freely, it becomes valueless.

Criticize constructively—although it is important to give praise and credit when deserved, it is equally important to identify mistakes and failures. It does not help to tell students they have made errors and not provide explanations. If a student has made an earnest effort but is told that the work is unsatisfactory, with no other explanation, frustration occurs. Errors cannot be corrected if they are not identified, and if they are not identified, they will probably be perpetuated through faulty practice. On the other hand, if the student is briefed on the errors and is told how to correct them, progress can be made.

Be consistent—students want to please their instructor. This is the same desire that influences much of the behavior of subordinates toward their superiors in industry and business. Naturally, students have a keen interest in knowing what is required to please the instructor. If the same thing is acceptable one day and unacceptable the next, the student becomes confused. The instructor's philosophy and actions must be consistent.

Admit errors—no one, including students, expects an instructor to be perfect. The instructor can win the respect of students by honestly acknowledging mistakes. If the instructor tries to cover up or bluff, students are quick to sense it. Such behavior tends to destroy student confidence in the instructor. If in doubt about some point, the instructor should admit it.

Flight Instructor Responsibilities

Learning to fly should provide students with an opportunity for exploration and experimentation. It should be a habit-building period during which students devote their attention, memory, and judgment to the development of correct habit patterns. All aviation instructors shoulder an enormous responsibility because their students will ultimately be flying, servicing, or repairing aircraft, but flight instructors have the additional responsibilities of evaluating student pilots and making a decision of when they are ready to solo. The flight instructor's job is to "mold" the student pilot into a safe pilot who takes a professional approach to flying. Other flight instructor responsibilities can be found in Title 14 of the Code of Federal Regulations (14 CFR) part 61 and FAA advisory circulars (ACs). *[Figure 7-5]*

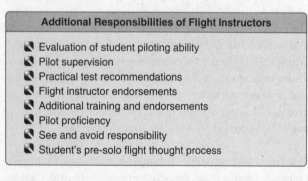

Additional Responsibilities of Flight Instructors

- Evaluation of student piloting ability
- Pilot supervision
- Practical test recommendations
- Flight instructor endorsements
- Additional training and endorsements
- Pilot proficiency
- See and avoid responsibility
- Student's pre-solo flight thought process

Figure 7-5. *The flight instructor has many additional responsibilities.*

Flight instructors must provide the most comprehensive ground and flight instruction possible. They should be current and proficient in the aircraft they use for flight instruction, encouraging each pilot to learn as much as he or she can and to continually "raise the bar." Flight instructors have the responsibility of producing the safest pilots possible with the overall focus on education and learning. It is also important to convey an understanding of why pilots are trained to standards and how they are set.

Instructors should not introduce the minimum acceptable standards for passing the check ride when introducing lesson tasks. The minimum standards to pass the check ride should

be introduced during the "3 hours of preparation" for the check ride. Keep the PTS in the proper perspective, with emphasis on the Practical Test Standard (PTS) increasing later in the training.

Physiological Obstacles for Flight Students

Although most student pilots have been exposed to air travel, they may not have flown in light, training aircraft. Consequently, students may react to unfamiliar noises or vibrations, or experience unfamiliar sensations due to G-force, or an uncomfortable feeling in the stomach. To teach effectively, instructors cannot ignore the existence of these negative factors, nor should they ridicule students who are adversely affected. These negative sensations can usually be overcome by understanding the nature of their causes. Remember, a sick student does not learn well.

Ensuring Student Skill Set

Flight instructors must ensure student pilots develop the required skills and knowledge prior to solo flight. The student pilot must show consistency in the required solo tasks: takeoffs and landings, ability to prioritize in maintaining control of the aircraft, proper navigation skills, proficiency in flight, proper radio procedures and communication skills, and traffic pattern operation. Student pilots should receive instruction to ask for assistance or help from the ATC system when needed.

Mastery of the skill set includes consistent use and continued growth as well as increased accuracy of performance. The instructor determines when a student is ready for his or her first solo flight. Generally this determination is made when the instructor observes the student from preflight to engine start to engine shutdown and the student performs consistently, without need of instructor assistance.

Flight instructors need to provide adequate flight and ground instruction for "special emphasis" items listed in each PTS for airplane, helicopter, and light sport aircraft. The student needs to be knowledgeable in these special emphasis areas because examiners and authorized instructors place special emphasis upon areas considered critical to flight safety. Special emphasis items include, but are not limited to:

1. Positive aircraft control

2. Procedures for positive exchange of flight controls

3. Stall and spin awareness (if appropriate)

4. Collision avoidance

5. Wake turbulence and low-level wind turbulence and wind shear avoidance

6. Runway incursion avoidance

7. Controlled flight into terrain (CFIT)

8. Aeronautical decision-making (ADM)/risk management

9. Checklist usage

10. Spatial disorientation

11. Temporary flight restrictions (TFR)

12. Special use airspace (SUA)

13. Aviation security

14. Wire strike avoidance

Flight instructors should be current on the latest procedures regarding pilot training, certification, and safety. It is the flight instructor's responsibility to maintain a current library of information. These sources are listed in the appropriate PTS, and other sources can be located on the Internet at www. faa.gov and www.faasafety.gov. The FAA website provides comprehensive information to pilots and instructors. Other aviation organizations also have excellent information. However, an instructor is bound to follow any procedures in the manner prescribed by the FAA. If an instructor needs any assistance, he or she should contact a more experienced instructor, an FAA Designated Pilot Examiner (DPE), or the local Flight Standards District Office (FSDO).

Aviator's Model Code of Conduct

The Aviator's Model Code of Conduct presents broad guidance and recommendations for General Aviation (GA) pilots to improve airmanship, flight safety, and to sustain and improve the GA community. The Code of Conduct presents a vision of excellence in GA aviation. Its principles both complement and supplement what is merely legal. The Code of Conduct is not a "standard" and is not intended to be implemented as such. The code of conduct consists of the following seven sections:

1. General Responsibilities of Aviators

2. Passengers and People on the Surface

3. Training and Proficiency

4. Security

5. Environmental Issues

6. Use of Technology

7. Advancement and Promotion of General Aviation

Each section provides flight instructors a list of principles and sample recommended practices. Successful instructor pilots continue to self-evaluate and find ways to make themselves safer and more productive instructors. The Aviator's Model Code of Conduct provides guidance and principles for the instructor to integrate into their own practices. More information about the Aviator's Model Code of Conduct can be found at www.secureav.com.

Safety Practices and Accident Prevention

Aviation instructors are on the front line of efforts to improve the safety record of the aviation industry. Safety, one of the most fundamental considerations in aviation training, is paramount. FAA regulations intended to promote safety by eliminating or mitigating conditions that can cause death, injury, or damage are comprehensive, but even the strictest compliance with regulations may not be sufficient to guarantee safety. Rules and regulations are designed to address known or suspected conditions detrimental to safety, but there is always a chance that some new combination of circumstances not contemplated by the regulations will arise. It is important for aviation instructors to be proactive to ensure the safety of flight or maintenance training activities.

The safety practices aviation instructors emphasize have a long-lasting effect on students. Generally, students consider their instructor to be a role model whose habits they attempt to imitate, whether consciously or unconsciously. The instructor's advocacy and description of safety practices mean little to a student if the instructor does not demonstrate them consistently. For example, if a maintenance student observes the instructor violating safety practices by not wearing safety glasses around hazardous equipment, the student probably will not be conscientious about using safety equipment when the instructor is not around. One of the best actions a flight or maintenance instructor can take to enhance aviation safety is to emphasize safety by example.

Another way for the instructor to advocate safety is to join the new FAA Safety Team (FAASTeam). The FAASTeam is dedicated to improving the aviation safety record by conveying safety principles and practices through training, outreach, and education. More information is available at FAASafety.gov.

Professionalism

The aviation instructor is the central figure in aviation training and is responsible for all phases of required training. The instructor, either pilot or aircraft maintenance technician, must be a professional. As professionals, aviation instructors strive to maintain the highest level of knowledge, training, and currency in the field of aviation. To achieve this goal, instructors need to commit themselves to continuous, lifelong learning and professional development through study, service, and membership in professional organizations such as the National Association of Flight Instructors (NAFI) and Professional Aviation Mechanics Association (PAMA). Professionals build a library of resources that keeps them in touch with their field through the most current procedures, publications, and educational opportunities. Being a professional also means behaving in a professional manner. *[Figure 7-6]* An aviation instructor should strive to practice the characteristics on the Instructor Do's list when teaching a student.

Instructor Do's

- Be professional at all times.
- Be sincere.
- Present a professional appearance and personal habits.
- Maintain a calm demeanor.
- Practice safety and accident prevention at all times.
- Avoid profanity.
- Define common terms.
- Continue professional development.
- Minimize student frustration.
- Motivate the student.
- Keep the student informed.
- Approach each student as an individual.
- Give credit when due.
- Criticize constructively.
- Be consistent.
- Admit errors.

Instructor Don'ts

- Ridicule the student's performance.
- Use profanity.
- Model irresponsible flight behaviors.
- Say one thing but do another.
- Forget personal hygiene.
- Disrespect the student.
- Demand unreasonable progress.
- Forget the student is new to aviation jargon.
- Set the student up for failure.
- Correct errors without an explanation of what went wrong.

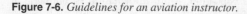

Figure 7-6. *Guidelines for an aviation instructor.*

Sincerity

An aviation instructor should be straightforward and honest. Attempting to hide inadequacy behind a smokescreen of unrelated instruction makes it impossible for the instructor to command the respect and full attention of a student. Teaching an aviation student is based upon acceptance of the instructor as a competent, qualified teacher and an expert pilot or aircraft maintenance technician. Any facade of instructor pretentiousness, whether it is real or mistakenly presumed by the student, causes the student to lose confidence in the instructor, and learning is adversely affected.

Acceptance of the Student

The instructor must accept students as they are, including all their faults and problems. The student is a person who wants to learn, and the instructor is a person who is available to help in the learning process. Beginning with this understanding, the professional relationship of the instructor with the student should be based on a mutual acknowledgement that the student and the instructor are important to each other, and that both are working toward the same objective.

Under no circumstance should the instructor do anything which implies degrading the student. Acceptance (rather than ridicule) and support (rather than reproof) encourage learning. Students must be treated with respect, regardless of whether they are quick to learn or require more time to absorb certain concepts. Criticizing a student who does not learn rapidly is similar to a doctor reprimanding a patient who does not get well as rapidly as predicted.

Personal Appearance and Habits

Personal appearance has an important effect on the professional image of the instructor. Today's aviation customer expects an instructor to be neat, clean, and appropriately dressed. Since the instructor is engaged in a learning situation, the attire worn should be appropriate to professional status. *[Figure 7-7]*

Figure 7-7. *The aviation instructor should always present a professional appearance.*

Personal habits have a significant effect on the professional image. The exercise of common courtesy is perhaps the most important of these. An instructor who is rude, thoughtless, and inattentive cannot hold the respect of a student, regardless of the instructor's ability as a pilot or aviation maintenance technician. Personal cleanliness is important to aviation instruction. Frequently, an instructor and a student work in close proximity, and even little annoyances such as body odor or bad breath can cause serious distractions from learning the tasks at hand.

Demeanor

The attitude and behavior of the instructor can contribute much to a professional image. The instructor should avoid erratic movements, distracting speech habits, and capricious changes in mood. The professional image requires development of a calm, thoughtful, and disciplined demeanor.

The successful instructor avoids contradictory directions, reacting differently to similar or identical errors at different times, demanding unreasonable performance or progress, or criticizing a student unfairly, and presenting an overbearing manner or air of flippancy. Effective instruction is best conducted in a calm, pleasant, thoughtful manner that puts the student at ease. The instructor must constantly demonstrate competence in the subject matter and genuine interest in the student's well being.

Proper Language

In aviation instruction, as in other professional activities, the use of profanity and obscene language leads to distrust or, at best, to a lack of complete confidence in the instructor. Many people object to such language. The professional instructor speaks normally, without inhibitions, and speaks positively and descriptively, without profanity.

Evaluation of Student Ability

Evaluation of a student's ability is an important element of instruction. Used in this context, evaluation refers to judging a student's ability to perform a maneuver or procedure.

Demonstrated Ability

Evaluation of demonstrated ability during flight or maintenance instruction is based upon established standards of performance, suitably modified to apply to the student's experience and stage of development as a pilot or mechanic. The evaluation considers the student's mastery of the elements involved in the maneuver or procedure, rather than merely the overall performance. For example, qualification of student pilots for solo and solo cross-country privileges depends upon demonstrations of performance.

Keeping the Student Informed

In evaluating student demonstrations of ability, it is important for the aviation instructor to keep the student informed of progress. This may be done as each procedure or maneuver is completed or summarized during a postflight or class critique. These critiques should be in a written format, such as notes, to aid the instructor in covering all areas that were noticed during the flight or lesson. When explaining errors in performance, instructors point out the elements in which the deficiencies are believed to have originated and, if possible, suggest appropriate corrective measures.

Correction of Student Errors

Correction of student errors does not include the practice of taking over from students immediately when a mistake is made. Safety permitting, it is frequently better to let students progress part of the way into the mistake and find a way out. For example, in a weight-shift control aircraft the bar is moved right to turn left. A student may show an initial tendency to move the bar in the direction of the desired turn. This tendency dissipates with time, but allowing the student to see the effect of his or her control input is a valuable aid in illustrating the stability of the aircraft. It is difficult for students to learn a maneuver properly if they seldom have the opportunity to correct an error.

On the other hand, students may perform a procedure or maneuver correctly but not fully understand the principles and objectives involved. If the instructor suspects this, students should be required to vary the performance of the maneuver or procedure slightly. The maneuver or procedure may also be combined with other operations, or the same elements could be applied to the performance of other maneuvers or procedures. Students who do not understand the principles involved will probably not be able to successfully complete the revised maneuver or procedure.

Aviation Instructors and Exams

Knowledge Test

When preparing a student or applicant for the private pilot certification or higher grade rating (i.e., commercial or instrument) a test is required to ensure the student has adequate aeronautical knowledge in those subject areas listed in 14 CFR part 61. The instructor may provide the student with an endorsement to certify he or she has the required knowledge to pass the test. Some additional ratings do not require a test. For information concerning additional aircraft certifications that do not require knowledge tests, refer to AC 61-65, Certification: Pilots and Flight and Ground Instructors. Flight instructors must take a short test for each additional category.

An instructor should remember he or she is held accountable for a deficient instructional performance. This is important for any instructor who signs recommendations for applicants who were not trained by that instructor.

If the applicant fails a test, the aviation instructor must sign the test after he or she has provided additional training in the areas the applicant failed. The applicant is given a retest. Prior to certification, the aviation instructor must make a statement that he or she gave the required training in the preceding 60 days and the instructor reviewed those areas of deficiency on the applicant's knowledge test.

Practical Test

Provision is made on the airman certificate or rating application form for the written recommendation of the flight instructor who has prepared the applicant for the practical test involved. Signing this recommendation imposes a serious responsibility on the flight instructor. A flight instructor who makes a practical test recommendation for an applicant seeking a certificate or rating should require the applicant to thoroughly demonstrate the knowledge and skill level required for that certificate or rating. This demonstration should in no instance be less than the complete procedure prescribed in the applicable PTS.

When the instructor endorses the applicant for the practical test, his or her signature on the FAA form 8710-1 Airman Certificate and/or Rating Application is valid for 60 days. This is also true with the flight proficiency endorsement that is placed in the applicant's logbook or training record (AC-61-65). These two dates should be the same.

Completion of prerequisites for a practical test is another instructor task that must be documented properly. Examples of all common endorsements can be found in the current issue of AC 61-65, appendix 1. This appendix also includes references to 14 CFR part 61 for more details concerning the requirements that must be met to qualify for each respective endorsement. The examples shown contain the essential elements of each endorsement. It is not necessary for all endorsements to be worded exactly as those in the AC. For example, changes to regulatory requirements may affect the wording, or the instructor may customize the endorsement for any special circumstances of the applicant. However, at a minimum, the instructor needs to cite the appropriate 14 CFR part 61 section that has been completed.

If a flight instructor fails to ensure a student pilot or additional rating pilot meets the requirements of regulations prior to making endorsements to allow solo flight or additional rating, that instructor is exhibiting a serious deficiency in performance. The FAA holds him or her accountable. Providing a solo endorsement for a student pilot who is not proficient for solo flight operations, or providing an endorsement for an additional rating for a pilot not meeting the appropriate regulatory requirements, is also a breach of faith with the student or applicant.

Professional Development

Aviation is changing rapidly, and aviation instructors must continue to develop their knowledge and skills in order to teach successfully in this environment. The aviation instructor is well respected by other technicians and pilots because instructors must meet additional training requirements in order to be certificated. Flight instructors undergo comprehensive evaluations and a practical test to obtain a flight instructor certificate. 14 CFR part 147 requires all instructors teaching maintenance subjects to hold an FAA certificate as an aircraft maintenance technician.

Successful, professional aviation instructors do not become complacent or satisfied with their own qualifications and abilities, and are constantly alert for ways to improve their qualifications, effectiveness, and the services they provide to students. Considered by their students to be a source of up-to-date information, instructors have the opportunity and responsibility of introducing new procedures and techniques both to their students and to other aviation professionals with whom they come in contact.

Continuing Education

A professional aviation instructor continually updates his or her knowledge and skills. This goal is attained in a variety of ways, such as reading an article in a technical publication or taking a course at a technical school. There are many different sources of information the aviation instructor can use in order to remain current in aviation knowledge and teaching.

Government

One of the first educational sources for the instructor is the FAA and other governmental agencies. The FAA either sponsors or collaborates in sponsoring aviation programs, seminars, and workshops for the public. For example, the FAA conducts safety seminars around the country in conjunction with the aviation industry. These seminars, although directed at pilots, can be a useful source of knowledge for aviation instructors.

The FAA is a rich source of information that can be used to enhance an instructor's knowledge. Regulations, advisory circulars, airworthiness directives, orders, and notices are some of the documents that can be downloaded from the FAA website at www.faa.gov.

As mentioned earlier in the chapter, participation in the Pilot Proficiency Awards Program is a good way for a flight instructor to improve proficiency and to serve as an example to students. Another way is to work toward the Gold Seal Flight Instructor Certificate. Accomplishing the requirements of the certificate is evidence the instructor has performed at a very high level as a flight instructor. See AC 61-65, Certification: Pilots and Flight and Ground Instructors, for a list of requirements for earning this certificate.

Similarly, the Aviation Maintenance Awards Program affords the aviation maintenance instructor the opportunity for increased education through attendance at FAA or industry maintenance training seminars. Details for the awarding of bronze through diamond pins can be found in AC 65-25, Aviation Maintenance Technician Awards Program.

The FAA approves the sponsors who conduct Flight Instructor Refresher Clinics (FIRCs) in accordance with AC 61-83. Nationally scheduled FAA-approved industry-conducted Flight Instructor Refresher Clinics (FIRC). These courses are available for flight instructors to complete the training requirements for renewal of flight instructor certificates.

The FAA cosponsors Inspection Authorization (IA) seminars. These seminars are open to all maintenance technicians, and are a good source of additional training and education for maintenance instructors.

Educational/Training Institutions

Professional aviation instructors can further increase their knowledge and skill in aviation specialties by attending classes at local community colleges, technical schools, or universities. These schools may offer complete degree programs in aviation subjects as well as single-subject courses of benefit to instructors.

Commercial Organizations

Commercial organizations are another important source of education/training for the aviation instructor. Some may be publishers of training materials while others may provide complete ground and flight training programs for professional pilots and instructors. These companies often provide a wide variety of study programs including videos, computer-based training, and printed publications. Many offer training that can be attended either at the home base of the company or in traveling classes/seminars so instructors can more easily attend.

There are numerous organizations around the country that offer courses of training for aviation instructors. These are generally courses that are available to all pilots and technicians, but are especially useful for instructors to improve their abilities. Examples of such courses include workshops for maintenance technicians to enhance their skills in subjects such as composites, sheet metal fabrication, and fabric covering. For pilots there are courses in mountain flying, spin training, and tail wheel qualification. Flight instructors also may increase their aviation knowledge and experience by adding additional category and class ratings to their certificates.

Industry Organizations

Other significant sources of ongoing education for aviation instructors are aviation organizations. These organizations not only provide educational articles in their publications, but also present training programs or cosponsor such programs.

Many industry organizations have local affiliated chapters that make it easy to meet other pilots, technicians, and instructors. These meetings frequently include presentations by industry experts, as well as formal training sessions. Some aviation industry organizations conduct their own training sessions on areas such as flight instructor refresher clinics and Inspection Authorization (IA) seminars. Properly organized safety symposiums and training clinics are valuable sources of refresher training. They are also an excellent opportunity to exchange information with other instructors.

Sources of Material

An aviation instructor should maintain access to current flight publications or maintenance publications. For the flight instructor, this includes current copies of regulations pertinent to pilot qualification and certification, Aeronautical Information Manual (AIM), appropriate Practical Test Standards (PTS), and pilot training manuals. The aviation maintenance instructor should have copies of applicable regulations, current knowledge and PTS, and maintenance training manuals. Aviation instructors must be thoroughly familiar with current certification and rating requirements in order to provide competent instruction. AC 00.2-15, Advisory Circular Checklist, is a listing of all current advisory circulars and other FAA publications sold by the Superintendent of Documents, U.S. Government Printing Office (GPO) or available online at www.faa.gov/. Many of the advisory circulars should be considered by the aviation instructor for inclusion in a personal reference library.

In addition to government publications, a number of excellent handbooks and other reference materials are available from commercial publishers. Aviation periodicals and technical journals from the aviation industry are other sources of valuable information for instructors. Many public and institutional libraries have excellent resource material on educational psychology, teaching methods, testing, and other aviation related subjects.

The aviation instructor has two reasons to maintain a source of current information and publications. First, the instructor needs a steady supply of fresh material to make instruction interesting and up to date. Second, instructors should keep themselves well informed by maintaining familiarity with what is being written in current aviation publications. Most of these publications are in printed form, but increasingly, information is available through electronic means. *[Figure 7-8]*

Figure 7-8. *Aviation instructors can improve their knowledge by becoming familiar with information on the Internet.*

Printed Material

In aviation, documentation in the form of flight publications or maintenance data must be immediately available for referral while flying or conducting maintenance. While the portability of printed material meets this need for immediate availability, printed material has two disadvantages. First, it takes up space for storage and second, it can be time consuming to keep printed material current. Many publishers of printed material now make their information available in electronic format. For example, most FAA regulations, standards, and guides are available either in electronic form or as hard copy.

Non-FAA publications are available through the GPO and from the National Technical Information Service (NTIS). Publications not printed by the U.S. Government Printing Office are available from the many publishers and suppliers of books. Commercial publishers usually provide catalogues and toll-free numbers or websites for ordering their products.

Electronic Sources

Access to the Internet via personal computers has opened up a vast storehouse of information for the aviation instructor. In the past, aviation instructors had limited access to information,

but the personal computer has greatly expanded sources of aviation information. This section lists some sources of information on the Internet. In the following discussion, several sites for accessing FAA materials are explored, and some non-FAA sites are included. Once instructors begin to navigate the Internet, they find sites which provide the information they use most frequently. Obviously, some FAA publications are more important to the aviation instructor than others. Many of the publications of interest to the aviation instructor can be accessed through the FAA website, www. faa.gov.

The FAA website is not the only source of aviation or education-related information on the Internet. The aviation instructor can access aviation-related publications at other government or non-government websites via published web addresses or by using the search function of the web browser. Keep in mind that most sites on the Internet are updated periodically, but some are not. In addition, new sites are added and old sites are discontinued on a regular basis. The aviation instructor can become more adept at obtaining information by entering and navigating around the Internet to become informed about the contents and how to best locate desired information. The more familiar aviation instructors become with the Internet, the better they are able to adapt to any changes that may occur.

Professional aviation instructors must continue to expand their knowledge and skills in order to be competent instructors. The field of aviation is advancing, and the instructor also must advance. Instructors can best do this by taking advantage of the wide variety of materials available from the FAA, other government agencies, commercial publishers and vendors, and from industry trade groups. These materials are available at training sessions and seminars, from printed books, papers, magazines, and from the Internet and other electronic sources. Instructors who commit to continuing education are able to provide the highest quality instruction to their students.

Chapter Summary

This chapter discussed the responsibilities of aviation instructors to the student, the public, and the FAA in the training process. The additional responsibilities of flight instructors who teach new student pilots as well as rated pilots seeking add-on certification, the role of aviation instructors as safety advocates, and ways in which aviation instructors can enhance their professional image and development were explored.

Chapter 8

Techniques of Flight Instruction

Introduction

Certificated flight instructor (CFI) Daniel decides his student, Mary, has gained enough confidence in flying that it is time for her to develop personal weather minimums. While researching the subject at the Federal Aviation Administration (FAA) website, he locates several sources that provide background information, such as the fact that, statistically, weather often poses some of the greatest risks to general aviation (GA) pilots, regardless of their experience level. He also finds charts and a lesson plan he can use.

Daniel's decision to help Mary develop personal weather minimums reflects a key component of the flight instructor's job: providing the student with the tools to ensure safety during a flight. Every flight instructor can agree that everyone wants to be safe, but what does "safety" really mean? How can a flight instructor ensure the safety of flight training activities, and also train clients to operate their aircraft safely after they leave the relatively protected flight training environment?

According to one definition, safety is the freedom from conditions that can cause death, injury, or illness; damage to/loss of equipment or property, or damage to the environment. FAA regulations are intended to promote safety by eliminating or mitigating conditions that can cause death, injury, or damage. These regulations are comprehensive, but there has been increasing recognition that even the strictest compliance with regulations may not be sufficient to guarantee safety. Rules and regulations are designed to address known or suspected conditions detrimental to safety, but there is always the probability that some new combination of circumstances not contemplated by the regulations will arise.

The recognition of aviation training and flight operations as a system led to a "system approach" to aviation safety. Since flight instructors are a critical part of the aviation safety system, this chapter introduces system safety—aeronautical decision-making (ADM), risk management, situational awareness, and single-pilot resource management (SRM)—in the modern flight training environment. It also provides methods flight instructors can teach students to use practical risk management tools and discusses how to evaluate student decision-making. The chapter begins with practical strategies flight instructors can use to enhance their instruction, the demonstration-performance training delivery method of flight instruction, integrated flight instruction, positive exchange of flight controls, use of distractions, obstacles to learning encountered during flight training, and how to evaluate students. After an intensive look at ADM, it closes with a discussion of CFI recommendations and endorsements.

Flight Instructor Qualifications

A CFI must be thoroughly familiar with the functions, characteristics, and proper use of all flight instruments, avionics, and other aircraft systems being used for training. This is especially important due to the wide variety in global positioning systems (GPS) and glass panel displays.

It is the personal responsibility of each flight instructor to maintain familiarity with current pilot training techniques and certification requirements. This may be done by frequent review of new periodicals and technical publications, personal contacts with FAA inspectors and designated pilot examiners (DPE), and by participation in pilot and flight instructor clinics. Additional information can be obtained from veteran flight instructors. *[Figure 8-1]* The application of outmoded instructional procedures or the preparation of students using obsolete certification requirements is inexcusable.

Practical Flight Instructor Strategies

During all phases of flight training, CFIs should remember they are role models for the student. The flight instructor should demonstrate good aviation sense at all times:

- Before the flight—discuss safety and the importance of a proper preflight and use of the checklist.

- During flight—prioritize the tasks of aviating, navigating, and communicating. Instill importance of "see and avoid" in the student.

Teaching Tips from Veteran Flight Instructors

1 | Use a tape recorder and/or video camera to rehearse preflight briefings until delivery is polished.

2 | Find a mentor to provide a second opinion on how well a student is performing during critical phases of flight training (such as first solo) for the first few PTs.

3 | Encourage a high standard of performance.

4 | Just because it's legal, doesn't make it safe. Maintain a high level of supervision of PT operations.

5 | Develop a safety-culture environment.

6 | Assign organized, specific, appropriate homework after each flight session.

7 | Use all available tools to supplement teaching and assignments: online sources, seminars, flight simulators, etc.

8 | Know the background, credentials, security issues, medications, etc., of the student before climbing into the cockpit with him or her.

9 | Thoroughly and carefully document all training events as though the National Transportation Safety Board (NTSB) were going to read them.

10 | Postflight debriefing after an FAA checkride is an excellent opportunity for additional learning.

11 | Encourage each student to establish personal minimums.

12 | Include a review of NTSB accident reports during advanced instructional activity.

Figure 8-1. *Teaching tips from veteran flight instructors.*

- During landing—conduct stabilized approaches, maintain desired airspeed on final, demonstrate good judgment for go-arounds, wake turbulence, traffic, and terrain avoidance. Use ADM to correct faulty approaches and landing errors. Make power-off, stall-warning blaring, on centerline touchdowns in the first third of runway.

- Always—remember safety is paramount.

Flight instructors have the responsibility of producing the safest pilots possible. For that reason, CFIs should encourage each student to learn as much as he or she is capable of and keep raising the bar. When introducing lesson tasks, flight instructors should not introduce the minimum acceptable standards for passing the checkride. The Practical Test Standard (PTS) is not a teaching tool. It is a testing tool. The overall focus of flight training should be on education, learning, and understanding why the standards are there and how they were set. The minimum standards to pass the checkride should not be introduced until the 3 hours of preparation for the checkride.

Obstacles to Learning During Flight Instruction

Certain obstacles are common to flight instruction and may apply directly to the student's attitude, physical condition, and psychological make-up. These include but are not limited to:

- Feeling of unfair treatment

- Impatience to proceed to more interesting operations

- Worry or lack of interest

- Physical discomfort, illness, fatigue, and dehydration

- Apathy due to inadequate instruction

- Anxiety

Unfair Treatment

Students who believe their instruction is inadequate, or that their efforts are not conscientiously considered and evaluated, do not learn well. In addition, their motivation suffers no matter how intent they are on learning to fly. Motivation also declines when a student believes the instructor is making unreasonable demands for performance and progress. *[Figure 8-2]*

Assignment of goals the student considers difficult, but possible, usually provides a challenge and promotes learning. In a typical flight lesson, reasonable goals are listed in the lesson objectives and the desired levels of proficiency for the goals are included in statements that contain completion standards.

Figure 8-2. *The assignment of impossible or unreasonable goals discourages the student, diminishes effort, and retards the learning process.*

Impatience

Impatience is a greater deterrent to learning pilot skills than is generally recognized. For a student, this may take the form of a desire to make an early solo flight, or to set out on cross-country flights before the basic elements of flight have been learned.

The impatient student fails to understand the need for preliminary training and seeks only the ultimate objective without considering the means necessary to reach it. With every complex human endeavor, it is necessary to master the basics if the whole task is to be performed competently and safely. The instructor can correct student impatience by presenting the necessary preliminary training one step at a time, with clearly stated goals for each step. The procedures and elements mastered in each step should be clearly identified in explaining or demonstrating the performance of the subsequent step.

Impatience can result from instruction keyed to the pace of a slow learner when it is applied to a motivated, fast learner. It is just as important that a student be advanced to the subsequent step as soon as one goal has been attained, as it is to complete each step before the next one is undertaken. Disinterest grows rapidly when unnecessary repetition and drill are requested on operations that have already been adequately learned.

Worry or Lack of Interest

Worry or lack of interest has a detrimental effect on learning. Students who are worried or emotionally upset are not ready to learn and derive little benefit from instruction. Worry or distraction may be due to student concerns about progress in the training course, or may stem from circumstances completely unrelated to their instruction. Significant emotional upsets may be due to personal problems, psychiatric disturbances, or a dislike of the training program or the instructor.

The experiences of students outside their training activities affect behavior and performance in training; the two cannot be separated. When students begin flight training, they bring with them their interests, enthusiasms, fears, and troubles. The instructor cannot be responsible for these outside diversions, but cannot ignore them because they have a critical effect on the learning process. Instruction must be keyed to the utilization of the interests and enthusiasm students bring with them, and to diverting their attention from their worries and troubles to learning the tasks at hand. This is admittedly difficult, but must be accomplished if learning is to proceed at a normal rate.

Worries and emotional upsets that result from a flight training course can be identified and addressed. These problems are often due to inadequacies of the course or of the instructor. The most effective cure is prevention. The instructor must be alert and ensure the students understand the objectives of each step of their training, and that they know at the completion of each lesson exactly how well they have progressed and what deficiencies are apparent. Discouragement and emotional upsets are rare when students feel that nothing is being withheld from them or is being neglected in their training.

Physical Discomfort, Illness, Fatigue, and Dehydration

Physical discomfort, illness, and fatigue will materially slow the rate of learning during both classroom instruction and flight training. Students who are not completely at ease, and whose attention is diverted by discomforts such as the extremes of temperature, poor ventilation, inadequate lighting, or noise and confusion, cannot learn at a normal rate. This is true no matter how diligently they attempt to apply themselves to the learning task.

A minor illness, such as a cold, major illness, or injury, interferes with the normal rate of learning. This is especially important for flight instruction. Most illnesses adversely affect the acuteness of vision, hearing, and feeling, all of which are essential to correct performance.

Airsickness can be a great deterrent to flight instruction. A student who is airsick or bothered with incipient airsickness is incapable of learning at a normal rate. There is no sure cure for airsickness, but resistance or immunity usually can be developed in a relatively short period of time. An instructional flight should be terminated as soon as incipient sickness is experienced. As the student develops immunity, flights can be increased in length until normal flight periods are practicable.

Keeping students interested and occupied during flight is a deterrent to airsickness. They are much less apt to become airsick while operating the controls themselves. Rough air and unexpected abrupt maneuvers tend to increase the chances of airsickness. Tension and apprehension apparently contribute to airsickness and should be avoided.

Fatigue

Fatigue is one of the most treacherous hazards to flight safety as it may not be apparent to a pilot until serious errors are made. Fatigue can be either acute (short-term) or chronic (long-term). Acute fatigue, a normal occurrence of everyday living, is the tiredness felt after long periods of physical and mental strain, including strenuous muscular effort, immobility, heavy mental workload, strong emotional pressure, monotony, and lack of sleep.

Acute fatigue caused by training operations may be physical or mental, or both. It is not necessarily a function of physical robustness or mental acuity. The amount of training any student can absorb without incurring debilitating fatigue varies. Generally speaking, complex operations tend to induce fatigue more rapidly than simpler procedures do, regardless of the physical effort involved. Fatigue is the primary consideration in determining the length and frequency of flight instruction periods and flight instruction should be continued only as long as the student is alert, receptive to instruction, and is performing at a level consistent with experience.

It is important for a CFI to be able to detect fatigue, both in assessing a student's substandard performance early in a lesson, and also in recognizing the deterioration of performance. If fatigue occurs as a result of application to a learning task, the student should be given a break in instruction and practice.

A CFI who is familiar with the signs indicative to acute fatigue will be more aware if the student is experiencing them. The deficiencies listed below are apparent to others before the individual notices any physical signs of fatigue.

Acute fatigue is characterized by:

- Inattention
- Distractibility
- Errors in timing
- Neglect of secondary tasks

- Loss of accuracy and control
- Lack of awareness of error accumulation
- Irritability

Another form of fatigue is chronic fatigue which occurs when there is not enough time for a full recovery from repeated episodes of acute fatigue. Chronic fatigue's underlying cause is generally not "rest-related" and may have deeper points of origin. Therefore, rest alone may not resolve chronic fatigue.

Chronic fatigue is a combination of both physiological problems and psychological issues. Psychological problems such as financial, home life, or job-related stresses cause a lack of qualified rest that is only solved by mitigating the underlying problems before the fatigue is solved. Without resolution, human performance continues to fall off, and judgment becomes impaired so that unwarranted risks may be taken. Recovery from chronic fatigue requires a prolonged and deliberate solution. In either case, unless adequate precautions are taken, personal performance could be impaired and adversely affect pilot judgment and decision-making.

Dehydration and Heatstroke

Dehydration is the term given to a critical loss of water from the body. Dehydration reduces a pilot's level of alertness, producing a subsequent slowing of decision-making processes or even the inability to control the aircraft. The first noticeable effect of dehydration is fatigue, which in turn makes top physical and mental performance difficult, if not impossible. Flying for long periods in hot summer temperatures or at high altitudes increases susceptibility to dehydration since dry air at high altitudes tends to increase the rate of water loss from the body. If this fluid is not replaced, fatigue progresses to dizziness, weakness, nausea, tingling of hands and feet, abdominal cramps, and extreme thirst.

Heatstroke is a condition caused by any inability of the body to control its temperature. Onset of this condition may be recognized by the symptoms of dehydration, but also has been known to be recognized only by complete collapse. To prevent these symptoms, it is recommended that an ample supply of water be carried and used at frequent intervals on any long flight, whether the pilot is thirsty or not. If the airplane has a canopy or roof window, wearing light-colored, porous clothing and a hat helps provide protection from the sun. Keeping the flight deck well ventilated aids in dissipating excess heat.

Apathy Due to Inadequate Instruction

Students can become apathetic when they recognize that the instructor has made inadequate preparations for the instruction being given, or when the instruction appears to be deficient, contradictory, or insincere. To hold the student's interest and to maintain the motivation necessary for efficient learning, well-planned, appropriate, and accurate instruction must be provided. Nothing destroys a student's interest as quickly as a poorly organized period of instruction. Even an inexperienced student realizes immediately when the instructor has failed to prepare a lesson. *[Figure 8-3]*

Let's see now, what did we do last time? Does anyone remember?

Figure 8-3. *Poor preparation leads to spotty coverage, misplaced emphasis, unnecessary repetition, and a lack of confidence on the part of the student. The instructor should always have a plan.*

Instruction may be overly explicit and so elementary it fails to hold student interest, or it may be so general or complicated that it fails to evoke the interest necessary for effective learning. To be effective, the instructor must teach for the level of the student. The presentation must be adjusted to be meaningful to the person for whom it is intended. For example, instruction in the preflight inspection of an aircraft should be presented quite differently for a student who is a skilled aircraft maintenance technician (AMT) compared to the instruction on the same operation for a student with no previous aeronautical experience. The instruction needed in each case is the same, but a presentation meaningful to one of these students might not be appropriate for the other.

Poor instructional presentations may result not only from poor preparation, but also from distracting mannerisms, personal untidiness, or the appearance of irritation with the student. Creating the impression of talking down to the student is one of the fastest ways for an instructor to lose student confidence and attention. Once the instructor loses student confidence, it is difficult to regain, and the learning rate is unnecessarily diminished.

Anxiety

Student anxiety may place additional burdens on the instructor. This frequently limits the student's perceptive ability and retards the development of insights. The student must be comfortable, confident in the instructor and the aircraft, and at ease if effective learning is to occur. Providing this atmosphere for learning is one of the first and most important tasks of the instructor. Although doing so may be difficult at first, successive accomplishment of recognizable goals and the avoidance of alarming occurrences or situations will rapidly ease the student's mind. This is true of all flight students, but special handling by the instructor may be required for students who are obviously anxious or uncomfortable.

Demonstration-Performance Training Delivery Method

The demonstration-performance training delivery method was discussed briefly in Chapter 4, The Teaching Process, but the following in-depth discussion is geared to the flight instructor. This training method has been in use for a long time and is very effective in teaching kinesthetic skills so flight instructors find it valuable in teaching procedures and maneuvers. The demonstration-performance method is divided into four phases: explanation, demonstration, student performance with instructor supervision, and evaluation. *[Figure 8-4]*

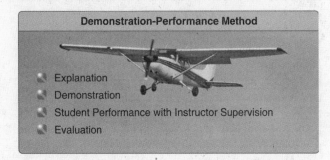

Demonstration-Performance Method

- Explanation
- Demonstration
- Student Performance with Instructor Supervision
- Evaluation

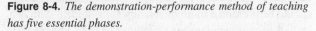

Figure 8-4. *The demonstration-performance method of teaching has five essential phases.*

Explanation Phase

The flight instructor needs to be well prepared and highly organized if complex maneuvers and procedures are to be taught effectively. The student must be intellectually and psychologically ready for the learning activity. The explanation phase is accomplished prior to the flight lesson with a discussion of lesson objectives and completion standards, as well as a thorough preflight briefing. Explanations must be clear, pertinent to the objectives of the particular lesson to be presented, and based on the known experience and knowledge of the students. Students need to know not only what they will learn, but also how they will learn it—that is, how the lesson will proceed and how they will be evaluated. In teaching a skill, the instructor must convey to the students the precise actions they are to perform. In addition to the necessary steps, the instructor should describe the end result of these efforts. The explanation phase also should include coverage of

appropriate safety procedures. Before leaving this phase, the instructor should encourage students to ask questions about any step of the procedure that they do not understand.

Demonstration Phase

The instructor must show students the actions necessary to perform a skill. As little extraneous activity as possible should be included in the demonstration if students are to clearly understand that the instructor is accurately performing the actions previously explained. If, due to some unanticipated circumstances the demonstration does not closely conform to the explanation, this deviation should be immediately acknowledged and explained.

Student Performance and Instructor Supervision Phases

As discussed in chapter 4, these two phases involve separate actions that are performed concurrently. The first of these phases is the student's performance of the physical or mental skills that have been explained and demonstrated. The second activity is the instructor's supervision.

Student performance requires students to act and do. To learn skills, students must practice. The instructor must, therefore, allot enough time for meaningful student activity. Through doing, students learn to follow correct procedures and to reach established standards. It is important that students be given an opportunity to perform the skill as soon as possible after a demonstration.

Then, the instructor reviews what has been covered during the instructional flight and determines to what extent the student has met the objectives outlined during the preflight discussion. The instructor should be satisfied that the student is well prepared and understands the task before starting. The instructor observes as the student performs, and then makes appropriate comments.

Evaluation Phase

In this phase, the instructor traditionally evaluates student performance, records the student's performance, and verbally advises the student of the progress made toward the objectives. Regardless of how well a skill is taught, there may still be performance deficiencies. When pointing out areas that need improvement, offer concrete suggestions that help. If possible, avoid ending the evaluation on a negative note.

As discussed in Chapter 5, Assessment, collaborative assessment (or learner centered grading (LCG)) is a form of authentic assessment currently used in aviation training with problem-based learning (PBL). PBL structures the lessons to confront students with problems that are encountered in real life and forces them to reach real-world solutions. Scenario-based training (SBT), a type of PBL, uses a highly structured script of real world experiences to address aviation training objectives in an operational environment. Collaborative assessment is used to evaluate whether certain learning criteria were met during the SBT.

Collaborative assessment includes two parts—learner self-assessment and a detailed assessment by the flight instructor. The purpose of the self-assessment is to stimulate growth in the learner's thought processes and, in turn, behaviors. The self-assessment is followed by an in-depth discussion between the instructor and the student which compares the instructor's assessment to the student's self-assessment.

The Telling-and-Doing Technique

The demonstration-performance method can be applied to the telling-and-doing technique of flight instruction in three steps. However, the telling-and-doing technique includes specific variations for flight instruction. *[Figure 8-5]*

Instructor Tells—Instructor Does

First, the flight instructor gives a carefully planned demonstration of the procedure or maneuver with accompanying verbal explanation. While demonstrating inflight maneuvers, the instructor should explain the required power settings, aircraft attitudes, and describe any other pertinent factors that may apply. This is the only step in which the student plays a passive role. It is important for the demonstration to conform to the explanation as closely as possible. In addition, it should be demonstrated in the same sequence in which it was explained so as to avoid confusion and provide reinforcement. Since students generally imitate the instructor's performance, the instructor must demonstrate the skill exactly the way the students are expected to practice it, including all safety procedures that the students must follow. If, due to some unanticipated circumstances, the demonstration does not closely conform to the explanation, this deviation should be immediately acknowledged and explained.

Most physical skills lend themselves to a sequential pattern where the skill is explained in the same step-by-step order normally used to perform it. When the skill being taught is related to previously learned procedures or maneuvers, the known to unknown strategy may be used effectively. When teaching more than one skill at the same time, the simple-to-complex strategy works well. By starting with the simplest skill, a student gains confidence and is less likely to become frustrated when faced with building skills that are more complex.

Another consideration in this phase is the language used. Instructors should attempt to avoid unnecessary jargon and technical terms that their students do not know. Instructors should also take care to clearly describe the actions students are expected to perform. Communication is the key. It is neither appropriate nor effective for instructors to try to impress students with their expertise by using language that is unnecessarily complicated.

As an example, a level turn might be demonstrated and described by the instructor in the following way:

- Use outside visual references and monitor the flight instruments.

- After clearing the airspace around the aircraft, add power slightly, turn the aircraft in the desired direction, and apply a slight amount of back pressure on the yoke to maintain altitude. Maintain coordinated flight by applying rudder in the direction of the turn.

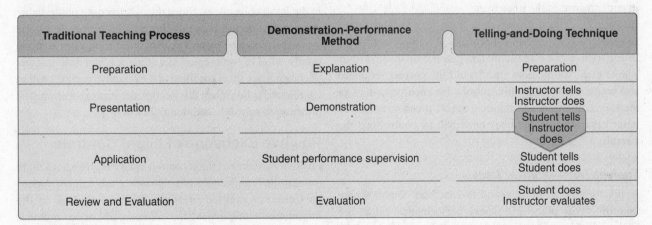

Traditional Teaching Process	Demonstration-Performance Method	Telling-and-Doing Technique
Preparation	Explanation	Preparation
Presentation	Demonstration	Instructor tells Instructor does
		Student tells Instructor does
Application	Student performance supervision	Student tells Student does
Review and Evaluation	Evaluation	Student does Instructor evaluates

Figure 8-5. *This comparison of steps in the teaching process, the demonstration-performance method, and the telling-and-doing technique highlights similarities as well as differences. The main difference in the telling-and-doing technique is the important transition, student tells—instructor does, which occurs between the second and third step.*

- Remember, the ailerons control the roll rate, as well as the angle of bank. The rate at which the aircraft rolls depends on how much aileron deflection is used. How far the aircraft rolls (steepness of the bank) depends on how long the ailerons are deflected, since the aircraft continues to roll as long as the ailerons are deflected. When the desired angle of bank is reached, neutralize the ailerons, and trim as appropriate.

- Lead the roll-out by approximately one-half the number of degrees of the angle of bank. Use coordinated aileron and rudder control pressures. Simultaneously begin releasing the back pressure so aileron, rudder, and elevator pressures are neutralized when the aircraft reaches the wings-level position.

- Leading the roll-out heading by one-half the bank angle is a good rule of thumb for initial training. However, keep in mind that the required amount of lead really depends on the type of turn, turn rate, and roll-out rate. As a pilot gains experience, he or she will develop a consistent roll-in and roll-out technique for various types of turns. Upon reaching a wings-level attitude, reduce power and trim to remove control pressures.

Student Tells—Instructor Does

Second, the student tells as the instructor does. In this step, the student actually plays the role of instructor, telling the instructor what to do and how to do it. Two benefits accrue from this step: the student, being freed from the need to concentrate on performance of the maneuver and from concern about its outcome, is able to organize his or her thoughts regarding the steps involved and the techniques to be used. In the process of explaining the maneuver as the instructor performs it, perceptions begin to develop into insights. Mental habits begin to form with repetition of the instructions previously received. Plus, the instructor is able to evaluate the student's understanding of the factors involved in performance of the maneuver.

According to the principle of primacy, it is important for the instructor to make sure the student gets it right the first time. The student should also understand the correct sequence and be aware of safety precautions for each procedure or maneuver. If a misunderstanding exists, it can be corrected before the student becomes absorbed in controlling the aircraft.

Student Tells—Student Does

Application is the third step in this method. This is where learning takes place and where performance habits are formed. If the student has been adequately prepared and the procedure or maneuver fully explained and demonstrated, meaningful learning occurs. The instructor should be alert during the student's practice to detect any errors in technique and to prevent the formation of faulty habits.

At the same time, the student should be encouraged to think about what to do during the performance of a maneuver, until it becomes habitual. In this step, the thinking is done verbally. This focuses concentration on the task to be accomplished, so that total involvement in the maneuver is fostered. All of the student's physical and mental faculties are brought into play. The instructor should be aware of the student's thought processes. It is easy to determine whether an error is induced by a misconception or by a simple lack of motor skills. Therefore, in addition to forcing total concentration on the part of the student, this method provides a means for keeping the instructor aware of what the student is thinking. The student is not only learning to do something, but he or she is also learning a self-teaching process that is highly desirable in development of a skill.

The exact procedures that the instructor should use during student practice depends on factors such as the student's proficiency level, the type of maneuver, and the stage of training. The instructor must exercise good judgment to decide how much control to use. With potentially hazardous or difficult maneuvers, the instructor should be alert and ready to take control at any time. This is especially true during a student's first attempt at a particular maneuver. On the other hand, if a student is progressing normally, the instructor should avoid unnecessary interruptions or too much assistance.

A typical test of how much control is needed often occurs during a student's first few attempts to land an aircraft. The instructor must quickly evaluate the student's need for help, and not hesitate to take control, if required. At the same time, the student should be allowed to practice the entire maneuver often enough to achieve the level of proficiency established in the lesson objectives. Since this is a learning phase rather than an evaluation phase of the training, errors or unsafe practices should be identified and corrected in a positive and timely way. In some cases, the student is not able to meet the proficiency level specified in the lesson objectives within the allotted time. When this occurs, the instructor should be prepared to schedule additional training.

Positive Exchange of Flight Controls

Positive exchange of flight controls is an integral part of flight training. It is especially critical during the demonstration-performance method of flight instruction. Due to the importance of this subject, the following discussion provides guidance on the recommended procedure to use for the positive exchange of flight controls between pilots when operating an aircraft.

Background

Incident/accident statistics indicate a need to place additional emphasis on the exchange of control of an aircraft by pilots. Numerous accidents have occurred due to a lack of communication or misunderstanding regarding who had actual control of the aircraft, particularly between students and flight instructors. Establishing the following procedure during initial training will ensure the formation of a habit pattern that should stay with students throughout their flying careers.

Procedure

During flight training, there must always be a clear understanding between students and flight instructors about who has control of the aircraft. The preflight briefing should include procedures for the exchange of flight controls. A positive three-step process in the exchange of flight controls between pilots is a proven procedure and one that is strongly recommended. When an instructor is teaching a maneuver to a student, the instructor normally demonstrates the maneuver first, then has the student follow along on the controls during a demonstration and, finally, the student performs the maneuver with the instructor following along on the controls. *[Figure 8-6]*

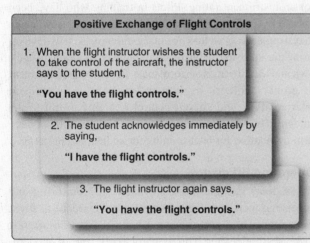

Positive Exchange of Flight Controls

1. When the flight instructor wishes the student to take control of the aircraft, the instructor says to the student,

   "You have the flight controls."

2. The student acknowledges immediately by saying,

   "I have the flight controls."

3. The flight instructor again says,

   "You have the flight controls."

Figure 8-6. *During this procedure, a visual check is recommended to see that the other person actually has the flight controls. When returning the controls to the instructor, the student should follow the same procedure the instructor used when giving control to the student. The student should stay on the controls and keep flying the aircraft until the instructor says, "I have the flight controls." There should never be any doubt about who is flying the aircraft.*

Flight instructors should always guard the controls and be prepared to take control of the aircraft. When necessary, the instructor should take the controls and calmly announce, "I have the flight controls." If an instructor allows a student to remain on the controls, the instructor may not have full and effective control of the aircraft. Anxious students can be incredibly strong and usually exhibit reactions inappropriate to the situation. If a recovery is necessary, there is absolutely nothing to be gained by having the student on the controls and having to fight for control of the aircraft. students should never be allowed to exceed the flight instructor's limits. Flight instructors should not exceed their own ability to perceive a problem, decide upon a course of action, and physically react within their ability to fly the aircraft.

Sterile Cockpit Rule

Commonly known as the "sterile cockpit rule," Title 14 of the Code of Federal Regulations (14 CFR) section 121.542 requires flight crewmembers to refrain from nonessential activities during critical phases of flight. As defined in the regulation, critical phases of flight are all ground operations involving taxi, takeoff, and landing, and all other flight operations below 10,000 feet except cruise flight. Nonessential activities include such activities as eating, reading a newspaper, or chatting. A series of aircraft accidents caused by flight crews who were distracted from their flight duties during critical phases of the flight caused the FAA to propose the rule. While the regulation grew out of accidents in the airline industry, it holds true for the entire aviation community. Pilots can improve flight safety significantly by reducing distractions during critical phases of flight. It is important the flight instructor not only teach the concept of a sterile cockpit, but also model such behavior during flight instruction.

Use of Distractions

National Transportation Safety Board (NTSB) statistics reveal that most stall/spin accidents occurred when the pilot's attention was diverted from the primary task of flying the aircraft. Sixty percent of stall/spin accidents occurred during takeoff and landing, and twenty percent were preceded by engine failure. Preoccupation inside or outside the flight deck while changing aircraft configuration or trim, maneuvering to avoid other traffic, or clearing hazardous obstacles during takeoff and climb could create a potential stall/spin situation. The intentional practice of stalls and spins seldom resulted in an accident. The real danger was inadvertent stalls induced by distractions during routine flight situations.

Pilots at all skill levels should be aware of the increased risk of entering into an inadvertent stall or spin while performing tasks that are secondary to controlling the aircraft. The FAA has established a policy for use of certain distractions on practical tests for pilot certification. The purpose is to determine that applicants possess the skills required to cope with distractions while maintaining the degree of aircraft control required for safe flight. The most effective training is the simulation of scenarios that can lead to inadvertent stalls by creating distractions while the student is practicing certain maneuvers.

Instructor responsibilities include teaching the student to divide his or her attention between the distracting task and maintaining control of the aircraft. The following are examples of distractions that can be used for this training:

- Drop a pencil. Ask the student to pick it up.

- Ask the student to determine a heading to an airport using a chart.

- Ask the student to reset the clock.

- Ask the student to get something from the back seat.

- Ask the student to read the outside air temperature.

- Ask the student to call the Automated Flight Service Station (AFSS) for weather information.

- Ask the student to compute true airspeed with a flight computer.

- Ask the student to identify terrain or objects on the ground.

- Ask the student to identify a field suitable for a forced landing.

- Have the student climb 200 feet and maintain altitude, then descend 200 feet and maintain altitude.

- Have the student reverse course after a series of S-turns.

It is a flight instructor's responsibility to teach the student how to take charge during a flight. A pilot in command (PIC) must know when to tell any passengers, even a DPE, when the PIC finds actions in the aircraft that distract and interfere with the safe conduct of the flight.

Integrated Flight Instruction

Integrated flight instruction is flight instruction during which students are taught to perform flight maneuvers both by outside visual references and by reference to flight instruments. For this type of instruction to be fully effective, the use of instrument references should begin the first time each new maneuver is introduced. No distinction in the pilot's operation of the flight controls is permitted, regardless of whether outside references or instrument indications are used for the performance of the maneuver. When this training technique is used, instruction in the control of an aircraft by outside visual references is integrated with instruction in the use of flight instrument indications for the same operations.

Development of Habit Patterns

It important for the student to establish the habit of observing and relying on flight instruments from the beginning of flight training. It is equally important for the student to learn the feel of the airplane while conducting maneuvers, such as being able to feel when the airplane is out of trim or in a nose-high or nose-low attitude. Students who have been required to perform all normal flight maneuvers by reference to instruments, as well as by outside references, develop from the start the habit of continuously monitoring their own and the aircraft's performance. The early establishment of proper habits of instrument cross-check, instrument interpretation, and aircraft control is highly useful to the student. The habitual attention to instrument indications leads to improved landings because of more precise airspeed control. Effective use of instruments also results in superior cross-country navigation, better coordination, and generally, a better overall pilot competency level.

General aviation accident reports provide ample support for the belief that reference to flight instruments is important to safety. The safety record of pilots who hold instrument ratings is significantly better than that of pilots with comparable flight time who have never received formal flight training for an instrument rating. Pilots in training who have been required to perform all normal flight maneuvers by reference to instruments, as well as by outside references, will develop from the start the habit of continuously monitoring their own and the aircraft's performance. The early establishment of proper habits of instrument cross-check, instrument interpretation, and aircraft control is highly useful to the student. The habits formed at this time also give him or her a firm foundation for later training for an instrument rating.

Operating Efficiency

As students become more proficient in monitoring and correcting their own flight technique by reference to flight instruments, the performance obtained from an aircraft increases noticeably. This is particularly true of modern, complex, or high-performance aircraft, which are responsive to the use of correct operating airspeeds.

The use of correct power settings and climb speeds and the accurate control of headings during climbs result in a measurable increase in climb performance. Holding precise headings and altitudes in cruising flight definitely increases average cruising performance.

The use of integrated flight instruction provides the student with the ability to control an aircraft in flight for limited periods if outside references are lost. In an emergency, this ability could save the pilot's life and those of the passengers.

During the conduct of integrated flight training, the flight instructor must emphasize to the students that the introduction to the use of flight instruments does not prepare them for operations in marginal weather or instrument meteorological conditions (IMC). The possible consequences, both to themselves and to others, of experiments with flight operations in weather conditions below visual flight rules (VFR) minimums before they are instrument rated should be constantly impressed on the students. According to NTSB accident data, inflight encounters with weather (attempting VFR flight into IMC) is one of the most lethal types of GA flying.

Procedures

Integrated flight instruction begins with the first briefing on the function of the flight controls. This briefing includes the instrument indications to be expected, as well as the outside references to be used to control the attitude of the aircraft.

Each new flight maneuver is introduced using both outside and instrument references with students developing the ability to maneuver an aircraft equally as well by instrument or outside references. They naturally accept the fact that the manipulation of the flight controls is identical, regardless of which references are used to determine the attitude of the aircraft. This practice should continue throughout the flight instruction for all maneuvers. To fully achieve the demonstrated benefits of this type of training, the use of visual and instrument references must be constantly integrated throughout the training. Failure to do so lengthens the flight instruction necessary for the student to achieve the competency required for a private pilot certificate.

See and Avoid

From the start of flight training, the instructor must ensure students develop the habit of looking for other air traffic at all times. If students believe the instructor assumes all responsibility for scanning and collision avoidance procedures, they do not develop the habit of maintaining a constant vigilance, which is essential to safety. Any observed tendency of a student to enter flight maneuvers without first making a careful check for other air traffic must be corrected immediately. Recent studies of midair collisions determined that:

- Flight instructors were onboard the aircraft in 37 percent of the accidents in the study.

- Most of the aircraft involved in collisions are engaged in recreational flying not on any type of flight plan.

- Most midair collisions occur in VFR weather conditions during weekend daylight hours.

- The vast majority of accidents occurred at or near nontowered airports and at altitudes below 1,000 feet.

- Pilots of all experience levels were involved in midair collisions, from pilots on their first solo, to 20,000 hour veterans.

- Most collisions occur in daylight with visibility greater than 3 miles.

It is imperative to introduce 14 CFR section 91.113 "Right-of-way" rules to the student. Practice the "see and avoid" concept at all times regardless of whether the training is conducted under VFR or instrument flight rules (IFR). For more information on how to reduce the odds of becoming involved in a midair collision, see www.faa.gov/about/office_org/headquarters_offices/ato/tracon/anchorage/pilots_info/mca/.

Assessment of Piloting Ability

Assessment is an essential component of the teaching process and determines how, what, and how well a student is learning. A well designed assessment provides a student with something constructive upon which he or she can work or build. An assessment should provide direction and guidance to raise the level of performance. Students must understand the purpose of the assessment; otherwise, they will be unlikely to accept the evaluation offered and little improvement will result. There are many types of assessment, but the flight instructor generally uses the review, collaborative assessment (LCG), written tests, and performance-based tests to ascertain knowledge or practical skill levels. Refer to chapter 5 for an in-depth discussion of the types of assessment available to the flight instructor.

An assessment can also be used as a tool for reteaching. Although not all assessments lend themselves to reteaching, the instructor should be alert to the possibility and take advantage of the opportunity when it arises. In assessing the ability of a student, the instructor initially determines if he or she understands the procedure or maneuver. Then, the instructor demonstrates the maneuver, allows the student to practice the maneuver under direction, and finally evaluates student accomplishment by observing the performance.

Demonstrated Ability

Assessment of demonstrated ability during flight instruction must be based upon established standards of performance, suitably modified to apply to the student's experience and stage of development as a pilot. The assessment must consider the student's mastery of the elements involved in the maneuver, rather than merely the overall performance.

In order for a student to be signed off for a solo flight, the CFI must determine that the student is qualified and proficient in the flight tasks necessary for the flight. The CFI bases this assessment on the student's ability to demonstrate consistent proficiency on a number of flight maneuvers. Also associated with pilot skill evaluations during flight training are the stage checks conducted in FAA-approved school courses and the practical tests for pilot certificates and ratings.

Postflight Evaluation

In assessing piloting ability, it is important for the flight instructor to keep the student informed of progress. This may be done as each procedure or maneuver is completed or summarized during postflight critiques. Postflight critiques should be in a written format, such as notes to aid the flight instructor in covering all areas that were noticed during the flight or lesson. Traditionally, flight instructors explained errors in performance, pointed out elements in which the deficiencies were believed to have originated and, if possible, suggested appropriate corrective measures. Traditional assessment depends on a grading scale of "excellent, good, fair, poor" or "exceeds standards, meets standards, needs more training" which often meets the instructor's needs but not the needs of the student.

With the advent of SBT, collaborative assessment is used whenever the student has completed a scenario. As discussed in chapters 4 and 5, SBT uses a highly structured script of real-world experiences to address aviation training objectives in an operational environment. During the postflight evaluation, collaborative assessment is used to evaluate whether certain learning criteria were met during the SBT.

Collaborative assessment includes learner self-assessment and a detailed assessment by the aviation instructor. The purpose of the self-assessment is to stimulate growth in the learner's thought processes and, in turn, behaviors. The self-assessment is followed by an in-depth discussion between the instructor and the student which compares the instructor's assessment to the student's self-assessment.

First Solo Flight

During the student's first solo flight, the instructor must be present to assist in answering questions or resolving any issues that arise during the flight. To ensure the solo

flight is a positive, confidence-building experience for the student, the flight instructor needs to consider time of day when scheduling the flight. Time of day is a factor in traffic congestion, possible winds, sun angles, and reflection.

If possible, the flight instructor needs access to a portable radio during any supervised solo operations. A radio enables the instructor to terminate the solo operation if he or she observes a situation developing. The flight instructor must use good judgment when communicating with a solo student. Keep all radio communications to a minimum. Do not talk to the student on short final of the landing approach.

Post-Solo Debriefing

During a post-solo debriefing, the flight instructor discusses what took place during the student's solo flight. It is important for the flight instructor to answer any questions the student may have as result of a solo flight. Instructors need to be involved in all aspects of the flight to ensure the student utilizes correct flight procedures. It is very important for the flight instructor to debrief a student immediately after a solo flight. With the flight vividly etched in the student's memory, questions about the flight will come quickly.

Correction of Student Errors

Correction of student errors should not include the practice of immediately taking the controls away when a mistake is made. Safety permitting, it is frequently better to let students progress part of the way into the mistake and find a way out. For example, in a weight-shift control aircraft the control bar is moved right to turn left. A student may show an initial tendency to move the bar in the direction of the desired turn. This tendency will dissipate with time, but allowing the student to see the effect of his or her control input is a valuable aid in illustrating the stability of the aircraft. It is difficult for students to learn a maneuver properly if they seldom have the opportunity to correct an error.

On the other hand, students may perform a procedure or maneuver correctly and not fully understand the principles and objectives involved. When the instructor suspects this, students should be required to vary the performance of the maneuver slightly, combine it with other operations, or apply the same elements to the performance of other maneuvers. Students who do not understand the principles involved will probably not be able to do this successfully.

Pilot Supervision

Flight instructors have the responsibility to provide guidance and restraint with respect to the solo operations of their students. This is by far the most important flight instructor responsibility. The flight instructor is the only person in a position to make the determination a student is ready for solo operations. Before endorsing a student for solo flight, the instructor should require the student to demonstrate consistent ability to perform all of the fundamental maneuvers.

Dealing with Normal Challenges

Instructors should teach students how to solve ordinary problems encountered during flight. Traffic pattern congestion, change in active runway, or unexpected crosswinds are challenges the student masters individually before being able to perform them collectively.

Visualization

SBT lends itself well to visualization techniques. For example, have a student visualize how the flight may occur under normal circumstances, with the student describing how he or she would fly the flight. Then, the instructor adds unforeseen circumstances such as a sudden change in weather that brings excessive winds during final approach. Other examples of SBT can have the instructor adding undesired landing sites for balloon student pilots, rope breaks for glider students, and radio outages for instrument airplane students. Now, the student must visualize how he or she will handle the unexpected change.

During this visualization, the flight instructor can ask questions to check the student's thought processes. The job of the instructor is to challenge the student with realistic flying situations without overburdening him or her with unrealistic scenarios.

Practice Landings

The FAA recommends that in all student flights involving landings in an aircraft, the flight instructor should teach a full stop landing. Full stop landings help the student develop aircraft control and checklist usage. Aircraft speed and control take precedence over all other actions during landings and takeoffs.

Stress landing in the first third of the runway to ensure there is stopping distance for the aircraft. If the student is unable to land in the first third, teach him or her to make an immediate go around. If the student bounces an airplane on landing, teach the student to make an immediate go around. By following these teaching guidelines, the student is better equipped to properly execute landings when he or she solos. Furthermore, by requiring the first solo flight to consist of landings to a full stop, the flight instructor has the opportunity to stop the flight if necessary.

In gliders, a low energy landing is the most desirable, based on current winds. This helps the student develop good off-field landings techniques. This is dependent on current weather, such as excess winds including crosswinds.

Practical Test Recommendations

Provision is made on the airman certificate or rating application form for the written recommendation of the flight instructor who has prepared the applicant for the practical test involved. Signing this recommendation imposes a serious responsibility on the flight instructor. A flight instructor who makes a practical test recommendation for an applicant seeking a certificate or rating should require the applicant to demonstrate thoroughly the knowledge and skill level required for that certificate or rating. This demonstration should in no instance be less than the complete procedure prescribed in the applicable PTS.

When the instructor endorses the applicant for the practical test, his or her signature on the FAA Form 8710-1, Airman Certificate and/or Rating Application, is valid for 60 days. This is also true with the flight proficiency endorsement that is placed in the applicant's logbook or training record (Advisory Circular (AC) 61-65). These two dates should be the same.

Completion of prerequisites for a practical test is another instructor task that must be documented properly. Examples of all common endorsements can be found in the current issue of AC 61-65, Appendix 1. This appendix also includes references to 14 CFR Part 61, Certification: Pilots, Flight Instructors, and Ground Instructors, for more details concerning the requirements that must be met to qualify for each respective endorsement. The examples shown contain the essential elements of each endorsement. It is not mandatory, but recommended for all endorsements to be worded exactly as those in the AC. For example, changes to regulatory requirements may affect the wording, or the instructor may customize the endorsement for any special circumstances of the applicant. However, at a minimum, the instructor needs to cite the appropriate 14 CFR part 61 section that has been completed.

FAA inspectors and DPEs rely on flight instructor recommendations as evidence of qualification for certification, and proof that a review has been given of the subject areas found to be deficient on the appropriate knowledge test. Recommendations also provide assurance that the applicant has had a thorough briefing on the PTS and the associated knowledge areas, maneuvers, and procedures. If the flight instructor has trained and prepared the applicant competently, the applicant should have no problem passing the practical test.

A flight instructor who fails to ensure a student meets the requirements of regulations prior to endorsing solo flight or additional rating exhibits a serious deficiency in performance. The FAA holds him or her accountable. Providing a solo endorsement for a student who is not fully prepared to accept the responsibility for solo flight operations, or providing an endorsement for an additional rating to a pilot not meeting the appropriate regulatory requirements, is also a breach of faith with the applicant.

Aeronautical Decision-Making

As discussed on page 8-2, aviation training and flight operations are now seen as a system rather than individual concepts. The goal of system safety is for pilots to utilize all four concepts (ADM, risk management, situational awareness, and SRM) so that risk can be reduced to the lowest possible level.

ADM is a systematic approach to the mental process used by aircraft pilots to consistently determine the best course of action in response to a given set of circumstances. Risk management is a decision-making process designed to systematically identify hazards, assess the degree of risk, and determine the best course of action associated with each flight. Situational awareness is the accurate perception and understanding of all the factors and conditions within the four fundamental risk elements that affect safety before, during, and after the flight. SRM is the art and science of managing all resources (both onboard the aircraft and from outside sources) available to a single pilot (prior and during flight) to ensure the successful outcome of the flight.

These key principles are often collectively called ADM. The importance of teaching students effective ADM skills can not be overemphasized. While progress is continually being made in the advancement of pilot training methods, aircraft equipment and systems, and services for pilots, accidents still occur. Despite all the changes in technology to improve flight safety, one factor remains the same—the human factor. It is estimated that approximately 80 percent of all aviation accidents are human factors related.

By taking a system approach to aviation safety, flight instructors interweave aeronautical knowledge, aircraft control skills, ADM, risk management, situational awareness, and SRM into the training process.

Historically, the term "pilot error" has been used to describe the causes of these accidents. Pilot error means that an action or decision made by the pilot was the cause of, or contributing factor to, the accident. This definition also includes the pilot's failure to make a decision or take action. From a broader perspective, the phrase "human factors related" more aptly describes these accidents since it is usually not a single decision that leads to an accident, but a chain of events triggered by a number of factors.

The poor judgment chain, or the error chain, describes this concept of contributing factors in a human factors related accident. Breaking one link in the chain is all that is usually necessary to change the outcome of the sequence of events. The best way to illustrate this concept to students is to discuss specific situations that lead to aircraft accidents or incidents. The following is an example of the type of scenario that can be presented to illustrate the poor judgment chain.

A private pilot with 100 hours of flight time made a precautionary landing on a narrow dirt runway at a private airport. The pilot lost directional control during landing and swerved off the runway into the grass. A witness recalled later that the aircraft appeared to be too high and fast on final approach, and speculated the pilot was having difficulty controlling the aircraft in high winds. The weather at the time of the incident was reported as marginal VFR due to rain showers and thunderstorms. When the aircraft was fueled the following morning, 60 gallons of fuel were required to fill the 62-gallon capacity tanks.

By discussing the events that led to this incident, instructors can help students understand how a series of judgmental errors contributed to the final outcome of this flight.

- Weather decision—on the morning of the flight, the pilot was running late and, having acquired a computer printout of the forecast the night before, he did not obtain a briefing from flight service before his departure.

- Flight planning decision/performance chart—the pilot calculated total fuel requirements for the trip based on a rule-of-thumb figure he had used previously for another airplane. He did not use the fuel tables printed in the pilot's operating handbook (POH) for the aircraft he was flying on this trip. After reaching his destination, the pilot did not request refueling. Based on his original calculations, he believed sufficient fuel remained for the flight home.

- Fatigue/failure to recognize personal limitations—in the presence of deteriorating weather, the pilot departed for the flight home at 5:00 p.m. He did not consider how fatigue and lack of extensive night flying experience could affect the flight.

- Fuel exhaustion—with the aircraft fuel supply almost exhausted, the pilot no longer had the option of diverting to avoid rapidly developing thunderstorms. He was forced to land at the nearest airfield available.

On numerous occasions during the flight, the pilot could have made decisions which may have prevented this incident.

However, as the chain of events unfolded, each poor decision left him with fewer and fewer options. On the positive side, the pilot made a precautionary landing at a time and place of his choosing. VFR into IMC accidents often lead to fatalities. In this case, the pilot landed his aircraft without loss of life.

Teaching pilots to make sound decisions is the key to preventing accidents. Traditional pilot instruction has emphasized flying skills, knowledge of the aircraft, and familiarity with regulations. ADM training focuses on the decision-making process and the factors that affect a pilot's ability to make effective choices.

Timely decision-making is an important tool for any pilot. The student who hesitates when prompt action is required, or who makes the decision to not decide, has made a wrong decision. Sometimes, sound ADM calls for going against procedure. For example, in the event of an engine fire, the pilot initiates an emergency descent. Some POHs call for mixture to be enriched during an emergency descent, but what if the powerplant is engulfed in flames? Emergencies require the pilot to think—assess the situation, choose and execute the actions that assure safety, not act in a rote manner.

It is important for flight instructors to teach students that declaring an emergency when one occurs is an appropriate reaction. Once an emergency is declared, air traffic control (ATC) gives the pilot priority handling. 14 CFR Section 91.3, Responsibility and Authority of the Pilot in Command, states that "In an inflight emergency requiring immediate action, the pilot in command may deviate from any rule of this part to the extent required to meet that emergency."

Flight instructors should incorporate ADM, risk management, situational awareness, and SRM throughout the entire training course for all levels of students. AC 60-22, Aeronautical Decision Making, provides background references, definitions, and other pertinent information about ADM training in the GA environment. *[Figure 8-7]*

The Decision-Making Process

An understanding of the decision-making process provides students with a foundation for developing ADM skills. Some situations, such as engine failures, require a pilot to respond immediately using established procedures with little time for detailed analysis. Traditionally, pilots have been well trained to react to emergencies, but are not as well prepared to make decisions, which require a more reflective response. Typically during a flight, the pilot has time to examine any changes that occur, gather information, and assess risk before reaching a decision. The steps leading to this conclusion constitute the decision-making process. When the decision-making process

is presented to students, it is essential to discuss how the process applies to an actual flight situation. To explain the decision-making process, the instructor can introduce the following steps with the accompanying scenario that places the students in the position of making a decision about a typical flight situation.

Defining the Problem

The first step in the decision-making process is to define the problem. This begins with recognizing that a change has occurred or that an expected change did not occur. A problem is perceived first by the senses, and then is distinguished through insight and experience. These same abilities, as well as an objective analysis of all available information, are used to determine the exact nature and severity of the problem.

One critical error that can be made during the decision-making process is incorrectly defining the problem. For example, failure of a landing-gear-extended light to illuminate could indicate that the gear is not down and locked into place or it could mean the bulb is burned out. The actions to be taken in each of these circumstances would be significantly different. Fixating on a problem that does not exist can divert the pilot's attention from important tasks. The pilot's failure to maintain an awareness of the circumstances regarding the flight now becomes the problem. This is why once an initial assumption is made regarding the problem, other sources must be used to verify that the pilot's conclusion is correct.

While on a cross-country flight, Brenda discovers her time en route between two checkpoints is significantly longer than the time she originally calculated. By noticing this discrepancy, she has recognized a change. Based on insight, cross-country flying experience, and knowledge of weather systems, she considers the possibility that she has an increased headwind. She verifies that the original calculations are correct and considers factors that may have lengthened the time between checkpoints, such as a climb or deviation off course. To determine if there is a change in the winds aloft forecast and to check recent pilot reports, she contacts Flight Watch. After weighing each information source, she concludes that the headwind has increased. To determine the severity of the problem, she calculates a new groundspeed and reassesses fuel requirements.

Choosing a Course of Action

After the problem has been identified, the pilot evaluates the need to react to it and determines the actions that may be taken to resolve the situation in the time available. The expected outcome of each possible action should be considered and the risks assessed before the pilot decides on a response to the situation.

Definitions
Aeronautical Decision-Making (ADM) is a systematic approach to the mental process used by pilots to consistently determine the best course of action in response to a given set of circumstances.
Attitude is a personal motivational predisposition to respond to persons, situations, or events in a given manner that can, nevertheless, be changed or modified through training as sort of a mental shortcut to decision-making.
Attitude Management is the ability to recognize hazardous attitudes in oneself and the willingness to modify them as necessary through the application of an appropriate antidote thought.
Crew Resource Management (CRM) is the application of team management concepts in the flight deck environment. It was initially known as cockpit resource management, but as CRM programs evolved to include cabin crews, maintenance personnel, and others, the phrase crew resource management was adopted. This includes single pilots, as in most general aviation aircraft. Pilots of small aircraft, as well as crews of larger aircraft, must make effective use of all available resources: human resources, hardware, and information. A current definition includes all groups routinely working with the cockpit crew who are involved in decisions required to operate a flight safely. These groups include, but are not limited to: pilots, dispatchers, cabin crewmembers, maintenance personnel, and air traffic controllers. CRM is one way of addressing the challenge of optimizing the human/machine interface and accompanying interpersonal activities.
Headwork is required to accomplish a conscious, rational thought process when making decisions. Good decision-making involves risk identification and assessment, information processing, and problem solving.
Judgment is the mental process of recognizing and analyzing all pertinent information in a particular situation, a rational evaluation of alternative actions in response to it, and a timely decision on which action to take.
Personality is the embodiment of personal traits and characteristics of an individual that are set at a very early age and extremely resistant to change.
Poor Judgment Chain is a series of mistakes that may lead to an accident or incident. Two basic principles generally associated with the creation of a poor judgment chain are: (1) One bad decision often leads to another; and (2) as a string of bad decisions grows, it reduces the number of subsequent alternatives for continued safe flight. ADM is intended to break the poor judgment chain before it can cause an accident or incident.
Risk Elements in ADM take into consideration the four fundamental risk elements: the pilot, the aircraft, the environment, and the type of operation that comprise any given aviation situation.
Risk Management is the part of the decision-making process which relies on situational awareness, problem recognition, and good judgment to reduce risks associated with each flight.
Situational Awareness is the accurate perception and understanding of all the factors and conditions within the four fundamental risk elements that affect safety before, during, and after the flight.
Skills and Procedures are the procedural, psychomotor, and perceptual skills used to control a specific aircraft or its systems. They are the airmanship abilities that are gained through conventional training, are perfected, and become almost automatic through experience.
Stress Management is the personal analysis of the kinds of stress experienced while flying, the application of appropriate stress assessment tools, and other coping mechanisms.

Figure 8-7. *Terms used in AC 60-22 to explain concepts used in ADM training.*

Brenda determines the fuel burn if she continues to her destination and considers other options: turning around and landing at a nearby airport, diverting off course, or landing prior to her destination at an airport en route. She now considers the expected outcome of each possible action and assesses the risks involved. After studying the chart, she concludes there is an airport which has fueling services within a reasonable distance along her route. She can refuel there and continue to her destination without a significant loss of time.

Implementing the Decision and Evaluating the Outcome

Although a decision may be reached and a course of action implemented, the decision-making process is not complete. It is important to think ahead and determine how the decision could affect other phases of the flight. As the flight progresses, the pilot must continue to evaluate the outcome of the decision to ensure that it is producing the desired result.

To implement her decision, Brenda plots the course changes and calculates a new estimated time of arrival. She also contacts the nearest AFSS to amend her flight plan and check weather conditions at the new destination. As she proceeds to the airport, she continues to monitor groundspeed, aircraft performance, and weather conditions to ensure no additional steps need to be taken to guarantee the safety of the flight.

Factors Affecting Decision-Making

It is important to stress to a student that being familiar with the decision-making process does not ensure he or she has the good judgment to be a safe pilot. The ability to make effective decisions as PIC depends on a number of factors. Some circumstances, such as the time available to make a decision, may be beyond the pilot's control. However, a pilot can learn to recognize those factors that can be managed, and learn skills to improve decision-making ability and judgment.

Recognizing Hazardous Attitudes

While the ADM process does not eliminate errors, it helps the pilot recognize errors, and in turn enables the pilot to manage the error to minimize its effects. Two steps to improve flight safety are identifying personal attitudes hazardous to safe flight and learning behavior modification techniques.

Flight instructors must be able to spot hazardous attitudes in a student because recognition of hazardous thoughts is the first step toward neutralizing them. CFIs should keep in mind that being fit to fly depends on more than just a pilot's physical condition and recency of experience. Hazardous attitudes contribute to poor pilot judgment and affect the quality of decisions.

Attitude can be defined as a personal motivational predisposition to respond to persons, situations, or events in a given manner. Studies have identified five hazardous attitudes that can affect a pilot's ability to make sound decisions and exercise authority properly. *[Figure 8-8]*

In order for a student to self-examine behaviors during flight, he or she must be taught the potential risks caused from hazardous attitudes and, more importantly, the antidote for each. *[Figure 8-9]* For example, if a student has an easy time with flight training and seems to understand things very quickly, there may be a potential for that student to have a "macho" hazardous attitude. A successful CFI points out

---

The Five Hazardous Attitudes

Anti-authority: "Don't tell me."
This attitude is found in people who do not like anyone telling them what to do. In a sense, they are saying, "No one can tell me what to do." They may be resentful of having someone tell them what to do, or may regard rules, regulations, and procedures as silly or unnecessary. However, it is always pilot prerogative to question authority if it seems to be in error.

Impulsivity: "Do it quickly."
This is the attitude of people who frequently feel the need to do something—anything—immediately. They do not stop to think about what they are about to do; they do not select the best alternative, and they do the first thing that comes to mind.

Invulnerability: "It won't happen to me."
Many people believe that accidents happen to others, but never to them. They know accidents can happen, and they know that anyone can be affected. They never really feel or believe that they will be personally involved. Pilots who think this way are more likely to take chances and increase risk.

Macho: "I can do it."
Pilots who are always trying to prove that they are better than anyone else are thinking, "I can do it, I'll show them." Pilots with this type of attitude will try to prove themselves by taking risks in order to impress others. While this pattern is thought to be a male characteristic, women are equally susceptible.

Resignation: "What's the use?"
Pilots who think, "What's the use?" do not see themselves as being able to make a great deal of difference in what happens to them. When things go well, the pilot is apt to think that it is good luck. When things go badly, the pilot may feel that "someone is out to get me," or attribute it to bad luck. The pilot will leave the action to others, for better or worse. Sometimes, such pilots will even go along with unreasonable requests just to be a "nice guy."

Figure 8-8. *Pilots should examine their decisions carefully to ensure that their choices have not been influenced by a hazardous attitude.*

Hazardous Attitude	Antidotes
Macho Steve often brags to his friends about his skills as a pilot and how close to the ground he flies. During a local pleasure flight in his single-engine airplane, he decides to buzz some friends barbecuing at a nearby park.	Taking chances is foolish.
Anti-authority Although he knows that flying so low to the ground is prohibited by the regulations, he feels that the regulations are too restrictive in some circumstances.	Follow the rules. They are usually right.
Invulnerability Steve is not worried about an accident since he has flown this low many times before and he has not had any problems.	It could happen to me.
Impulsivity As he is buzzing the park, the airplane does not climb as well as Steve had anticipated and, without thinking, he pulls back hard on the yoke. The airspeed drops and the airplane is close to stalling as the wing brushes a power line.	Not so fast. Think first.
Resignation Although Steve manages to recover, the wing sustains minor damage. Steve thinks to himself, "It doesn't really matter how much effort I put in—the end result is the same whether I really try or not."	I'm not helpless. I can make a difference.

Figure 8-9. *Students in training can be asked to identify hazardous attitudes and the corresponding antidotes when presented with flight scenarios.*

the potential for the behavior and teaches the student the antidote for that attitude. Hazardous attitudes need to be noticed immediately and corrected with the proper antidote to minimize the potential for any flight hazard.

Stress Management

Learning how to recognize and cope with stress is another effective ADM tool. Stress is the body's response to demands placed upon it. These demands can be either pleasant or unpleasant in nature. The causes of stress for a pilot can range from unexpected weather or mechanical problems while in flight to personal issues unrelated to flying. Stress is an inevitable and necessary part of life; it adds motivation and heightens an individual's response to meet any challenge.

Everyone is stressed to some degree all the time. A certain amount of stress is good since it keeps a person alert and prevents complacency. However, the effects of stress are cumulative and, if not coped with adequately, they

eventually add up to an intolerable burden. Performance generally increases with the onset of stress, peaks, and then begins to fall off rapidly as stress levels exceed a person's ability to cope. The ability to make effective decisions during flight can be impaired by stress. Factors, referred to as stressors, can increase a pilot's risk of error in the flight deck. *[Figure 8-10]*

Stressors
Physical Stress Conditions associated with the environment, such as temperature and humidity extremes, noise, vibration, and lack of oxygen.
Physiological Stress Physical conditions, such as fatigue, lack of physical fitness, sleep loss, missed meals (leading to low blood sugar levels), and illness.
Psychological Stress Social or emotional factors, such as a death in the family, a divorce, a sick child, or a demotion at work. This type of stress may also be related to mental workload, such as analyzing a problem, navigating an aircraft, or making decisions.

Figure 8-10. *Three types of stressors that can affect pilot performance.*

One way of exploring the subject of stress with a student is to recognize when stress is affecting performance. If a student seems distracted, or has a particularly difficult time accomplishing the tasks of the lesson, the instructor can query the student. Was the student uncomfortable or tired during the flight? Is there some stress in another aspect of the student's life that may be causing a distraction? This may prompt the student to evaluate how these factors affect performance and judgment. The instructor should also try to determine if there are aspects of pilot training that are causing excessive amounts of stress for the student. For example, if the student consistently makes a decision not to fly, even though weather briefings indicate favorable conditions, it may be due to apprehension regarding the lesson content. Stalls, landings, or an impending solo flight may cause concern. By explaining a specific maneuver in greater detail or offering some additional encouragement, the instructor may be able to alleviate some of the student's stress.

To help students manage the accumulation of life stresses and prevent stress overload, instructors can recommend several techniques. For example, including relaxation time in a busy schedule and maintaining a program of physical fitness can help reduce stress levels. Learning to manage time more effectively can help pilots avoid heavy pressures imposed by getting behind schedule and not meeting deadlines. While these pressures may exist in the workplace, students may also experience the same type of stress regarding their flight training schedule. Instructors can advise students to self-assess to determine their capabilities and limitations and then set realistic goals. In addition, avoiding stressful situations and encounters can help pilots cope with stress.

Use of Resources

To make informed decisions during flight operations, students must be made aware of the resources found both inside and outside the flight deck. Since useful tools and sources of information may not always be readily apparent, learning to recognize these resources is an essential part of ADM training. Resources must not only be identified, but students must also develop the skills to evaluate whether they have the time to use a particular resource and the impact that its use would have upon the safety of flight. For example, the assistance of ATC may be very useful if a pilot is lost. However, in an emergency situation when action needs be taken quickly, time may not be available to contact ATC immediately. During training, CFIs can routinely point out resources to students.

Internal Resources

Internal resources are found in the flight deck during flight. Since some of the most valuable internal resources are ingenuity, knowledge, and skill, pilots can expand flight deck resources immensely by improving their capabilities. This can be accomplished by frequently reviewing flight information publications, such as 14 CFR and the Aeronautical Information Manual (AIM), as well as by pursuing additional training.

A thorough understanding of all the equipment and systems in the aircraft is necessary to fully utilize all resources. For example, advanced navigation and autopilot systems are valuable resources flight instructors must ensure students know how to use. If students do not fully understand how to use the equipment, or if they rely on it so much that they become complacent, it can become a detriment to safe flight. With the advent of advanced avionics with glass displays, GPS, and autopilot, flying might seem inherently easier and safer, but in reality it has become more complex. With the update of the Instrument Practical Test Standards (PTS) to include electronic flight instrument displays, flight management systems, GPS, and autopilot usage, knowledge of internal resources becomes an important component of flight training. As discussed in the section on flight instructor qualifications, instructors must be familiar with the components of each aircraft in which they instruct to ensure students understand the operation of the equipment.

Checklists are essential flight deck resources for verifying that the aircraft instruments and systems are checked, set,

and operating properly, as well as ensuring that the proper procedures are performed if there is a system malfunction or inflight emergency. Students reluctant to use checklists can be reminded that pilots at all levels of experience refer to checklists, and that the more advanced the aircraft is, the more crucial checklists become. With the advent of electronic checklists, it has become easier to develop and maintain personal checklists from the manufacturer's checklist with additions for specific aircraft and operations.

In addition, the AFM/POH, which is required to be carried onboard the aircraft, is essential for accurate flight planning and for resolving inflight equipment malfunctions. Other valuable flight deck resources include current aeronautical charts and publications, such as the Airport/Facility Directory (A/FD).

It should be pointed out to students that passengers can also be a valuable resource. Passengers can help watch for traffic and may be able to provide information in an irregular situation, especially if they are familiar with flying. A strange smell or sound may alert a passenger to a potential problem. The PIC should brief passengers before the flight to make sure that they are comfortable voicing any concerns.

External Resources

Possibly the greatest external resources during flight are air traffic controllers and flight service specialists. ATC can help decrease pilot workload by providing traffic advisories, radar vectors, and assistance in emergency situations. AFSS can provide updates on weather, answer questions about airport conditions, and may offer direction-finding assistance. The services provided by ATC can be invaluable in enabling pilots to make informed inflight decisions. Instructors can help new students feel comfortable with ATC by encouraging them to take advantage of services, such as flight following and Flight Watch. If students are exposed to ATC as much as possible during training, they feel confident asking controllers to clarify instructions and are better equipped to use ATC as a resource for assistance in unusual circumstances or emergencies.

Throughout training, students can be asked to identify internal and external resources, which can be used in a variety of flight situations. For example, if a discrepancy is found during preflight, what resources can be used to determine its significance? In this case, the student's knowledge of the aircraft, the POH, an instructor or other experienced pilot, or an AMT can be a resource which may help define the problem.

During cross-country training, students may be asked to consider the following situation. On a cross-country flight, you become disoriented. Although you are familiar with the area, you do not recognize any landmarks, and fuel is running low. What resources do you have to assist you? students should be able to identify their own skills and knowledge, aeronautical charts, ATC, flight service, and navigation equipment as some of the resources that can be used in this situation.

Workload Management

Effective workload management ensures that essential operations are accomplished by planning, prioritizing, and sequencing tasks to avoid work overload. As experience is gained, a pilot learns to recognize future workload requirements and can prepare for high workload periods during times of low workload. Instructors can teach this skill by prompting their students to prepare for a high workload. For example, when en route, the student can be asked to explain the actions that need to be taken during the approach to the airport. The student should be able to describe the procedures for traffic pattern entry and landing preparation. Reviewing the appropriate chart and setting radio frequencies well in advance of need helps reduce workload as the flight nears the airport. In addition, the student should listen to the Automatic Terminal Information Service (ATIS), Automated Surface Observing Systems (ASOS), or Automated Weather Observing System (AWOS), if available, and then monitor the tower frequency or Common Traffic Advisory Frequency (CTAF) to get a good idea of what traffic conditions to expect. Checklists should be performed well in advance so there is time to focus on traffic and ATC instructions. These

procedures are especially important prior to entering a high-density traffic area, such as Class B airspace.

To manage workload, items should be prioritized. This concept should be emphasized to students and reinforced when training procedures are performed. For example, during a go-around, adding power, gaining airspeed, and properly configuring the aircraft are priorities. Informing the tower of the balked landing should be accomplished only after these tasks are completed. students must understand that priorities change as the situation changes. If fuel quantity is lower than expected on a cross-country flight, the priority can shift from making a scheduled arrival time at the destination, to locating a nearby airport to refuel. In an emergency situation, the first priority is to fly the aircraft and maintain a safe airspeed.

Another important part of managing workload is recognizing a work overload situation. The first effect of high workload is that the pilot begins to work faster. As workload increases, attention cannot be devoted to several tasks at one time, and the pilot may begin to focus on one item. When the pilot becomes task saturated, there is no awareness of inputs from various sources; decisions may be made on incomplete information, and the possibility of error increases. [Figure 8-11]

During a lesson, workload can be gradually increased as the instructor monitors the student's management of tasks. The instructor should ensure that the student has the ability to recognize a work overload situation. When becoming overloaded, the student should stop, think, slow down, and

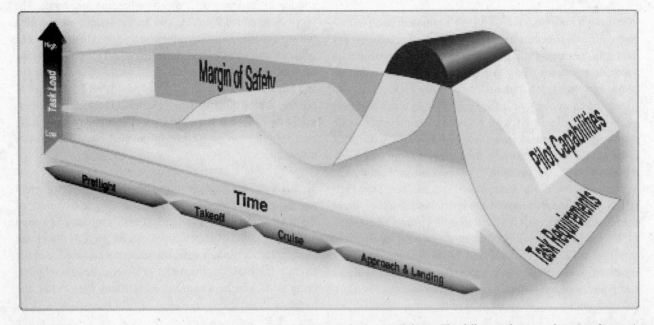

Figure 8-11. *Accidents often occur when flying task requirements exceed pilot capabilities. The difference between these two factors is called the margin of safety. Note that in this idealized example, the margin of safety is minimal during the approach and landing. At this point, an emergency or distraction could overtax pilot capabilities, causing an accident.*

prioritize. It is important that the student understand options that may be available to decrease workload. For example, locating an item on a chart or setting a radio frequency may be delegated to another pilot or passenger, an autopilot (if available) may be used, or ATC may be enlisted to provide assistance.

Chapter Summary

This chapter discussed the demonstration-performance and telling-and-doing training delivery methods of flight instruction, SBT techniques, practical strategies flight instructors can use to enhance their instruction, integrated flight instruction, positive exchange of flight controls, use of distractions, obstacles to learning encountered during flight training, and how to evaluate students. After an intensive look at ADM with suggestions for how to interweave ADM, risk management, and SRM into the teaching process, it closes with a discussion of CFI recommendations. Additional information on recommendations and endorsements can be found in Appendix E, Flight Instructor Endorsements.

APPENDIX C
GROUND SCHOOL COURSE SUGGESTIONS

(10 pages of outline)

The purpose of this appendix is to suggest ideas concerning marketing, organization, and presentation of ground schools for pilot knowledge tests. We will appreciate any comments or suggestions you may have after reading this material, as will other aviation professionals when we incorporate this information into subsequent editions. Please jot down notes on the last page of this book and send these to us at your convenience, or email us at aviation@gleim.com. Thank you.

RATIONALE FOR CONDUCTING A GROUND SCHOOL

1. **Aid to the industry.** General aviation (including flight instruction), while more financially sound than it has been in years past, is still not normally a high-profit enterprise. A ground school is the first step into aviation for many students who will one day become aircraft renters and owners--the people who sustain GA. While it will not generate large profits for a business on its own, a ground school sets the stage for a lasting relationship between a flight school/FBO and its students.

2. **Maintaining a professional level of currency and familiarity with aviation subjects.** Obtaining your flight and/or ground instructor certificate will keep you up to date on the CFRs and all other academic areas of flight. Additionally, teaching will challenge you to learn and understand a wide variety of material.

3. **Finding new customers.** Many flight instructors use ground schools as a source of student pilots.

4. **Public service.** Many flight and/or ground instructors provide ground schools to Civil Air Patrol (CAP) chapters, high school classes, etc., as a public service to young people.

5. **Personal employment.** Obtaining your flight and/or ground instructor certificate can lead to opportunities for part-time work at FBOs, community colleges, and adult education programs.

POTENTIAL SPONSORS OF GROUND SCHOOLS

1. **Community colleges.** Call your local junior college and ask if a ground school is offered. Ask what division it is in and call the Dean or Director to indicate your interest in teaching the ground school. While talking to the Dean or Director, you should obtain a course outline, as well as information on the cost and class schedule. The college may already have an instructor, but you should make known your interest in teaching in case there should be an opening.

    a. Send us the Dean or Director's name and address and your own name and address. We will send him/her a complimentary copy of *Private Pilot FAA Knowledge Test* or *Sport Pilot FAA Knowledge Test* and explain that it was at your suggestion. We will reiterate your interest in presenting a ground school.

2. **Local high school adult education centers.** Call all local high schools for more information.

3. **FBOs.** Inquire at your local airport, or search on the Internet (e.g., www.airnav.com).

4. **Civil Air Patrol units.** Inquire at your local armed forces recruiting or training station for the name and telephone number of local CAP unit commanders (see the U.S. Government section of your telephone book). You can also find information about the CAP's aerospace education program at the Civil Air Patrol National Headquarters website (gocivilairpatrol.com).

MARKETING GROUND SCHOOLS

The objective of marketing a ground school is to contact interested students if you are beginning a new ground school and to increase enrollment if you are associated with an existing ground school. The following are only a few suggestions.

1. **Classified ads in local newspapers.** Ads usually cost only a few dollars a day for a brief description that might read

    "Private Pilot/Sport Pilot Ground School. 6 weeks in length, Tuesday and Thursday evenings, 7:00-9:00 p.m. Offered at [course location]. Tuition, books, etc., $[your price]. Call [instructor or sponsor name] at [phone number] after 7 p.m."

2. **Radio ads.** Call your local radio station and pay for an advertisement or, preferably, have it broadcast as a public service announcement. Provide the same information stated in the sample ad above.

3. **Posters.** Prepare posters and provide a telephone number, again with the above information. Post them at your local community college, university, airport, in stores, etc.

4. **Internet.** Create a simple website or have one builty for you to advertise your services, schedule, location, etc. Gleim can provide you with buttons leading directly to our products in our aviation store.

GROUND SCHOOL COURSE ORGANIZATION

We hope you will use *Pilot Handbook*, as well as *Private Pilot FAA Knowledge Test*, *FAA Test Prep* Software Download/Test Prep for Windows Mobile, and/or *Gleim Online Ground School* for your ground school. Based on that presumption, it is probably easiest to follow our study unit organization, which is the same in both *Pilot Handbook* and *Private Pilot FAA Knowledge Test*.

We recommend that you incorporate a Sport Pilot ground school with your Private Pilot ground school to help you maximize the number of students interested in the course. Sport pilots need to know approximately 70% of the required material for Private Pilot to pass their FAA knowledge test. It is beneficial for them to learn more than what is required for them to pass the FAA knowledge test; therefore, we include additional study units in *Sport Pilot FAA Knowledge Test*.

Make sure that you are aware of the differences between Sport Pilot and Private Pilot and make it clear to your students which information they may omit for Sport Pilot.

Private Pilot FAA Knowledge Test

Study Unit 1 • Airplanes and Aerodynamics
Study Unit 2 • Airplane Instruments, Engines, and Systems
Study Unit 3 • Airports, Air Traffic Control, and Airspace
Study Unit 4 • Federal Aviation Regulations
Study Unit 5 • Airplane Performance and Weight and Balance
Study Unit 6 • Aeromedical Factors and Aeronautical Decision Making (ADM)
Study Unit 7 • Aviation Weather
Study Unit 8 • Aviation Weather Services
Study Unit 9 • Navigation: Charts and Publications
Study Unit 10 • Navigation Systems
Study Unit 11 • Cross-Country Flight Planning

Sport Pilot FAA Knowledge Test

Study Unit 1 • Airports
Study Unit 2 • Airspace
Study Unit 3 • Federal Aviation Regulations - Parts 1 through 71
Study Unit 4 • Federal Aviation Regulations - Parts 91.3 through 91.131
Study Unit 5 • Federal Aviation Regulations - Parts 91.155 through 91.417 and NTSB Part 830
Study Unit 6 • Aeromedical Factors and Aeronautical Decision Making (ADM)
Study Unit 7 • Aviation Weather
Study Unit 8 • Weather Services
Study Unit 9 • Sectional Charts and Airspace
Study Unit 10 • Navigation and Preflight Preparation
Study Unit 11 • Airplanes and Aerodynamics
Study Unit 12 • Airplane Instruments
Study Unit 13 • Airplane Engines and Systems
Study Unit 14 • Airplane Performance and Weight and Balance

The *Pilot Handbook* is $24.95 retail, and the *Private Pilot FAA Knowledge Test* and *Sport Pilot FAA Knowledge Test* books are each $19.95 retail. *FAA Test Prep* Software Download retails for $54.95 and *Gleim Online Ground School* retails for $99.95. Quantity discounts are available. For example, a 40% discount is available on prepaid orders of four or more items. Thus, with a class as small as two students, you could sell the books and software at your cost of $47.94 per set (or more if you wish), or include them in the cost of the ground school. Finally, you may wish to recommend the appropriate Gleim Pilot Kit, which contains everything: books, Test Prep Software Download, Test Prep for Windows Mobile, Audio CDs (Private only) Gleim Online Ground School, and additional online courses (Private Pilot, retail $249.95; Sport Pilot, retail $199.95). Other purchase options are also available, including having your students order directly from us. To place an order or to obtain additional information, visit www.gleim.com, or call us at (800) 874-5346.

You will probably not have exactly 11 class sessions, which may necessitate combining study units for various classes. Approximately 12, 2-hr. sessions should be adequate if your course objective is to get your students ready for their pilot knowledge test. Even if you have 11 sessions, you may still want to combine certain study units and spend more time on other units. As an example of how study units might be combined for Private Pilot, if you have a 5-week program that meets for 10 sessions, you might want to combine Study Units 9, 10, and 11. You could easily cover the Introduction in Session 1 and still use a good part of the session to get into Study Unit 1. Then spend another entire meeting to finish Study Unit 1.

If your course objective is to cover all the subjects in the amount of detail needed by proficient pilots (rather than simply to "teach the test"), 16 to 18, 2-hr. sessions should be adequate. More time is needed for this comprehensive course because the FAA does not test every topic that your students need to know in order to be safe, capable pilots. Having 16 to 18 sessions will allow you to spend more than one session on the largest and most important study units in *Pilot Handbook* (Study Units 1 through 4) and will allow you to spend extra time on challenging concepts like airspace and radio navigation. A comprehensive course outline for Private Pilot might entail 2 sessions for the Introduction and Study Unit 1, 2 sessions for Study Unit 2, 2 sessions for Study Unit 3, 1 to 2 sessions for Study Unit 4 (depending on how detailed you wish to get), 1 to 2 sessions for Study Unit 5, and 1 session each for Study Units 6 through 11. Any extra time left in the course can be spent reviewing difficult topics and engaging in test-specific preparation.

Regardless of your course objective, you may wish to reserve 5 or 10 minutes at the end of each session for an overview and introduction of the material to be covered in the next session. That will help your students study for the next session and help them understand it.

COURSE SYLLABUS AND HANDOUTS

1. At the beginning of the course, you should distribute an outline of the material to be covered in the course. It should show the meeting times, quiz schedule, and reading assignments for each session.

2. A suggested syllabus for a 9-week class (whose objective is to prepare students for the test) that meets for 3 hours one night per week is presented on the following page.

   a. Undoubtedly, you will have to change the scheduling of topics. The topics have been overlapped so that you can talk about the same topic during two periods, i.e., you can provide double exposure. Introducing the topic the week before provides 3 weeks' coverage, which may be useful to your students.

3. Of course, the six study units in this book will be helpful to you as general background in preparing and presenting your ground school.

GLEIM PILOT KITS

The Gleim Private Pilot Kit and Sport Pilot Kit are designed to simplify and facilitate your students' flight and ground training. The Pilot Kits include

- *FAA Knowledge Test*
- *Flight Maneuvers and Practical Test Prep*
- *Pilot Handbook*
- *FAR/AIM*
- *Syllabus*
- Deluxe *Pilot Logbook* (hard cover)
- Training Record

- Online Ground School
- *FAA Test Prep* Software Download
- Test Prep for Windows Mobile
- Audio CDs (Private Pilot only)
- Navigational plotter
- Flight computer
- Flight bag

For ground training, your students will need to have at least a textbook *(Pilot Handbook)*, a *FAR/AIM*, a means of test preparation (*Private Pilot FAA Knowledge Test* or *Sport Pilot FAA Knowledge Test*, *FAA Test Prep* Software Download, and/or *Gleim Online Ground School*), a navigational plotter, and a flight computer. These items make up most of the Pilot Kits; the remaining items are primarily concerned with flight training. Because most people who take ground school courses intend to undertake flight training, it makes sense for your students to go ahead and obtain everything they will need at one time (at substantial savings) by purchasing the Pilot Kit.

SAMPLE COURSE SYLLABUS

COURSE SYLLABUS

Jonesville Community College
Evening Education Course 1121

Tuesday evenings, 7:00 - 10:00 p.m.
North Campus, Building C, Room 171

PRIVATE PILOT/SPORT PILOT GROUND SCHOOL
Summer Term A, 200X
June 1 - July 27

INSTRUCTOR: Mr. Harold Gray, AGI
Office: (111) 555-5252
Home: (111) 555-2525

COURSE OBJECTIVE: Learn the material required by the FAA for the private pilot knowledge test (airplane) and sport pilot knowledge test with the objective of each student passing the test.

CLASSROOM PROCEDURE: Lecture and guided discussion.

1. Each class will begin with a review and questions from the last class (approximately 5-15 minutes).

2. Next, there will be a brief overview and core concepts for the current evening's assignment, followed by class discussion and questions.

3. When appropriate, after the class break, an in-class quiz will be administered, self-graded, and analyzed through class discussion.

4. The last 15-30 minutes of each class session will be directed toward an overview and discussion of the next class's assignment.

5. Visual aids and handouts will be used as appropriate.

REQUIRED TEXT: *Private Pilot FAA Knowledge Test*, by Irvin N. Gleim and Garrett W. Gleim, or *Sport Pilot FAA Knowledge Test*, by Irvin N. Gleim and Garrett W. Gleim

RECOMMENDED TEXT: *Pilot Handbook*, by Irvin N. Gleim and Garrett W. Gleim

These texts are available in the College Bookstore on the North Campus, which is open until 8:00 p.m. each Tuesday.

SCHEDULE

Class	Date	PPKT* Study Units	SPKT** Study Units	Topic
1	June 1	Introduction, 1	Introduction, 11	Introduction, Aerodynamic Theory
2	June 8	1, 2	11, 13	Aerodynamics and Airplane Systems
3	June 15	2, 3	1, 2, 13	Airplane Systems, Airports, ATC
4	June 22	3, 4	2-5	Airspace, FARs
5	June 29	4, 5	3-5, 14	FARs, Airplane Performance
6	July 6	5, 6	6, 14	Weight and Balance, Aeromedical Factors
7	July 13	7, 8	7, 8	Aviation Weather and Weather Services
8	July 20	9, 10, 11	9, 10	Navigation, Cross-Country Flight
9	July 27			Review for pilot knowledge test

* PPKT = *Private Pilot FAA Knowledge Test*
** SPKT = *Sport Pilot FAA Knowledge Test*

You may photocopy this syllabus and change it in any way you like.

ENROLLMENT PROCEDURES

1. You should make a list of the students and their telephone numbers so you can contact them in the event the classes need to be changed, rescheduled, etc.

    a. Note the form and date of their payment.

2. As each student enrolls, you can sell him/her a book(s), software, and/or online course access (or give to him/her if the materials are included in the cost of the ground school course).

3. If you have a syllabus ready, distribute copies to your students and encourage them to do some study in advance.

4. With respect to requiring or recommending *Pilot Handbook* and *Aviation Weather and Weather Services*, you may proceed as follows:

    a. For each student, put one copy of each title on reserve in the bookstore of your choice.

    b. Get one copy of each book and pass them around to the class; indicate they can purchase another one from you, a local FBO, the bookstore you are using, or by calling Gleim Publications, Inc.

    c. Alternatively, have them order the materials by calling us at (800) 874-5346, or online at www.gleim.com.

5. Note that you may wish to encourage each person who enrolls or even inquires about the program to invite friends to take the course with him/her. The idea is to build enrollment through enthusiasm for and interest in aviation.

THE FIRST CLASS SESSION

1. Preliminaries

    a. Arrive early with a supply of books, handouts, and your lecture notes for the first lecture.

    b. Begin by enrolling any students who show up at the first class without having already enrolled.

    c. Go over the roll and pass out the syllabus.

    d. Introduce yourself.

2. Student-Instructor Interaction

    a. Tell the students about your background, the origin of the course, your reasons for teaching, and any other relevant personal things.

    b. Tell the class that you need to learn more about them in order to teach effectively.

        1) Ask people to introduce themselves.
        2) Unless the class is too large, make notes on your roster to individualize participants and help you learn their names.
        3) Ask them why they are taking the course, if they have any flying experience, if they know anyone else who flies, if they have ever flown before in a small aircraft, etc.

    c. Such interaction is an ice-breaker, allowing you to get to know your students, and allowing them to get to know you and one another.

3. Discussion of Course Objective (FAA Pilot Knowledge Test)

    a. Display *Private Pilot FAA Knowledge Test* and *Sport Pilot FAA Knowledge Test*.

    b. Point out that the textbooks have the FAA questions reorganized by topic, with answer explanations next to them.

    c. Indicate that the areas tested on the exams will be the topics specified on your syllabus (course outline), that the test will be only 60 questions for private and 40 questions for sport, and that the students need to get at least 42 questions correct for private and 28 questions correct for sport in order to pass.

        1) This will be very easy because they will have gone over all possible test questions during your course (all of which appear in *Private Pilot FAA Knowledge Test* and *Sport Pilot FAA Knowledge Test*), as well as additional material to help them learn how to fly safely.

    d. Explain the content of *Private Pilot FAA Knowledge Test* and/or *Sport Pilot FAA Knowledge Test*.

        1) Explain that the Introduction is the current topic of discussion.

        2) Show them the organization of Study Units 1 through 11 for Private Pilot and Study Units 1 through 14 for Sport Pilot.

            a) Each study unit begins with an outline, subunit by subunit (topic by topic).

            b) Following the outlines are questions and answer explanations organized in the same subunits and presented in the same order.

            c) Thus, the students are able to study and try to learn the material before they answer the questions. This format provides an extra level of reinforcement as they study the material.

4. Discussion of Course Objective (Comprehensive Coverage)

    a. Display *Pilot Handbook* and *Private Pilot FAA Knowledge Test* or *Sport Pilot FAA Knowledge Test*.

    b. Explain that both *Pilot Handbook* and *Private Pilot FAA Knowledge Test* have the same study unit numbers and titles, which means that the content of each study unit number in both books will correspond (for *Sport Pilot FAA Knowledge Test*, they will need to refer to the index).

        1) Explain that, because the study units of these books are complementary, Study Units 1 through 4 of *Pilot Handbook* are disproportionately larger than their counterparts in *Private Pilot FAA Knowledge Test* and *Sport Pilot FAA Knowledge Test*. Explain that this is because there is a lot of material that the FAA does not test, but with which a pilot must be familiar in order to fly safely (much of this untested material happens to fit into the first 4 study units).

        2) Explain that more time will therefore be spent on Study Units 1 through 4 of *Pilot Handbook*.

    c. Explain that, while your students will be well prepared for their pilot knowledge test at the completion of this course, it is not your goal to simply "teach the test," and that you plan to give them a solid background in aviation topics.

        1) Explain that they will be expected to follow the progress of the course in *Private Pilot FAA Knowledge Test* or *Sport Pilot FAA Knowledge Test* on their own and that you will primarily be teaching out of *Pilot Handbook*.

        2) Provide additional background about how to use *Private Pilot FAA Knowledge Test* or *Sport Pilot FAA Knowledge Test* based on item 3. of this list.

LECTURE PRESENTATION

1. There are many ways to present a lecture, and you should use the method with which you feel most comfortable. The best method for you will be the best method for your students because you will perform better.

2. One approach to keep in mind is the idea of hitting the high points or key concepts.

    a. What are the basic or major concepts within any topic? These are generally outlined at the opening of each study unit in *Private Pilot FAA Knowledge Test* and *Sport Pilot FAA Knowledge Test.*

    b. To amplify these concepts and provide additional discussion, consult *Pilot Handbook*, after which you can use additional examples from other textbooks, including the FAA/government textbooks.

3. A major objective of your lecture presentation is to make it interactive: The students must respond to you and participate.

    a. Learning is **not** a one-way communication from you to your students.

    b. You need to ask questions of individual students and of the class as a whole so that they can react and commit to an answer (silently or orally), and then get immediate feedback about the accuracy of their responses.

4. Have them work examples, e.g., provide them with a calculation and ask them to determine the answer.

    a. You could present a series of questions from the FAA knowledge test (current or earlier test), take away the alternative answers, and have them work through a couple of exercises.

    b. You might also put these on overhead projectors.

5. Your preparation before class is very important. You should consult the lesson plan discussed in Appendix B of this book and review Study Unit 4, "Teaching Methods," beginning on page 51.

VISUAL AIDS

1. Visual aids include small model airplanes, film strips, slides, blackboard presentations, overhead projector pictures, etc.

2. Visual aids are most helpful in explaining ideas that are abstract when presented verbally (e.g., airspace).

3. You can bring items to class and pass them around, such as navigation tools/charts and operating manuals from airplanes.

4. Experiment with visual aids. Use them as attention-getters or to break the pace of the normal presentation.

5. If using presentation software (such as Microsoft PowerPoint), avoid reading from slides. Use this tool to present important (i.e., tested) concepts as well as images, animations, and/or video.

COURSE EVALUATIONS

1. At the end of the course, but before the session set aside for the FAA knowledge test, you should administer a course evaluation.

    a. Your objective is to obtain feedback from your students about how the course can be improved in several aspects, including:

        1) Course organization
        2) Textbook(s)
        3) Lecture presentation
        4) Physical facilities

    b.   Let the students know that you are seeking constructive criticism across many areas.

    c.   Tell them that you do not want to make them ill at ease, so you are going to ask one member (tell them who) to hold the evaluations until the course is over.

    d.   If the course is for grade credit, the evaluations should be held until after you have turned in the grades.

2.   Please feel free to photocopy and modify the course evaluation illustrated below. Note that you should leave the back blank for additional written comments.

3.   Remember that, at the conclusion of the last class session prior to your students taking the FAA pilot knowledge test, you need to complete the Instructor Certification Form at the back of *Private Pilot FAA Knowledge Test* or *Sport Pilot FAA Knowledge Test* for each student.

Date _____

(NAME OF COURSE)
GROUND SCHOOL EVALUATION FORM

This Ground School is being presented to aid you in your preparation for the FAA knowledge test. Please help us by answering the following questions, keeping in mind our objective: to help you prepare for the FAA knowledge test. Please check one response for each line. Return the completed form to the person designated to hold the evaluations until the completion of the last class (or after grades have been turned in).

Instructor	Excellent	Good	Adequate	Poor
1. Instructor presentation of material	___	___	___	___
2. Instructor knowledge of subject	___	___	___	___
3. Allocation of time to topics	___	___	___	___
4. Use of slides, boards, visual aids, etc.	___	___	___	___
5. Use of handouts, problems, etc.	___	___	___	___
Other questions				
6. Overall rating of instructor	___	___	___	___
7. Classroom comfort	___	___	___	___
8. Progress of class as a whole	___	___	___	___
9. Outlines in *FAA Knowledge Test*	___	___	___	___
10. Answer explanations in *FAA Knowledge Test*	___	___	___	___
11. Overall rating of *FAA Knowledge Test*	___	___	___	___

12. **Other comments.** Please explain poor responses and make any other suggestions you feel may be relevant in the space provided below and on the back of this sheet. **Thank you.**

HELPING YOUR STUDENTS SELECT A COMPUTER TESTING CENTER

1.   Since most computer testing centers have limited seating, it is unlikely that you will be able to have all of your students take the test at the same time and place.

    a.   Thus, you will need to help your students in the selection of a computer testing center.

2.   Call each testing service to determine if any discounts are being offered and the payment policy. Explain your class situation (number of students, etc.)

    a.   Some students may not have a credit card, so they need to select a computer testing center that will accept a check or cash at the time of the test.

       1)   Some computer testing services may require that a check or money order be sent before the student can take the test.

    b.   Make yourself available to assist your students as necessary.

3. Provide your students with the contact information for the following computer testing services and the results of your inquiries.

   CATS   (800) 947-4228 or www.catstest.com
   LASERGRADE   (800) 211-2754 or www.lasergrade.com

4. Discuss the examination process and demonstrate testing procedures by using the Gleim *FAA Test Prep* Software Download.

5. You, as a flight instructor, are required to maintain a record of each person for whom you sign a certification for a pilot knowledge test, including the kind of test, date of test, and the test result (FAR 61.189).

   a. An efficient way of obtaining test results is to pre-address and stamp one postcard for each student (include the student's name on the card) and explain why you need these returned.

      1) Hand them out on the exam day.
      2) Ask students to mail their numerical scores to you.
      3) List the student scores on your roster as they come in the mail.
      4) Call any individuals who have not submitted cards.

   b. Email is another simple method for obtaining this information.

   c. You can use these pass rates in future advertising.

AN ALTERNATIVE APPROACH: EXPANDING YOUR MARKET

1. You may wish to broaden your ground school course so that it appeals to aviation enthusiasts interested in doing more than passing the FAA private pilot (airplane) or sport pilot knowledge test. If so, you need to

   a. Diversify your marketing plan and advertisements.
   b. Edit the suggested syllabus (make it more general).
   c. Prepare fewer class assignments focused on the FAA pilot knowledge test.

2. Can you prepare student pilots for the FAA pilot knowledge test **and** provide a general-interest aviation course?

   a. Many ground schools are so directed, especially at community colleges where a considerable number of enrollees do not take the FAA pilot knowledge test.

   b. One approach is to emphasize discussion of FAA test questions at the end (optional part) of each class; e.g., in a 100-minute class.

      1) The last 30 minutes might be restricted to discussion of FAA questions in *Private Pilot FAA Knowledge Test* and/or *Sport Pilot FAA Knowledge Test*.
      2) The first 70 minutes would involve lecture discussion.

   c. Occasional questions might be discussed, but the emphasis would be on learning about airplanes, weather, and navigation rather than passing the FAA pilot knowledge test.

   d. In such a course, *Pilot Handbook* would be the required text instead of *Private Pilot FAA Knowledge Test* or *Sport Pilot FAA Knowledge Test*, which can be optional.

3. With these general guidelines, we trust you will take the plunge and **start your class** (or at least begin to prepare for it) **right now**! It is fun, and it provides a valuable service -- teaching new aviation enthusiasts to **ENJOY FLYING -- SAFELY!**

CROSS-REFERENCES TO
THE FAA LEARNING STATEMENT CODES

Pages 153 and 154 contain a listing of the FAA fundamentals of instructing questions from the flight and ground instructor knowledge test bank. The questions are in FAA Learning Statement Code (LSC) sequence. (Refer to page 10 in the Introduction for a complete listing and description of each.) To the right of each LSC, we present our study unit/question number and our answer. For example, look below and note that PLT204 is cross-referenced to 3-13, which represents our Study Unit 3, question 13; the correct answer is B.

The first line of each of our answer explanations in Study Units 1 through 6 contains the correct answer and a reference for the answer explanation, e.g., *AIH Chap 1*. If this reference is not useful, use the following chart to identify the learning statement code to determine the specific reference appropriate for the question.

FAA Learning Code	Gleim SU/ Q. No.	Gleim Answer	FAA Learning Code	Gleim SU/ Q. No.	Gleim Answer	FAA Learning Code	Gleim SU/ Q. No.	Gleim Answer
PLT204	3-13	B	PLT229	3-33	C	PLT270	5-26	A
PLT204	3-14	A	PLT229	3-34	B	PLT295	2-15	B
PLT204	3-15	C	PLT230	2-18	C	PLT295	3-20	C
PLT204	3-16	C	PLT230	2-20	A	PLT295	3-21	C
PLT204	3-17	B	PLT230	3-25	C	PLT295	5-1	A
PLT204	3-18	C	PLT230	3-26	B	PLT295	5-2	B
PLT204	3-19	C	PLT230	3-27	B	PLT295	5-27	C
PLT227	4-27	A	PLT231	1-16	A	PLT306	1-3	C
PLT227	4-28	C	PLT231	1-17	A	PLT306	1-19	B
PLT227	4-29	C	PLT231	1-21	A	PLT306	1-30	B
PLT227	4-30	A	PLT231	2-11	B	PLT306	1-31	C
PLT228	5-14	B	PLT231	2-12	B	PLT306	1-32	A
PLT228	5-15	A	PLT231	2-13	B	PLT306	1-33	A
PLT228	5-16	A	PLT231	2-14	A	PLT306	1-34	B
PLT228	5-17	B	PLT232	2-16	B	PLT306	1-35	A
PLT228	5-18	C	PLT232	2-17	B	PLT306	1-36	C
PLT228	5-19	C	PLT232	2-19	B	PLT307	1-2	C
PLT228	5-20	C	PLT233	2-3	C	PLT307	1-22	C
PLT228	5-21	C	PLT233	2-4	C	PLT307	1-23	A
PLT228	5-23	C	PLT233	2-5	A	PLT307	1-24	A
PLT228	5-24	C	PLT233	2-6	B	PLT307	1-25	C
PLT228	5-28	B	PLT233	2-7	A	PLT307	1-26	A
PLT228	5-29	C	PLT233	2-8	B	PLT307	1-27	C
PLT229	3-28	A	PLT233	2-9	B	PLT307	1-28	C
PLT229	3-29	B	PLT233	2-10	B	PLT307	1-29	B
PLT229	3-30	A	PLT270	3-1	B	PLT308	1-1	A
PLT229	3-31	C	PLT270	3-2	A	PLT308	1-4	B

FAA Learning Code	Gleim SU/ Q. No.	Gleim Answer	FAA Learning Code	Gleim SU/ Q. No.	Gleim Answer	FAA Learning Code	Gleim SU/ Q. No.	Gleim Answer
PLT308	1–5	C	PLT482	6–19	A	PLT489	5–12	B
PLT308	1–6	A	PLT482	6–20	B	PLT489	5–13	B
PLT308	1–7	A	PLT482	6–21	A	PLT490	1–13	A
PLT308	1–8	A	PLT482	6–22	C	PLT490	1–14	A
PLT308	1–9	C	PLT482	6–23	A	PLT490	3–4	B
PLT308	1–10	B	PLT482	6–24	B	PLT490	3–5	B
PLT308	1–11	A	PLT482	6–25	B	PLT490	3–6	A
PLT308	1–12	A	PLT482	6–26	C	PLT490	3–7	A
PLT308	1–15	B	PLT482	6–27	A	PLT490	3–8	B
PLT308	1–18	A	PLT482	6–28	C	PLT490	3–9	B
PLT308	1–37	B	PLT482	6–29	B	PLT490	3–10	C
PLT308	1–38	C	PLT482	6–30	A	PLT490	3–11	A
PLT308	1–39	C	PLT482	6–31	C	PLT490	4–31	B
PLT308	1–40	A	PLT482	6–32	B	PLT490	4–32	B
PLT308	1–41	B	PLT482	6–33	C	PLT490	5–22	A
PLT308	1–42	C	PLT482	6–34	B	PLT491	5–3	C
PLT308	2–1	C	PLT482	6–35	A	PLT491	5–4	B
PLT308	2–2	A	PLT482	6–36	B	PLT491	5–5	C
PLT481	1–20	C	PLT482	6–37	B	PLT491	5–6	A
PLT481	1–43	B	PLT487	4–19	C	PLT491	5–7	C
PLT481	1–44	B	PLT487	4–20	C	PLT491	5–8	B
PLT481	3–22	C	PLT487	4–21	B	PLT491	5–9	C
PLT481	3–23	C	PLT487	4–22	B	PLT491	5–10	A
PLT481	3–24	B	PLT487	4–23	C	PLT491	5–11	A
PLT482	6–1	A	PLT488	4–1	A	PLT491	5–25	A
PLT482	6–2	C	PLT488	4–2	A	PLT504	4–24	C
PLT482	6–3	B	PLT488	4–3	B	PLT504	4–25	B
PLT482	6–4	C	PLT488	4–4	C	PLT504	4–26	B
PLT482	6–5	B	PLT488	4–5	C	PLT504	5–30	B
PLT482	6–6	C	PLT488	4–6	B	PLT504	5–33	A
PLT482	6–7	C	PLT488	4–7	B	PLT505	5–31	C
PLT482	6–8	B	PLT488	4–8	A	PLT505	5–32	B
PLT482	6–9	C	PLT488	4–9	C			
PLT482	6–10	B	PLT488	4–10	A			
PLT482	6–11	C	PLT488	4–11	B			
PLT482	6–12	A	PLT488	4–12	B			
PLT482	6–13	A	PLT488	4–13	A			
PLT482	6–14	B	PLT488	4–14	B			
PLT482	6–15	A	PLT488	4–15	A			
PLT482	6–16	A	PLT488	4–16	B			
PLT482	6–17	B	PLT488	4–17	C			
PLT482	6–18	A	PLT488	4–18	C			

LESSON:

STUDENT: _____ **DATE:** _____

OBJECTIVE

CONTENT

SCHEDULE

EQUIPMENT

INSTRUCTOR'S ACTIONS

STUDENT'S ACTIONS

COMPLETION STANDARDS

INSTRUCTOR CERTIFICATION FORM
FUNDAMENTALS OF INSTRUCTING KNOWLEDGE TEST
FOR SPORT PILOT INSTRUCTORS

Name: _____

I certify that I have reviewed the above individual's preparation for the FAA Fundamentals of Instructing knowledge test [covering the topics specified in 14 CFR 61.407(a)(1) through (6)] using the *Fundamentals of Instructing FAA Knowledge Test* book, software, and/or online course by Irvin N. Gleim and find him/her competent to pass the knowledge test.

_____   _____   _____   _____   _____
Signed   Date   Name   CFI or CGI   Expiration Date
                                                                Number   N/A if CGI

158

AUTHORS' RECOMMENDATIONS

The Experimental Aircraft Association, Inc. is a very successful and effective nonprofit organization that represents and serves those of us interested in flying, in general, and in sport aviation, in particular. We personally invite you to enjoy becoming a member. Visit their website at www.eaa.org.

Types of EAA Memberships:

$40 - Individual (plus choice of *EAA Sport Aviation Magazine* or *EAA Sport Pilot Magazine*) - add a second magazine subscription for $20

$50 - Family (extends all benefits to member's spouse and children under 18, except for an additional EAA magazine subscription)

$10 - Student (for those age 17 or under; includes Student Membership kit & access to student members-only website)

$975 - Lifetime

Write: EAA Aviation Center   *Call:* (920) 426-4800
3000 Poberezny Rd.   (800) JOIN-EAA
Oshkosh, Wisconsin 54902   *Email:* membership@eaa.org

The Annual EAA Oshkosh AirVenture is an unbelievable aviation spectacular with over 10,000 airplanes at one airport! Virtually everything aviation-oriented you can imagine! Plan to spend at least 1 day (not everything can be seen in a day) in Oshkosh (100 miles northwest of Milwaukee). Visit the AirVenture website at www.airventure.org.

Convention dates: 2009 -- July 27 through August 2
2010 -- July 26 through August 1
2011 -- July 25 through July 31

The annual Sun 'n Fun EAA Fly-In is also highly recommended. It is held at the Lakeland, FL (KLAL) airport (between Orlando and Tampa). Visit the Sun 'n Fun website at www.sun-n-fun.org.

Convention dates: 2010 -- April 13 through April 18
2011 -- April 5 through April 10
2012 -- April 17 through April 22

AIRCRAFT OWNERS AND PILOTS ASSOCIATION

AOPA is the largest, most influential aviation association in the world, with more than 415,000 members--two thirds of all pilots in the United States. AOPA's most important contribution to the world's most accessible, safest, least expensive, friendliest, easiest-to-use general aviation environment is their lobbying on our behalf at the federal, state, and local levels. AOPA also provides legal services, advice, and other assistance to the aviation community.

We recommend that you become an AOPA member, which costs only $39 annually. To join, call 1-800-USA-AOPA or visit the AOPA website at www.aopa.org.

LET'S GO FLYING!

The Aircraft Owner's and Pilot's Association (AOPA) hosts an informational web page on getting started in aviation. "Let's Go Flying!" contains information for those still dreaming about flying, those who are ready to begin, and those who are already making the journey.

The goal of this program is to encourage people to experience their dreams of flying through an introductory flight. Interested individuals can order a FREE DVD that explains how amazing it is to be a pilot. Other resources are available, such as a flight school finder, a guide on what to expect throughout training, an explanation of pilot certification options, a FREE monthly flight training newsletter, and much more. To learn more about "Let's Go Flying!," visit www.aopa.org/letsgoflying.

ABBREVIATIONS AND ACRONYMS IN
FUNDAMENTALS OF INSTRUCTING FAA KNOWLEDGE TEST

A/FD	*Airport/Facility Directory*		NOTAM	notice to airmen
AC	Advisory Circular		NPRM	Notice of Proposed Rulemaking
AD	Airworthiness Directive		NTSB	National Transportation Safety Board
ADF	automatic direction finder		OAT	outside air temperature
AFSS	Automated Flight Service Station		OBS	omnibearing selector
AGL	above ground level		PAPI	precision approach path indicator
AIM	*Aeronautical Information Manual*		PCL	pilot-controlled lighting
AIRMET	Airman's Meteorological Information		PIC	pilot in command
AME	aviation medical examiner		PIREP	pilot weather report
ANDS	accelerate north, decelerate south		RB	relative bearing
AOE	airport of entry		SFC	surface
ARTS	Automated Radar Terminal System		SIGMET	Significant Meteorological Information
ASEL	airplane single-engine land		SM	statute mile
ATA	actual time of arrival		STC	supplemental type certificate
ATC	Air Traffic Control		SVFR	special VFR
ATIS	Automatic Terminal Information Service		TACAN	Tactical Air Navigation
CDI	course deviation indicator		TAF	terminal aerodrome forecast
CDT	central daylight time		TAS	true airspeed
CFI	certificated flight instructor		TC	true course
CG	center of gravity		TH	true heading
CH	compass heading		TWEB	Transcribed Weather Broadcast
CT	control tower		UHF	ultra high frequency
CTAF	Common Traffic Advisory Frequency		UTC	Coordinated Universal Time
DME	distance measuring equipment		V_A	maneuvering speed
DT	daylight time		VASI	visual approach slope indicator
DUAT	Direct User Access Terminal		V_{FE}	maximum flap extended speed
DVFR	defense VFR		VFR	visual flight rules
EFAS	En Route Flight Advisory Service		VHF	very high frequency
ELT	emergency locator transmitter		VHF/DF	VHF direction finder
ETA	estimated time of arrival		VIP	video integrated processor
ETD	estimated time of departure		V_{LE}	maximum landing gear extended speed
FA	area forecast		V_{NE}	never-exceed speed
FAA	Federal Aviation Administration		V_{NO}	maximum structural cruising speed
FAR	Federal Aviation Regulation		VOR	VHF omnidirectional range
FBO	fixed-base operator		VORTAC	collocated VOR and TACAN
FCC	Federal Communications Commission		VOT	VOR test facility
FD	winds and temperatures aloft forecast		VR	visual route
FL	flight level		V_{S0}	stalling speed or the minimum steady flight speed in the landing configuration
FSDO	Flight Standards District Office			
FSS	Flight Service Station		V_{S1}	stalling speed or the minimum steady flight speed obtained in a specific configuration
GPH	gallons per hour			
Hg	mercury		V_X	speed for best angle of climb
HP	horsepower		V_Y	speed for best rate of climb
IAS	indicated airspeed		WCA	wind correction angle
ICAO	International Civil Aviation Organization		Z	Zulu or UTC time
IFR	instrument flight rules			
IR	instrument route			
ISA	International Standard Atmosphere			
LLWAS	low-level wind-shear alert system			
mb	millibar			
MB	magnetic bearing			
MC	magnetic course			
MEF	maximum elevation figure			
METAR	aviation routine weather report			
MH	magnetic heading			
MOA	Military Operations Area			
MSL	mean sea level			
MTR	military training route			
MVFR	marginal VFR			
NDB	nondirectional radio beacon			
NFCT	nonfederal control tower			
NM	nautical mile			

INDEX

164

Convert "downtime" into study time

with GLEIM *FAA Audio Review*

GLEIM Complete Pilot Kits

Sport Pilot	$199.95 _____
Private Pilot	$249.95 _____
Instrument Pilot	$249.95 _____
Commercial Pilot	$174.95 _____
Instrument/Commercial Pilot	$341.95 _____
Sport Pilot Flight Instructor	$174.95 _____
Flight/Ground Instructor	$174.95 _____
ATP	$189.95 _____

Also Available:

Flight Engineer Test Prep Software	$64.95 _____
Flight Engineer Online Ground School	$99.95 _____

Shipping (nonrefundable): **$20 per kit** $ _____
(Alaska and Hawaii please call for shipping price)
Add applicable sales tax for shipments within the state of Florida. $ _____
For orders outside the United States, please visit our website at
www.gleim.com/aviation/products.php to place your order.   TOTAL $ _____

Reference Materials and Other Accessories Available by Contacting Gleim.

TOLL FREE: 800.874.5346
INTERNET: gleim.com

LOCAL: 352.375.0772
FAX: 352.375.6940
EMAIL: sales@gleim.com

Gleim Publications, Inc.
P.O. Box 12848
Gainesville, FL 32604

NAME (please print) _____

ADDRESS _____ Apt. _____
          (street address required for UPS)

_____

CITY _____ STATE _____ ZIP _____

_____ MC/VISA/DISC _____ Check/M.O.   Daytime Telephone (_____) _____ - _____

Credit Card # _____ - _____ - _____ - _____

Exp. ____ / ____   Signature _____
        Mo./Yr.

Email Address _____

1. We process and ship orders daily, within one business day over 98.8% of the time. Call by 3:00 pm for same day service.
2. Gleim Publications, Inc. guarantees the immediate refund of all resalable texts, unopened and un-downloaded Test Prep Software, and unopened audios returned within 30 days. Online courses may be canceled within 30 days if no more than the first study unit or lesson has been accessed. This only applies to products that are purchased directly from Gleim Publications, Inc. No refunds will be provided on opened or downloaded Test Prep Software or audios, partial returns of package sets, or shipping and handling charges. Any freight charges incurred for returned or refused packages will be the customer's responsibility.
3. Please PHOTOCOPY this order form for others.
4. No CODs. Orders from individuals must be prepaid.
5. Shipping and handling charges are nonrefundable.

Prices subject to change without notice.   7/09

Please forward your suggestions, corrections, and comments concerning typographical errors, etc., to **Irvin N. Gleim • c/o Gleim Publications, Inc. • P.O. Box 12848 • University Station • Gainesville, Florida • 32604.** Please include your name and address so we can properly thank you for your interest.

1. _____

2. _____

3. _____

4. _____

5. _____

6. _____

7. _____

8. _____

9. _____

10. _____

11. _____

12. _____

13. _____

14. _____

15. _____

16. _____

17. _____

18. _____

We need your help identifying which questions the FAA is pretesting (but not grading -- see page 5). After you take your exam, please email, fax, or mail us a description of these questions so we can anticipate their future use by the FAA.

Remember, for superior service: Mail, email, or fax questions about our materials.
Telephone questions about orders, prices, shipments, or payments.

Name: _____

Address: _____

City/State/Zip: _____

Telephone: Home: _____   Work: _____   Fax: _____

Email: _____